GW00994512

Genesis

in the 1970s

Bill Thomas

sonicbondpublishing.com

Sonicbond Publishing Limited
www.sonicbondpublishing.co.uk
Email: info@sonicbondpublishing.co.uk

First Published in the United Kingdom 2021
First Published in the United States 2021

British Library Cataloguing in Publication Data:
A Catalogue record for this book is available from the British Library

Copyright Bill Thomas 2021

ISBN 978-1-78952-146-7

Typeset in ITC Garamond & ITC Avant Garde
Printed and bound in England

Graphic design and typesetting: Full Moon Media

DECADES

Genesis
in the 1970s

Bill Thomas

sonicbondpublishing.com

Acknowledgements

If you're writing a book on Genesis, then the first people to thank are all those involved in the story. That extends to not just the band themselves, but the crew, the record producers and engineers, management, sleeve designers, record company believers, supportive journalists and the early adopters, all of whom played their part in the background in helping get the show on the road and then keeping it there. Some are namechecked within these pages, many are not, but on behalf of the Genesis community, my thanks go to them all.

Naturally, those thanks extend to all the members of Genesis across the 1970s, but in connection with this book, most particularly to Steve Hackett and Anthony Phillips, who were both unfailingly helpful and charming when being asked all those questions one more time. Thanks too to Jerry Marotta for much enlightenment on the early Peter Gabriel solo years.

And finally, thanks to Stephen Lambe for being brave enough to think there might still be something left worth saying about Genesis in the Seventies. I think he was right. I hope you do too.

DECADES | Genesis in the 1970s

Contents

Introduction

In the interests of full disclosure, I suppose I should say from the outset that Genesis are my Beatles. Having been born just too late to appreciate the Fabs as anything other than the Old Testament, it was the newer miracles of the Genesis canon that really fired my imagination and sparked a lifelong love affair with music. That's not to say that all the gospels are holy writ – 'Illegal Alien' surely transgresses against several of the commandments and if it doesn't, it can only be because Moses left a couple of tablets behind – but that Genesis' music has always been my touchstone, the records I have always gone back to.

That Beatles analogy holds more water than just being a shorthand for favourite band, best band or whatever. For just as The Beatles were a hothouse for incredible songwriters, so too were Genesis, as this book will, I hope, illustrate. It made for a combustible, heady brew when those talents were all harnessed in the service of the band, but by the end of the 1970s, we'd also had genuinely impressive and exciting solo albums from Steve Hackett, Peter Gabriel, Anthony Phillips and Tony Banks, while Mike Rutherford's *Smallcreep's Day* was finished and ready for release in the early months of the 1980s, a decade which would go on to become the private property of Phil Collins.

I'm not in the camp that thinks Genesis were finished once Phillips, Gabriel or Hackett (delete as applicable) left. The classic three-man line-up, and the one with Ray Wilson for that matter, were often still sublime and the same goes for the solo material the assorted members went on to produce away from the mothership in the 1980s and beyond.

But together and apart, when you look back at the consistently high standards of the material they produced across the 1970s, it is simply astonishing. I know what I like, and this is plenty of it…

Author's note. Unless attributed otherwise in the text, quotes from Anthony Phillips (April 2015), Steve Hackett (May 1988 and May 2013) and Jerry Marotta (March 2015) come from interviews conducted by the author.

Prologue: In the Beginning

Take a little trip back to the 1960s, the decade when British pop and rock music took over the world, when The Beatles, the Stones, The Who, The Kinks et al. established the template for how a rock band should perform, how it should behave, what it should look like. The rules tended to revolve around playing up a band's working class roots, adopting an aggressive pose, wearing a perpetual sneer on your upper lip, acting like a harbinger of the revolution.

Nowhere in those templates was there much about forming at public school where you had been sent to be trained to become leaders of the Establishment, captains of industry, upholders of the ruling class. But Charterhouse public school, the alma mater of politicians, diplomats, bishops, judges and winners of the Victoria Cross, was the primordial swamp from which two groups evolved, The Garden Wall, featuring singer and flautist Peter Gabriel (born 13 February 1950) and pianist Tony Banks (born 27 March 1950), and Anon which included budding guitarists Anthony Phillips (born 23 December 1951) and Michael Rutherford (born 2 October 1950), Phillips also popping up in The Garden Wall.

Those two pairs eventually joined forces when Phillips and Rutherford spent a school holiday trying to record some of the songs they'd written and, needing a pianist and organist to augment their sound, invited Banks along. He persuaded them to bring Gabriel along because they, too, had been writing songs and wanted to try out one of theirs.

In the Easter holidays of 1967, they decamped to a small home studio set up operated by school friend Brian Roberts to record some demos. Gabriel was late arriving, so they began by recording the songs Phillips and Rutherford had in hand, with Phillips singing before Banks chimed in with, 'We should really wait for Peter because he's got an awful lot better voice.' To his credit, Phillips agreed, Rutherford saying later in the video that accompanied the 1970-75 box set, 'If Ant hadn't realised that [Peter was a better singer] we might have missed the moment.'

It was a decision that brought almost immediate dividends. As well as filling the ranks of the civil service, Charterhouse had produced itself a pop sensation earlier in the 1960s; Jonathan King reached number four in the UK charts with his single, 'Everyone's Gone to the Moon', in 1965 and was quickly an established figure in the music scene. When word circulated that he was returning to Charterhouse for an 'old boys' day, they hatched a plot to get a tape of their songs into his hands, though their collective nerve failed them and schoolfriend John Alexander had to do the deed, leaving the tape in his Austin Healey Sprite.

King was sufficiently taken by the tape to get in touch, arrange a meeting and put them into a real studio to record four songs. Happy with the results of that, he then signed them to a ten-year publishing deal – later reduced to a year thanks to the intervention of the band's parents – for this fledgling four saw themselves as songwriters for other people in best Brill Building tradition. For all his contacts, not even King could find any takers for the songs, particularly for the second batch of material that they provided him with, songs that veered away from the more obvious pop of the initial tape. To recapture King's waning attention, Banks and Gabriel famously crafted 'The Silent Sun' in the style of the Bee Gees, sufficiently successful that he took them into the studio to record it as a single – with schoolfriend Chris Stewart (born 27 March 1951) on drums – arguing that they might be better off recording the songs themselves.

It was a sensible suggestion, for while there were occasional glimpses of what Genesis might become musically during that Decca Records era, the thing that really distinguishes them at that point wasn't the songwriting or the musicianship, it was Peter Gabriel's voice. That was the hook.

To issue a single, the band still needed a name, having toyed with such disastrous ideas as The Champagne Meadow. King suggested Gabriel's Angels, which found favour with the singer but not the rest of the group, strangely enough, before settling on Genesis, King seeing the band as the beginning of his production career. 'The Silent Sun' was released to a wave of public apathy on 2 February 1968, as was 'A Winter's Tale' on 10 May. Refusing to be disheartened, King suggested they record an album, stipulating that they should improve the rhythm section ahead of making the album. Rutherford, still finding his way on bass, was going nowhere, so Chris Stewart was eased out of the line-up; Rutherford sent off as the hangman. Stewart was to be replaced by another Charterhouse alumnus, John Silver (born 22 February 1949), a jazz fan in the main, who Gabriel later credited with being an important factor in encouraging Genesis to follow a more idiosyncratic path and to craft their own personality away from the demands of the record company.

That the newly christened Genesis were a musically ambitious bunch was immediately evident as they chose their subject matter for this debut album, using the Book of Genesis and the Book of Revelations as loose themes for the two sides of the vinyl. 'Absolutely pathetic', said Banks later in the band's *Chapter & Verse* book, 'but it did give us something to hang everything around'.

Recording took place during the school holidays in August 1968 at Regent Sound Studios in London, Banks playing organ for the first time, the band recording their parts inside two days under King's supervision as producer. Once they had finished their work, King sat on the tapes for a time, wondering if what he had was suitable for release. Concluding that it wasn't, in December, he drafted in Arthur Greenslade and Lou Warburton to add string and horn arrangements, the band mixed onto one stereo channel, these new embellishments, added without their knowledge, on the other.

From Genesis to Revelation was released by Decca in a pre-Spinal Tap jet black sleeve with gothic gold lettering at the top on 7 March 1969. There was no band name, research having uncovered an already existing Genesis in the United States. 'Revelation' was toyed with as an alternative until an English band of that name was unearthed. And so briefly, they were the band with no name with a record that, based on its sleeve, found its way into the religious section of most record shops, not the best way to launch a career. Famously, on release, it sold just 650 copies, Phillips ruefully admitting, 'Between us, I think we knew everybody who bought one'.

Largely ignored as part of the Genesis canon, not least because the rights still reside with King rather than the group and so it has never come under the band's umbrella, it has a certain period charm and some enjoyable songs, but it's a pretty naïve offering, one that, for the most part, is the sum of its influences and of King's contribution. Overall, the record is in thrall to the sounds of the time, the Stones, the Small Faces, even film soundtracks of the era worming their way into the songs. Noel Gallagher of Oasis has become a latter-day champion of the record, admitting his own song 'If Love Is the Law' is based on 'The Conqueror'.

There have been many re-releases over the years, perhaps the best a double CD on Edsel Records in 2005, which offers thirteen additional tracks. There is also a digital-only release from 2017, *50 Years Ago*, which, while not the album itself, acts as a fine companion piece, including as it does material taken from the multi-tracks that were previously thought lost in a fire. It's a fascinating glimpse into the making of the record and one that deserves a wider release.

With the commercial failure of *From Genesis to Revelation*, their association with King drifted to a close and Genesis were left to their own devices as they reached the summer of 1969. This was a significant period for them, for decisions on continuing with their education or plugging into the band had to be made. Ultimately, the music won out, not least because over the latter part of 1968 and into '69, they had been finding their own sound, one that hadn't really found favour with King. Songs were getting longer, more complex, and in particular, the sound of two, sometimes three, 12-string guitars was something that gave Genesis an identity. Phillips was very much the moving force behind it:

At Charterhouse, I was in a house called Duckites, but I had pockets of friends in other houses too. Each house had its own style. The Robinites were rather cool, not exactly rebels, but among them was this guy, Tony Henderson. We were coming back from the Glade, where we used to go and smoke illegally, it was the summer of 1966, and he was in a field playing this 12-string and I just thought, 'Bloody hell, that's a great sound!' I would have heard a 12-string before that, The Beatles used an electric 12-string quite a lot, The Byrds were around, there was the odd pop track with an acoustic, but it wasn't normally in a picking, arpeggio way, it was more a strumming thing, so you didn't get the full timbre. To hear him playing that way, solo, outside in the summer, it had a magical quality to it. You have this strange, harmonic thing going on which is very, very different, and I was captivated by it and then so was Mike. In early 1969, Mike and I started playing and then writing on them in tandem, and with the two 12-strings, we found a sound that we thought was fascinating. It's still a very underused sound and I'm very happy about that!

Genesis were a man down that summer though, John Silver heading off to study in America at Cornell University, leading to a spell of auditions from which John Mayhew (born 27 March 1947) emerged as the new drummer as Genesis got down to some serious writing and rehearsing, initially at the home of Phillips' parents before moving to Christmas Cottage for six months in the early autumn of '69. It was a weekend retreat owned by the parents of Richard Macphail, former lead singer with Anon. They were preparing to sell it the following spring, so it was lying empty. Macphail, the band's greatest early cheerleader, was determined to do all he could to ensure they persisted with their music, and so he arranged for Genesis to move in. There followed a largely monastic period where the band devoted themselves to their music, writing and refining material that was a far cry from the simpler style that had brought them to Jonathan King's attention, much more in the mould of the songs that had turned him off prior to 'The Silent Sun'.

By the turn of the year, they had also played their first eight gigs. Genesis were ready for the 1970s.

1970: The Crusade Has Begun

There were to be many pivotal years in the Genesis story, but 1970 lays down a pretty strong case for being the most important of them all. It began with no record deal, no fan base, the band still 'getting it together in the country', and surviving on homemade bread, muesli and yoghurt. By the time it was over, they had recorded their first BBC radio session, were signed to Tony Stratton Smith's famous Charisma label, had released a well-received second album, were beginning to build a strong live following, especially in and around London, and had recruited the man who was to become perhaps progressive rock's greatest drummer. It turned out he could sing a bit too.

For a group that had been so heavily cocooned through 1969, concentrating upon writing rather than getting out onto the gig circuit, Genesis were already remarkably well regarded as the new decade began. Amongst the first work they did was to soundtrack a film for the BBC, the first of two collaborations with the corporation in the decade's first two months.

Genesis Plays Jackson

Personnel: Tony Banks, Peter Gabriel, John Mayhew, Anthony Phillips, Mike Rutherford
Recorded at BBC Shepherd's Bush Studios, January 1970.
Produced by Paul Samwell-Smith.
Released as part of the Genesis 1970-1975 box set, 10 November 2008.
Running time: 14:42
Tracklisting: 1. Provocation 2. Frustration 3. Manipulation 4. Resignation.
All songs by Banks/Gabriel/Phillips/Rutherford

Based upon the work of painter Michael Jackson, the documentary was to be a 'silent' film that required accompanying music, *Metropolis* by Fritz Lang being the template. The session took place as early as 9 January according to the note on the tape box, though Peter Gabriel's explanation of the session within the 1970-1975 box set suggests this might be too early – just to add to the confusion, the *Extra Tracks* booklet puts the Jackson material down as being demos from 1969, though this seems highly unlikely.

The session was produced by Paul Samwell-Smith, former bass player of The Yardbirds, then working with Cat Stevens on the *Mona Bone Jakon* album. Gabriel's sleeve notes say that he had already provided flute on 'Katmandu' on that album and from there had asked Samwell-Smith to produce the *Jackson* session for Genesis. Given that sessions for *Mona Bone Jakon* didn't start until 5 January 1970, while possible, it would seem a tight time frame for Gabriel to have recorded a flute overdub so early on in the sessions and have then found a gap in Samwell-Smith's schedule to produce Genesis by the 9th. An earlier interview with Gabriel, published in Hugh Fielder's *The Book of Genesis*, notes that Samwell-Smith had heard the demos that the band had recorded over the course of the second half of 1969. They'd been passed on to him by Marcus Bicknell, a television producer who was a fan of the group and had expressed an interest in managing them. That offers a more likely chronology, Samwell-Smith hearing the demo in late '69 and then recruiting Genesis for the *Jackson* project and offering Gabriel the Cat Stevens gig at roughly the same time.

The Jackson documentary was swiftly aborted, but not before Genesis had spent a valuable couple of hours in the BBC studios, a great experience for a band still so limited in that regard. Gabriel recalled in the *Extra Tracks* booklet that most of the time allotted was spent on the instrumental track, and, 'I never had time to do a proper vocal. Unfortunately, my guide track was recorded, a lot of it undeveloped and out of tune, merely a sketch for ideas and never intended to be heard by anyone else. Consequently, the instrumental sounds fine, and I think Paul did a great job in making Genesis sound good, but it's a terrible vocal track....'

You can see his point, the vocal veering from vaguely structured lyric to what he later termed 'Gabrielese', noises and made-up words that gave an idea of the melody and rhythm for a lyric yet to be completed. For Gabriel, having such work in progress published might be embarrassing – though his interest in charting the songwriting process was later illustrated when he put out the *So DNA* album on similar lines – but the real value of *Genesis Plays Jackson* is to chart the quantum leap forward that the band had taken since recording *From Genesis to Revelation*, not just as writers but more particularly as musicians. The diffidence of that album has been replaced by a group that seems very much more assured, with a real sense of direction. No longer are they working on pop songs for others to record but producing work that's more challenging, idiosyncratic, with a character all its own. The intensive work that had gone on in Christmas Cottage had clearly borne fruit and, having just begun to play live too, there's a harder edge appearing. Genesis had a sense of purpose. They had become a real band.

And a prolific band at that, for none of the music that found its way into the *Jackson* project was being played on stage at that point. That made some sense, for it needed some relationship to the visuals, existing songs and lyrics not necessarily fitting. So it was that, for the most part, the session was filled with musical ideas and fragments, some that would go on to see the light of day on future albums, as was evidenced on the first track, 'Provocation'. What immediately leaps out – and continues to do so across the four tracks – is the advance made by Tony Banks, who has begun to be the fulcrum of the Genesis sound. Where he was very much a pianist who occasionally switched to organ on *From Genesis to Revelation*, he was now much more at home on the electric instrument, playing in a similar style to that which Hugh Banton was exploring with Van der Graaf Generator. It combines a real grandeur with a soulfulness influenced by an area all too often ignored in reviews of early Genesis – hymns and church music in general. Gabriel spoke in Armando Gallo's early biography, *Genesis: Evolution of a Rock Band*, of how at Charterhouse, pupils would go into the Memorial Chapel and 'Everyone would stand up and scream their heads off. It would be as moving as a Negro spiritual and people would come out of the Chapel feeling like they were on top of the world!' That music and especially that emotion informed much of their early work, Anthony Phillips and Mike Rutherford later going so far as to write a hymn, 'Take This Heart', for *Beyond an Empty Dream*, the Charisma album of modern hymns that was released in 1975.

'Provocation' begins with the organ part that would ultimately develop into 'The Fountain of Salmacis' from 1971's *Nursery Cryme*. It's a piece Banks had written at Sussex University in the academic year 1968/69, demonstrating how quickly the style of his music was changing. He was not the only one, for it evolves into a later instrumental section that would form part of 'Looking for Someone' on *Trespass* later in the year, featuring an angular piece of guitar from Phillips.

'Frustration' sees Banks back on piano, very much in the classical mould and again playing a piece that would go on to feature later in the Genesis story as 'Anyway' from *The Lamb Lies Down on Broadway*. Given it took nearly five years before it finally made it to vinyl, it's surprisingly fully formed, Gabriel singing the melody as it would be heard in the final version, albeit with different words. There follows a section from 'Hair on the Arms & Legs', one of the clutch of 1968 demos, the original version of which is on the *Archive 1967-75* box set, before heading off into a brief section driven by acoustic guitar with a flute melody which has the same kind of atmosphere that would go on to colour much of *Trespass*.

The acoustic side of the band came to the fore in the opening moments of 'Manipulation', which is, initially, the forerunner of 'The Musical Box'. It's a piece written by Phillips and Rutherford, which had a working title of 'F Sharp' after Rutherford tuned the top three pairs of strings on his 12-string down to F sharp to create that chiming effect. Banks adds an organ figure which muddies the waters somewhat before the more familiar keyboard section comes in and it becomes more aggressive, though it lacks the howling electric guitar that Steve Hackett would add on *Nursery Cryme*, and then fades into a later section that is more in the pastoral mould of *Trespass* featuring a bank of choral voices. A demo of 'F Sharp' was released on Phillips' *The Archive Collection Volume One*. It was recorded at Send Barns, his parents' house, while Genesis were working there in September 1969, prior to moving on to Christmas Cottage.

A second instrumental follows, 'Resignation' opening with echoes of 'In Hiding' from *From Genesis to Revelation* before heading into a more acoustic section, very much from the Phillips wing of the band, with nods in the direction of what would later become *The Geese & The Ghost*. A flute-led passage from the 'Stagnation' / 'Let Us Now Make Love' area of their music follows before a more aggressive final burst. While 'Resignation' doesn't jump out at the listener in the way of the three other tracks, largely because there's nothing immediately identifiable from the later canon bar a slight hint again at 'The Fountain of Salmacis', it is perhaps the most interesting piece because it's groping towards a Genesis trademark. Here, it's a little bit forced and awkward, but the employment of dynamics within a song was a quality that always marked Genesis out from so many contemporaries.

The band were back at the BBC on 22 February, perhaps as a result of their exposure on *Genesis Plays Jackson*, to record a session for Jon Curle's *Nightride* radio show, a programme known for featuring new, up and coming rock bands. Getting a slot on there was a coup for Genesis and they performed six songs: 'Shepherd', 'Pacidy', 'Let Us Now Make Love', 'Dusk', 'Looking for Someone' and 'Stagnation'. The material was a reflection of their live set at the time, an eccentric list that saw the band opening with acoustic numbers before gradually building up to the more aggressive songs later in the gig.

A little like *Genesis Plays Jackson*, the first three tracks in that list are the most intriguing now given that they didn't make it onto *Trespass* and so became long lost songs from their body of work until they were aired again on the BBC in the 1990s by Alan Freeman, though by that time the tapes of 'Dusk' had gone missing. 'Shepherd' opens in a similar vein to 'Looking for Someone', though Gabriel's vocal here is preceded by a piano introduction. There's also a brief Banks solo vocal on the song, singing a couple of verses in the pastoral opening as Gabriel plays flute, and then a backing line to Gabriel later too. It's quite a slight song and it's Gabriel's dramatic performance that really grabs the attention, the guitar accompaniment that comes in midway so low down in the mix as to be barely audible, with Banks' piano part lacking in character by his increasingly impressive standards – it's nothing like as strong as his playing on 'Frustration' for instance. It has a touch of the 'singer/songwriter' about it, no surprise at a time when people like Joni Mitchell, James Taylor and Neil Young were becoming so significant.

'Pacidy' is a much stronger track, beginning around a 12-string part but gradually building across its near six minutes, illustrating Banks' growing mastery of the organ as an instrument while Rutherford is getting to grips with his role on bass guitar. At this stage, it must have been a strong contender for their next album, although it doesn't have the same strength of atmosphere as 'White Mountain', which was probably the song it ended up competing with by that time.

The importance of Gabriel as a flautist has been undervalued, but it's illustrated in his melody, which opens 'Let Us Now Make Love'. The song develops into quite the best of the three that didn't make it to *Trespass*, deftly illustrating an improving understanding of a song's internal dynamics compared with 'Resignation' on *Genesis Plays Jackson*. The choruses swell to an effective crescendo, Gabriel swathed in blocks of backing vocals that bear similarity to the later recorded version of 'Visions of Angels' and giving a nod to another important influence, Crosby, Stills & Nash. Its biggest weakness is in its title, forever tethering it to the kaftans, beads, incense and Woodstock era – which, in fairness, they were then living through – in the same way that the putative band name The Champagne Meadow would have done.

With 'Dusk' having disappeared, we are left with just two of the early *Trespass* songs still available. 'Looking for Someone' is essentially the same as the album version, though Gabriel's vocal is more bluesy, giving an indication of the influence of Roger Chapman, singer with Family, while when the whole band comes in, it's with a real crash; John Mayhew is particularly prominent, making the most of a rare opportunity to shine on the session. The lyrics aren't quite finished and we're treated to more Gabrielese, but the song does a better job of conjuring up the *Trespass* sound than any of the others, Phillips underscoring his importance to the band with some terrific lead playing that really cuts through. Thanks to the best-known elements of his solo work, especially *The Geese & The Ghost* and the *Private Parts & Pieces* series, history has characterised Phillips as essentially an acoustic and 12-string guitarist but had things worked out differently, here was a potential guitar hero in the making.

Of the five pieces that have survived from the session, the best song is 'Stagnation', in hindsight the obvious pointer to how Genesis would develop. Initially, it's the same song that made it to the album in terms of its structure though the playing is rather different, especially the guitars. Banks' keyboard solo, which acts as the bridge from acoustic to electric, hasn't yet crystallised into the familiar version, and it becomes clear this is a work in progress with more thought required on the final section after the 'I want a drink' vocal. There's a staccato breakdown, a device they were clearly toying with since it's apparent on *Genesis Plays Jackson* too, but one which didn't really work. Then, going into the final minute, there's a very awkward and unconvincing join of two distinct sections to let them return to the opening 'Here today' melody. Joining lots of disparate bits was to become a forte with the band, but not on this occasion. The final verse that follows, one that didn't make it to the final version, has Gabriel's lead line drenched in backing vocals, something used rather more effectively later on 'Visions of Angels' and wisely discarded here.

These recordings early in 1970 showcase a very different Genesis to the Decca band, not surprisingly according to Anthony Phillips:

There was an awful lot going into the pot in those early Genesis records, especially by the time we got to 1969, which was when we started to do probably more complicated music. Tony was bringing in his classical background, his knowledge of the lighter classical pieces, Holst and Rimsky-Korsakov and so on, so there were elements of that. Remember, we'd been through not just the more complicated Beatles albums by then, which we'd all listened to and absorbed, but very importantly, you had Procol Harum, Fairport Convention, Family, all those bands in that more progressive area, who were writing longer songs, bringing forward more complicated ideas. 'Looking for Someone', I thought Peter sounded like Steve Winwood, and the 12-string sound, I was quite influenced by John Whitney in Family – I remember Tony being very shocked when he first heard one of their things, he said, 'Bloody hell, you've cribbed that!' The first King Crimson album was a huge influence. Then Tony and Peter were influenced more by Tamla Motown than Mike and I were, they were very keen on that, so there was so much going on, all kinds of influences. I think because there was so much feeding into the band, being processed by all of us in our different ways, by the time it came out into the songs, it was a reasonably original sound with its own identity. I don't think we were slavish to anyone.

Genesis had become increasingly busy as a live act since the turn of the year, and music industry people were beginning to take note. They were invited to do demos for the Moody Blues' Threshold label as part of a ridiculously busy few days in early March. They checked in to do that session at De Lane Lea Studios in London on 8 March, finishing up at 6 am the following morning. That night, 9 March, they played in Sunderland, and then the following evening, they were back in London to continue their residency in the upstairs room at Ronnie Scott's. Then on 11 March, it was over to the Roundhouse in London's Chalk Farm to play as part of the *Atomic Sunrise* festival which was being staged with the co-operation of Yoko Ono. David Bowie was also on the bill, the acts playing to a tiny audience.

The Threshold session, supervised by Mike Pinder of the Moody Blues, did not go especially well, although the label retained some interest in them, as did Island Records, Gabriel's preferred destination. But in the end, fate smiled on them, for they were to find the perfect home in Charisma Records. Charisma producer and A&R man John Anthony saw them in action at Ronnie Scott's and was so impressed that he chased across to one of the nearby Soho watering holes to find label boss Tony Stratton Smith (known to everyone as Strat) and dragged him along to see the end of their set. He was instantly impressed and quickly concluded that Genesis would slot in perfectly on Charisma alongside Van der Graaf Generator, The Nice, Rare Bird and Lindisfarne.

Genesis continued playing live until the middle of April, at which point Phillips was struck down by bronchial pneumonia, particularly nasty coming on top of a bout of glandular fever the previous year, creating a six-week hiatus as he was given time to recover. Even by then, no more than 50 gigs into their career, the live circuit had wrought dramatic changes on their music, for already the more acoustic, delicate pieces such as 'Shepherd', 'Pacidy' and others that never saw a release such as 'Little Leaf' had begun falling by the wayside.

When you're an unknown band, unless you're specifically playing folk clubs – which they weren't – tinkling 12-string guitars don't cut through the noise from the bar and so gradually it was the louder songs that survived, including 'Going Out To Get You', a slightly lumpen, very Stones-influenced rocker, a demo of which was released in the *1970-1975* box. It worked onstage, but it's not a song that survives too many plays and, quite rightly, when the band came to work out the songs that would make it to *Trespass*, it lost out to 'The Knife'. If in concert all the softest acoustic stuff had been trampled beneath the sound of punters going to the bar, 'The Knife' had its revenge and pinned them to the walls. The songs were selecting themselves for their forthcoming record.

Trespass (1970)

Personnel: Tony Banks, Peter Gabriel, John Mayhew, Anthony Phillips, Mike Rutherford
Producer: John Anthony
Engineer: Robin Cable
Cover art: Paul Whitehead
Recorded at Trident Studios, London, June – July 1970.
Released: 23 October 1970
Label: Charisma Records
Running time: 42:56
Tracklisting: 1. Looking for Someone 2. White Mountain 3. Visions of Angels 4. Stagnation 5. Dusk 6. The Knife
All songs by Banks/Gabriel/Mayhew/Phillips/Rutherford.

Genesis returned to the boards in June, just prior to going into Trident Studios to work on their first Charisma album. An article in *Sounds* early the following year suggested that they spent two months in there, honing the record, but that's something the band themselves now deny. Two weeks was nearer the mark, all that the budget would stretch to for such a new band. Even that was a luxury for a band of such little studio experience, and the nervousness that that created was something producer John Anthony quickly picked up on. He told *Melody Maker*,

'Often I go down and sing with the bands in the studio. Like with Genesis singer Peter Gabriel, who lacks confidence when he goes into the studio. It helps him to build confidence in his singing.'

If Gabriel was lacking in confidence, then John Anthony certainly built it up for the album opener, 'Looking for Someone'. Although Gabriel is backed by Banks playing organ, that is so low down in the mix that it feels as though he's singing the first couple of lines a cappella, channelling Otis Redding this time rather than the blues inflections of the BBC version. It institutes what became a real Genesis strength over the next few years, opening an album not merely with one of the best songs in the set, but one of the most arresting and idiosyncratic – think 'The Musical Box', 'Watcher of the Skies' and 'Dancing With the Moonlit Knight', which has a similarly naked vocal opening to 'Looking for Someone'.

Their ability to 'join the bits' had clearly improved over the first half of 1970 because 'Looking for Someone' was very much a jigsaw but one which held together seamlessly, their use of dynamics considerably improved from the *Genesis Plays Jackson* sessions at the beginning of the year. It's a song that started with Gabriel and it quickly became plain on this, and on 'The Knife' too, that he had very different preoccupations to the others in the band. Banks, Phillips and Rutherford were very concentrated on music for its own sake, that was their focus in life, where for Gabriel, while he loved music, it was as much about what it could do and what it symbolised that energised him.

Reflecting on growing up in the late 1960s as part of the Genesis box set interviews, he said, 'There was so much going on, *IT* [International Times] and *Oz* magazines, there was this cultural explosion happening. There was this sense that youth for the very first time, was taking over the world and that every barrier was being smashed. In our small, isolated little cell, we definitely felt connected to that, me probably more than anybody else.' Gabriel's later life, in solo songs such as 'Biko', 'Wallflower' and many others, his involvement with political causes such as Amnesty International and The Elders and his work with WOMAD underscored that wider interest, but even in a song as early as 'Looking for Someone', his disdain for the Establishment was evident in lines such as 'Keep on a straight line / I don't believe I can' and 'Your mumbo-jumbo never tells me anything'.

The song ends in an extended group improvised passage, each of them getting a moment in the spotlight before the piece quickly moves onto the next idea, nothing outstaying its welcome but equally, none of the moments getting too long to shine. As time went on, they would gradually move towards sitting with a mood, an atmosphere, an idea for longer, as they did on sections in *The Lamb Lies Down on Broadway*.

The cliché says that progressive rock is all about hobbits and fairies and dungeons and dragons. Genesis weren't often to be found working in that area, they were generally earthier than that, but they had their moments. Even then, 'White Mountain' had a lyric written by Banks based on characters from *White Fang*, a book by Jack London, an author well known for socialist leanings that wouldn't have found favour among the Charterhouse hierarchy of the time. It's the allegorical tale of One-Eye, leader of the wolf pack, hunting down and eventually killing Fang, seen as a traitor for venturing into territory forbidden to him, the rest of the pack trading the search for knowledge for a quiet life under One-Eye's reign.

Musically, it's the work of Phillips and Rutherford, a beautiful depiction of their combined 12-string playing, giving the song, and the album, a character apart from any other band of the time. The faster sections, featuring a galloping organ part, evoke the chase and the fight sequences followed by a more pastoral section in the aftermath, flute and guitars combining beautifully. It was something of a forgotten song from the Gabriel years, undeservedly so, until the band exhumed it for the *A Trick of the Tail* tour in 1976. Like a number of the songs on *Trespass*, it's a compromise between the acoustic and electric worlds, those dynamic shifts the root of its appeal.

The world might have heard 'Visions of Angels' rather earlier than it did, for it was slated to appear on *From Genesis to Revelation* before missing the cut, much to the dismay of its writer, Anthony Phillips, who composed it on piano. It had dropped off the radar but reappeared in time for *Trespass*, the only song from that early period to survive, albeit that it was revisited for this recording, Banks, in particular, working with Phillips on the majestic instrumental section in the middle that really elevates the song, further showcasing the way in which Phillips and Rutherford were so in sync on guitar. The arrival of the Mellotron in the final run is especially effective and an indicator of just how important it was going to be over the coming years. Phillips was complimentary about the way in which John Mayhew's drumming had contributed to improving it from the original version, and it does need saying that as a player on the album, Mayhew is holding his own despite the demands of the music – this was not straight rock'n'roll drumming. If you had listened to *Trespass* at the time, unaware of what was to come, you wouldn't necessarily leave the album with the thought that the drummer was holding them back. As Phillips was to point out later, Mayhew was to be the victim of one of fate's crueller tricks – he was succeeded on the drum stool by a genius who made most drummers' efforts, not least his predecessor's, pale by comparison.

The 'Visions of Angels' lyric has survived a little less well, the lovelorn poetry identifiably of its time, both in terms of the calendar (1968) and Phillips' age, just 16 when he penned it. Yet it's honest and heartfelt and if it still carries that slightly naïve quality that was so prevalent on *From Genesis to Revelation*, that brings with it a certain charm.

Opening the second side is 'Stagnation', the most important track on the record, a bona fide Genesis classic, far more so than the more celebrated 'The Knife'. It began to come together at the same time as 'F Sharp', Phillips and Rutherford demoing a whole host of 12-string pieces at Send Barns in 1969, some of which found their way into the first Genesis epic, a 30-minute song called 'The Movement'. That never made it to the recording studio, but sections from it did within 'Stagnation' where they were worked on further by the whole band, group written pieces very often the strongest material rather than those that were essentially the work of one or a pair of songwriters.

That opening section where the 12-strings weave in and out of one another certainly betrayed the fact that they'd been listening to early Fairport Convention as well as Family, but there is a uniquely Genesis voice to it. The grasp of dynamics is masterly, a meandering acoustic instrumental section involving the guitars and a muted organ part following on from the opening verse building a tension that is suddenly smashed when Banks comes in with an organ solo playing off the guitars to create something genuinely thrilling. The temperature cools again for what starts off as a quieter vocal section before Gabriel gradually builds up to a full-throated performance in the 'I want a drink' section.

The problems evident in the final section on the *Nightride* recording had all been resolved by now, a flute melody – which they later incorporated into live performances of 'I Know What I Like' – carrying 'Stagnation' to a much more satisfying conclusion. But it isn't merely musically that the song acts as a signpost towards the motherlode they would so successfully mine in the future, for Gabriel's darkly surreal story of the fate of Thomas S. Eiselberg points to not just future lyrics, but the stories that he would come to tell onstage as he adopted the otherworldly persona that helped him overcome his shyness and become such an extravagant front man. As noted on the sleeve, Eiselberg's post-apocalyptic tale is of a man 'who was wise enough to spend all his fortunes in burying himself many miles beneath the ground. As the only surviving member of the human race, he inherited the whole world.' Not exactly 'In the Summertime', the Mungo Jerry hit that was number one in the UK all the time the band were in the studio recording *Trespass*.

Using thick blocks of supporting vocals was very much a characteristic of the album, the rest of the band chiming in as a heavenly choir throughout proceedings, sometimes even taking over the lead from Gabriel as they do on alternate verses on 'Dusk', Phillips the leading voice. In some respects, this was the sound element that changed the most between *Trespass* and its follow up, for while Phillips' acoustic side was lost to a certain extent on his departure, Rutherford was still there to fight that corner. But with the advent of Phil Collins as a singer as well as a drummer, it made perfect sense for Banks and Rutherford to now leave backing vocals well alone.

Pared down by a couple of minutes from the August 1969 demo version that was later released on the *Archive 1967-75* set, 'Dusk' continues that delicate combination of 12-string and classical guitar, Phillips' lyric this time looking at life, rather than love, slipping away, a meditation on a life already lived from the viewpoint of an elderly man. It could be dismissed as being maudlin, as teenagers often are, but there's some striking imagery in there, while in the couplet 'If a leaf has fallen / Does the tree lie broken?' it's tempting to speculate if, subconsciously, he might have already been beginning to wonder if his time in Genesis was coming towards a close.

After their debut album had been so deeply rooted in stories from the Bible, even to the extent of the album title, it would have been reasonable to expect that, still saddled with the name Genesis, they might do everything possible to distance themselves from those connections. But no, from the mention of a Damascene conversion on 'Looking for Someone' and 'Visions of Angels' itself, the record was full of such references, 'Dusk' as much as any, speaking of 'A false move by God' and 'Once a Jesus suffered'. It extended to the album name, a nod to The Lord's Prayer as well as the theme of 'White Mountain', and to the cover artwork by Paul Whitehead, which looked as though it might have been taken from an illustrated version of the King James Bible, decorated further with angels, and a dove of peace. That slightly fey symbolism was then subverted with a heavy dose of violence as the canvas was slashed through the middle by a knife, its jewelled handle still sticking out from the wound.

That knife made its presence felt in the title of the album's final track, the military stomp that was also the final song in their live set. Born out of Gabriel's determination to get something more ballsy onto the album, it had begun with the working title of 'The Nice', a nod to his appreciation of Keith Emerson's band of the time, an enthusiasm shared by Banks, the two of them often catching their shows at the Marquee in London. As Gabriel was at pains to point out later, this was Emerson prior to ELP where, for some tastes, including the singer's, things got a little too pretentious. The Nice, in contrast, were a band sufficiently hip for Jimi Hendrix to ask if he could join them at one point.

'The Knife' opens with a real attack, the opening section penned by Gabriel, and there was a hit single in there struggling to get out had they chosen to condense it – a 1971 single release that featured the song in two parts on either side of a 45 met with no takers – and they did play it that way as an encore in later days around the time of the *Duke* tour and just beyond. After the aggression of the first three minutes, there's a meandering atmospheric section that dissolves into a lovely flute melody before all hell breaks loose again with a musical depiction of a riot that catches the febrile mood of the late '60s and early '70s, evoking the civil rights protests, anti-Vietnam demos and the then-recent Kent State University shootings that took place at the start of May 1970.

Gabriel's lyric – with a little help from Phillips – was intended as a parody of a protest song but it cuts deeper than that. Following the Marxist dictum (Groucho not Karl), it pointed the finger at those who would replace the leaders, noting that those who want to lead are, by definition, unfit to do so: 'Some of YOU are going to die' indeed. 'The Knife' warned against the zeitgeist in much the same way that Woody Allen's film *Bananas* did the following year – revolutions against dictators often simply beget new dictators.

'The Knife' bowed out on a ferocious guitar solo from Anthony Phillips, which, as it turned out, was his swansong. He admitted that he had pretty much coasted through the making of the record, having all but made the decision that he was not able to continue with the band any longer:

I suddenly started to get paralytically nervous before the gigs, then I got physically ill with bronchial pneumonia. I just got very depressed as you tend to when you're ill and I had to ask myself, 'Why am I doing this, it was supposed to be fun?' It suddenly became a job. It was very all-consuming – it was great to be committed and not dilettante about it, but

I felt it was becoming threatening. I was blitzed, I didn't feel I could talk to anyone about it and I just felt that my whole position with them was untenable. Even aside from the stage-fright aspect, which was grim, the experience on the road was not great, we were just going through the same thing every night, playing the same set all the time. We didn't have time to rehearse any new material and we had no life outside the group. We used to literally do the gig, pack up the gear, go all the way home, unload the gear, do it again. There was no thought of going out socialising with anyone. People say now, 'You knew Nick Drake, he came to your gigs, you played with him, what was he like?' I have no idea, because we hardly ever talked to him. We were getting in the van and leaving as quick as we could! It wasn't glamorous at all, it was a terribly isolated existence and of course, we made the mistake of working too hard and living on top of one another, so everybody got on each other's nerves. We would fall out and things could get a bit frosty. We used to get at Peter quite a bit, which was terribly unfair, because although his ideas were ahead of their time as was to be shown, he wasn't very good at explaining them! He didn't have an instrument to demonstrate things, a lot of his stuff was conceptual, so we tended to get frustrated with him and it just became a bit unpleasant really. They realised later that they couldn't live together, they needed space from each other and that improved things. What that intense and intensive period did do was turn us into a much more professional fighting force, but in hindsight, maybe it could have been done in a different way. It was sad in a way, we did become distant from each other, we weren't having a great time, to be honest. We were young and we didn't know how to deal with it all. There was the odd gig where we would go down really well and get the surge of adrenalin and that was great, but a lot of gigs weren't like that. It was a real mish-mash of weird gigs, we did some absolutely ridiculous things. We genuinely did play to an audience of one in a pub in the East End, and Peter said, 'Any requests?'

For all that's been written about Genesis and about Phillips' departure across the years, one thing seems to have been ignored – just how young he was, even compared with the others. Wind back a year to the playback of *From Genesis to Revelation*. When Phillips heard how Jonathan King had smothered their album with strings and how that had affected the stereo mix, in particular, he stormed out in horror, later wondering just how it was that the others had been so much more mature. The simple answer? Look at the calendar.

On his final departure after a show at Hayward's Heath on 18 July 1970, Phillips was just 18 years old. Banks and Gabriel were comparatively old men at 20, Rutherford just two months away from joining them at that milestone. At that age, that age gap is very significant, probably even more so among a group of ex-public schoolboys 50 years ago, for they had been brought up to clamp on the stiff upper lip. Back then, they were also living in a culture where mental health was barely ever discussed. Phillips' entirely natural response in that environment was not to admit to the problem, to show no sign of 'weakness' and to just get on with it. Thankfully, things have progressed a bit since those days, but in 1970 it meant Anthony Phillips really had no option but to throw in the towel.

It was a huge shame, both for him personally and for the band, for all their later successes and for all that they were able to replace him with another brilliant and highly original guitarist in Steve Hackett. His legacy was that without his early drive, without the obsessive zeal that he brought to Genesis – which was ultimately to prove his downfall – the group might never have got off the ground. He was the one who pushed them to turn professional in 1969 when the others were embarking on further education, he was the one who wanted them to become a live band. If you look at the tracks on those first two records, his songwriting is all over it, and the 12-string sound was very much his creation, Rutherford a supportive and talented partner in that endeavour. He was absolutely crucial to Genesis.

The departure of the man the others looked upon as the closest thing they had to a leader was a serious and potentially fatal blow. Initially, it looked as if the band would implode and the various members go their separate ways, but gradually they came to the conclusion that they would press on after all. The different nature of Genesis as an entity played a huge part here because they were a band apart from so many contemporaries who were comprised of players who dabbled in songwriting. The Nice, for example, was impossible to think of without Keith Emerson and his musical fireworks. But Banks, Gabriel and Rutherford were writers and even if Phillips had been perhaps the most important, the bulk of that songwriting collective was still in harness. In addition, although he was a fine musician and imaginative guitarist, Phillips was not a showman; he wasn't the axe hero that the audience had come to see the way they might go to see Jimmy Page, Jeff Beck or Ritchie Blackmore. He was one of the four men studiously sitting at their instruments while Gabriel tried to inject a bit of movement into things.

And, having yet to release *Trespass*, Genesis had no real following and so the existing five-piece was not set in stone in the mind of the public. In short, hindsight tells us that having launched the ship, if Phillips had to get into the lifeboat and return to shore, he went at the point where it would do the least damage to the band.

Actually, that wasn't quite true in the case of drummer John Mayhew, for Banks, Gabriel and Rutherford concluded that if they were going to carry on, they needed a new drummer. Mayhew's performance on *Trespass* had been perfectly solid, notwithstanding a flat drum sound in the studio, pretty typical for the time, but they all found that he was a slow learner and didn't offer enough creatively at the arrangement stage on new songs. Mayhew was out, and then there were three…

The search for replacements started out in the back pages of *Melody Maker*, as was the way at the time, and their anonymous advert, which stood out among the classifieds by virtue of being boxed in, caught the eye of Flaming Youth's drummer, Phil Collins (born 30 January 1951). A former child actor – a period that history has distilled down into playing the Artful Dodger in *Oliver!*, storming off the set in *Calamity the Cow* and posing for knitting patterns – Collins was becoming increasingly disenchanted with his band who, despite having released the album *Ark 2* in November 1969, were struggling to get much live work. The advert explained that Tony Stratton Smith was looking for a drummer and guitarist 'sensitive to acoustic music' and that piqued Collins' interest given that he already knew Strat pretty well from frequenting the bar at the Marquee and other drinking dens in Soho. Thinking the job would be his simply for the asking, he was surprised to find that he'd have to go and audition for it, but was at least encouraged to hear that it was Genesis who were looking, having regularly seen their name in the gig guides.

In early August 1970, he and Flaming Youth's guitarist Ronnie Caryl headed to Peter Gabriel's parents' house to audition, arriving well ahead of time. Collins had the opportunity to listen to a number of other drummers trying out the audition pieces the band had set, so when it was his turn, he breezed through it, quickly making the job his own, something Gabriel confirmed to him in a phone call on 8 August. Caryl was not so fortunate, though he was asked back to rehearse with the band on several occasions that month.

The four settled in to rehearse with Collins across the next six weeks in between auditioning for a new guitar player, but when they returned to the live arena on 2 October 1970, Rutherford's 20th birthday, it was as a four-piece, with Banks trying to cover some of the lead guitar parts, Rutherford using bass pedals extensively to allow him to play guitar throughout the set too. It proved a valuable learning experience for both, particularly Banks, though, at Collins' behest, Caryl did feature on their final show in October when they opened for Medicine Head. It was the day that *Trespass* was released to a largely disinterested world – it reputedly sold around 6,000 copies on its initial release.

Guitarist Mick Barnard was at that gig. He had played in an Aylesbury band called The Farm and auditioned twice for Genesis in late October before playing his first gig in Barnet on 3 November. But it was an uneasy alliance and when Gabriel noticed an ad in *Melody Maker* in mid-December, he thought they might have found their man. 'Imaginative guitarist/writer seeks involvement with receptive musicians determined to strive beyond existing stagnant music forms.' It was the same edition of the paper that featured a review of *Trespass* in which Michael Watt wrote, 'It's tasteful, subtle and refined but with enough spunk in the music to prevent the album from becoming a self-indulgent wallow in insipidity'. A good omen?

Banks and Gabriel went to meet the advert's author, Steve Hackett (born 12 February 1950) and were impressed with what they found, to the point where they invited him to come and watch them play a free lunchtime show at the Lyceum in London on 28 December 1970. On seeing that show, he was as intrigued by them as they were with him. The famous five was complete.

1971: The Winding Stream, and In Between

There were to be two more shows for the band with Mick Barnard in tow, at Manchester Arts Club on the third and then in High Wycombe on 5 January 1971. After that one, Peter Gabriel took the guitarist aside and told him his time with Genesis was up. Quoted in Mario Giammetti's *Genesis: 1967 to 1975 – The Peter Gabriel Years*, Barnard said, 'I didn't feel cheated by anything. It was just not a very nice experience at that time. I do feel that they could have been a little bit more honest with the situation, instead of just keep saying, 'We'll let you know'.'

Genesis played four shows as a four-piece again before Steve Hackett made his debut at University College, London, on 14 January. The gig was not a roaring success, Phil Collins admitting, 'That was the night I decided to see how many pints of Newcastle Brown you could drink and still be able to play. I know I had too many!' Hackett weathered that storm, for reserved and sometimes insecure as he was in the company of the rest of Genesis early on, there was a steely determination within him too. Having joined Quiet World and released an album with them, *The Road,* in 1969, he had parted company when there was a disagreement over the final mix, albeit that the band was very much a 'don't give up the day job' operation.

Genesis, in contrast, was the day job, the night job, the weekend job, the holiday job. Although they now all had their own space and were no longer living on top of each other, the workload remained intense. Hackett's first real test came in their first properly organised tour of England, comprising seven shows in the final week of January and a couple more the following month.

The brainchild of Tony Stratton Smith, harking back to the rock'n'roll package tours that did the rounds in the 1950s and 1960s, the *Charisma Six Bob Tour* gave audiences the chance to watch three Charisma acts on the same bill for the princely sum of six shillings as it was until decimalisation kicked in in the UK on 15 February, a couple of days after the final show – the 'Charisma 30p Tour' wouldn't have had quite the same ring to it. Genesis opened the show, followed by Lindisfarne and then Van der Graaf Generator, a great opportunity to reach new fans given that the other two acts commanded a bigger following at that point. The combined pulling power of the three allowed them to play some prestigious venues, including Birmingham Town Hall, Manchester Free Trade Hall and Newcastle City Hall, among others, playing to packed houses throughout.

Lindisfarne's Rod Clements recalls in a YouTube clip from *Tyneidols. com* the pecking order on the tour bus:

> Van der Graaf Generator were at the back, getting up to all sorts of strange, exotic practices that we knew nothing about at all. Chemistry sets and things! Genesis were occupying the front seats, with bottles of sherry and mineral water and cameras to take pictures of the countryside, pointing out cathedrals. We were in the middle, but eventually, everything got mixed up. But it was a very interesting cross-cultural exercise.

Gabriel remembers something akin to Beatlemania:

> Lindisfarne especially were attracting a lot of fans at this point and the tour manager got it into his head that we needed some security. At one point, he had the whole tour crawl out the bathroom window at the back of some theatre and straight onto the tour bus!

The tour was a success, so much so that it was repeated in April, and for Genesis, it meant playing to bigger crowds than ever before and winning plenty of new fans as they went. It was also an important opportunity for Collins and especially the less naturally gregarious Hackett to get to know their new colleagues. 'I think both Phil and I found it hard at first. The band had grown up together and it seemed like they had their own language and were on a different wavelength. I didn't always know what they were talking about.'

The spring and summer saw the band working the UK's club circuit, clocking up the miles up and down the country, as well as experiencing their first trip abroad when they played a gig in Belgium on 7 March, capitalising on the fact that *Trespass* had reached number one in the charts there. The gig was followed by a couple of days in a TV studio there, recording material that was never screened in the end. The live set they played in Brussels featured a lot of hitherto unrecorded material, including the hardy perennial 'Going Out To Get You', along with 'Happy the Man' and 'Twilight Alehouse', which would later get released on singles. They also played 'The Light', an early Collins tune and another track that fell by the wayside but which was cannibalised later, forming part of 'Lilywhite Lilith' on *The Lamb Lies Down on Broadway*. That aside, there was little to really commend it, underlining the problem that besets any working band – finding the opportunity to write new material while spending so much time on the road is never easy.

Gabriel resolved the issue in fairly spectacular fashion. Reaching the encore of 'The Knife' at a show in Aylesbury on 19 June, the singer was so caught up in the moment that he jumped off the stage, the crowd parted and he fell and broke his ankle. The band were still able to play a handful of shows with Gabriel on crutches or in a wheelchair, including a slot at the Reading Festival, but July and August were largely given over to writing more new material to add to 'The Musical Box'. That was well played in by now and was already broadly in its finished state when showcased on another BBC session, recorded for *Sounds of the Seventies* on 10 May, a few minor differences in the arrangement notwithstanding. They also had a version of 'Harlequin', a leftover from Anthony Phillips' time in the band and the most *Trespass* sounding song that made it onto the next album, and elements of 'The Fountain of Salmacis' which had been further refined since the *Genesis Plays Jackson* session, mutating into a song called 'Ketch'.

Off the road for the summer, they decamped to Tony Stratton Smith's country home, Luxford House in Crowborough, to write, luxuriating in the acquisition of a new Mellotron and a Gibson Les Paul. With producer John Anthony on board again, able to visit them on-site and listen to the songs and make suggestions before they headed back to Trident Studios in August, the pre-production phase was ideal and while Mike Rutherford has since said that he found writing the album quite difficult, some strong new material emerged. More than that, Genesis became a sonically different prospect with the addition of Collins and Hackett, who were certainly the two most proficient players in the band on a technical level at that point, bringing a new edge to the music, as Hackett noted:

I got the impression they had grown up as songwriters and, whilst I'd written stuff, I regarded myself as a player, although that changed as I developed and started to write more. By the time I met Genesis, it seemed as if the band frowned on blues, saw it as overly simplistic. They didn't want to sound anything like Deep Purple, whereas I suspect I would have been perfectly happy to sound either like Deep Purple or Procol Harum. I didn't have any prejudice in that same sense.

Nursery Cryme

Personnel: Tony Banks, Phil Collins, Peter Gabriel, Steve Hackett, Mike Rutherford
Producer: John Anthony
Engineer: David Hentschel

Cover art: Paul Whitehead
Recorded at Trident Studios, London, August 1971.
Released: 12 November 1971
Label: Charisma Records
Running time: 39:26
Tracklisting: 1. The Musical Box 2. For Absent Friends 3. The Return of the Giant Hogweed 4. Seven Stones 5. Harold the Barrel 6. Harlequin 7. The Fountain of Salmacis
All songs by Banks/Collins/Gabriel/Hackett/Rutherford.

When *Nursery Cryme* was released 13 months after *Trespass*, it showcased a band that had subtly changed the terrain on which it operated. Genesis still had its contrasts, its light and shade, its serenity and its chaos, but while the acoustic element remained, there was a very definite shift towards the electric end of things. Further, the arrival of Collins meant that backing vocals were now very much his domain, the thicker blocks of harmony vocal replaced by something a little lighter, something that didn't take up so much of the sound spectrum.

Beyond that, more of the identifiably Genesis personality began to seep into the music, a peculiarly English sensibility, more so than any of the contemporaries with whom they were linked. Within Genesis, there was a surrealism that clothed a taste for the macabre particularly evident in Gabriel's lyrics and in concert stories, as well as the kind of suppressed rage that nobody endures the way an Englishman does, especially one that's been through the public school system. Yet at the same time, there's a lyrical, romanticism there too, sometimes expressed in a Molesworthian 'hello clouds, hello sky' tweeness it's true, but done that way to avoid the risk of exposing deeper feelings, which takes us back to the top of the circle where it feeds into that suppressed rage again. If you think of it in that way, the act that was closest to Genesis wasn't Yes or the Moody Blues, it was Monty Python. There is the suffocating frustration that ate away at Basil Fawlty on the one hand, the doomed heroism and romantic daring-do of *Ripping Yarns* on the other. They were a genuinely funny band when they chose to be, too, something that legions of critics missed but which was blazingly obvious to their supporters. Little wonder that the Pythons ended up on Charisma Records as well.

'The Musical Box' is a beautiful illustration of all those strands, from the gentle opening 12-string through to the demonic denouement when the band is hurling a showroom full of kitchen sinks at it. It's a genuinely harrowing musical moment and that's before Gabriel got to acting it out on stage. The lyric is one of his very best for Genesis, carrying those slightly malevolent tones that were a hallmark of his early work, while the story is concise and doesn't lose its way under the weight of imagery that other pieces could. Young Cynthia, taking the sport of croquet a little too seriously, using her mallet over-enthusiastically, separates her little brother Henry's head from his neck. Returning to the house after her game, Cynthia finds Henry's musical box and in opening it, she unleashes her brother's spirit, like the genie from the lamp, only to find that he has taken on the form of an old man with 70 years' worth of unfulfilled desires raging through his veins and other extremities. Little Cynthia finds herself the object of these desires as the song reaches its raging climax, if you'll pardon the pun. It's questionable whether a band could write a song like that nowadays without igniting a Twitter storm, but I'm sure we all have our views on whether the policing of art represents progress or not.

Powerful as the song is, it's given further potency by the album sleeve, which is largely derived from the lyric, Cynthia holding her mallet aloft on a croquet lawn full of decapitated heads, a subversion of *Alice in Wonderland* in its way. I must confess that along with *Wind and Wuthering*, it's my favourite album cover, to the point where I've got a lithograph of it above my desk as I write this. There is something about this Paul Whitehead sleeve that captures the essence of that early period Genesis. It's funny, darkly surreal, has more than a hint of the Gothic about it and is full of intricate little details such as the hogweed on the back cover, the scene from 'Harold the Barrel' in the background and the dead flies stuck to the varnish, the painting dated 1871. It conjures up the Victorian setting of 'The Musical Box' perfectly and that carries through to the inner gatefold where the lyrics are placed within a scrapbook, each song depicted by a little vignette that brings it further to life. In the days when vinyl was the only real format in town, the *Nursery Cryme* sleeve took full advantage of that huge canvas and gave the listener something to luxuriate in as they contemplated these new Genesis sounds.

And what sounds they were on 'The Musical Box', not merely destined to become one of their greatest songs but another starter that drew you in, its delicate, jangling 12-string opening followed by Gabriel's murmured first lines forcing the listener to give the song their full attention, leaning into the speakers once again to better hear what was going on. The song had been constructed across a year or more, its origins in a brief demo put together by Anthony Phillips and Mike

Rutherford. The material was then worked upon by the four-piece Genesis in rehearsals at the Maltings in Farnham in the latter part of 1970 before Mick Barnard joined, the guitarist then adding much of the song's guitar solo during his brief spell in the band.

That it should have passed through so many hands before completion is extraordinary, for if anything underlined the potential of the new five-piece and their ensemble playing, it was 'The Musical Box'. Where sonically *Trespass* had been shrouded by fine mist, by the time the opening song had gone through all its changes, it was clear that on *Nursery Cryme*, they had burned that off. There was instantly more punch and presence to the sound and the fresh influence of Collins and Hackett was quickly apparent. Building on what they'd already done with 'Stagnation', the song built gradually through an opening acoustic passage, Collins injecting some telling backing harmonies, giving way to an electric section featuring a call and response between keyboards and guitar that was to become something of a Genesis feature – you'd even find it as late as 'Abacab' for instance. Hackett flexes his muscles with a guitar solo over the top of the keyboard chords, introducing the world to tapping on the guitar, a technique he was to pioneer over the coming records and which would be heard to greater effect on 'The Return of the Giant Hogweed' later on the album.

The song crescendos on a typically majestic chord sequence from Banks, over which Gabriel conjures little Henry back to life with an explosively commanding vocal, much to Banks' initial dismay as he felt he was detracting from the music, but the singer was right, the two elements together creating something more powerful between them. Little wonder it was an instant stage classic.

One of the great benefits that early Genesis enjoyed was the opportunity to have distinct writing sessions away from being on the road. Though that could lead to fractious living arrangements, it also gave them the time to dedicate themselves to the work without being interrupted by having to get in the van and trundle off to Darlington, Southport or Truro to play a gig. It also meant that they could experiment with different ideas and writing set-ups, as was the case on 'For Absent Friends', a song that came mostly from Hackett but which he completed with Collins, the two new boys bringing forward a song for the village elders to consider. Hackett admitted later that he was probably too unsure of himself to offer up a lyric for Gabriel, the perceived star of the show, to sing, but it's a tune that better lends itself to Collins anyway. Hackett:

I keep coming back to The Beatles in general and specifically to 'Eleanor Rigby'. Four young guys from Liverpool, writing about the plight of an elderly woman, shortly to meet with her demise, all of that contained inside a couple of minutes of song, bringing in all the old instruments, downing their own out of reverence for the character, so much so that you feel you can smell the dust. For me, it's a character sketch, yet it becomes a full-blown portrait within those two minutes and that is the challenge for any contemporary writer in any field – can you engage people with those little snippets, those vignettes, those little moments in her life that we get to follow?

It's a brief thing, clocking in at well under two minutes, but lyrically and musically, it offers plenty and hints at more. 'Eleanor Rigby' catches the 'Tumbleweed Connection' on the way to 'Blood on the Rooftops', it's a little slice of life, two elderly widowers on their way to and from church on a Sunday evening, thinking back to the days when they both had partners. All the lonely people... Vocally, it's Collins in James Taylor mode, backed by Hackett and Rutherford on 12-string guitars, Banks on Pianet, a folky edge to a quintessentially English piece.

If you had turned up the volume to hear the lyrics better on this little acoustic number, you were quickly back across the room to turn it down again as 'The Return of the Giant Hogweed' fired up. This album's version of 'The Knife', it was the one real hard rocker they had, for all that *Nursery Cryme* was generally more aggressive than *Trespass*. Opening with Hackett's tapping technique playing in unison with Banks on electric piano, as with all Genesis' longer songs, it goes through distinct sections, dancing around Gabriel's lyric that is part *Day of the Triffids*, part Livingstone meets Stanley. Tapping into the mood of baroque Victoriana that pervades so much of the album, the tale of the hogweed, vengeful after being taken from its home in the Russian hills, spreading its seed and running rampant across England, suffocating the nation, is another of those stories that set Genesis apart from their contemporaries – it was far closer to the dark whimsy of the already passed Pink Floyd of Syd Barrett than the one that Roger Waters would lead through the 1970s for example. It was educational too – who amongst us hasn't found themselves shouting 'heracleum mantegazziani' at the TV whenever *Gardener's World* mentions the hogweed? It's okay, you're among friends.

The constraints of vinyl lead to *Nursery Cryme* being a slightly unbalanced album, the second side featuring three more muted numbers before going out in a blaze of glory on 'The Fountain of Salmacis'. Side two begins with 'Seven Stones', betraying those church influences again in the gradual keyboard swell to a crescendo before Gabriel adds a flute melody in a quietly atmospheric middle section. It's a song that adds just a little more to the audience's perception of the singer, this strange character who found it so hard to communicate in interviews, so introspective that in order to come through on stage, he was increasingly wrapping himself in different characters. The masks were to come later, but the monologues between songs, initially conjured up to cover the interminable tuning of 12-string guitars, were already building the perception of an other-worldly character, what Collins later described in many interviews as 'this mysterious, cosmic traveller', while Roy Carr saw him as a 'macabre entrepreneur' in the *New Musical Express*.

As a persona, it was increasingly useful, for it laid out the sense of him as a seer and sage, come amongst us to share his wisdom, though he was always ready, willing and able to undercut any creeping pomposity with a joke or an excruciating pun. Lyrics like 'I heard the old man tell his tale' from 'Seven Stones' only added to that, the singer cast as a bringer of ancient truths. In fact, it was mostly a lyric written by Banks, though the persistent references to changes and to chance are said to come from Gabriel dabbling in the *I Ching* at that time.

In contrast with much of the album where Banks' playing is often dominant, on 'Seven Stones', a song he largely wrote alone, it's much more restrained, the importance of the Mellotron they'd acquired from King Crimson becoming evident. Collins' lightness of touch across the song is an early indicator of just how important an influence he would become in colouring songs that might otherwise have been rather stiff, and again, his backing vocals are a delight.

He moved closer to the front of stage on 'Harold the Barrel', where he and Gabriel are often singing the lead lines in unison, the lighter tones in the drummer's voice ensuring that it's him that you hear rather better than the lead singer. For all that, it's a characteristically Gabriel song, drenched in his preoccupations with repressed English society. On the one hand, you have Harold, the seaside restaurant owner, crushed by the demands of convention and the rat race, eventually driven sufficiently mad by it all that he chops his own toes off and serves them up for his customers as a Bognor version of frogs' legs. Fleeing the scene and eventually deciding to end it all in time-honoured fashion by jumping off a high building, he is then confronted by various parties trying to stop him, not out of love and concern – that wouldn't be British – but because it would be a disreputable thing to do, especially given he's not wearing a clean shirt, thereby bringing disgrace on his family. And all in front of the BBC too!

Gabriel – with a little help from Collins on a couple of lines – was tapping into the deep vein of irritation that the younger generation had with their elders and their attachment to the British reserve and stiff upper lip that won an Empire, in much the same way that Monty Python did with the 'Pepperpots', the old ladies that they played themselves, forever muttering, 'Oh dear, there goes the neighbourhood!' whenever anything changed. Ironically, he was confronting the generation gap in that most British of styles, the Victorian comic operetta of Gilbert & Sullivan, the chorus of intellectually challenged policemen mumbling 'We can help you!' straight out of *The Pirates of Penzance*. It was a style that was rich with possibilities and one that he would return to subsequently in yet darker tones on 'Get 'Em Out by Friday' and 'The Battle of Epping Forest'.

'Harlequin' dials the pace down a little, its sweet, acoustic temperament in sharp contrast to the rollicking 'Harold the Barrel', recapturing that summery shimmer that was so apparent on *Trespass. Nursery Cryme* is, by and large, a much more claustrophobic record than its predecessor, Gabriel saying later that it was an album that took the band indoors, but 'Harlequin' is a break from that, a shaft of sunlight, all 12-strings out on the croquet lawn and not a severed head in sight. Other things might have been severed, however, for as well as Gabriel and Collins, Banks and Rutherford were pressed into vocal service on what Banks termed 'the castrati chorus'. In its time, 'Harlequin' suffered from the fact that Genesis were beginning to play bigger, louder venues. The accompanying winnowing out from the live set of the softer songs had begun prior to recording *Trespass*, so it rarely got much exposure in concert and has been rather forgotten as a consequence, even by the band. But on going back to the material for the remasters, remixes and 5.1 mixes for the box sets around 2007, Banks 'realised it was pretty good'. That's a typical understatement from the keyboard wizard, for it's an exquisite performance in which the guitars chime beautifully with the voices. Like so much of The Beatles' work, it's deceptively simple on the surface, but just below there are all kinds of little embellishments wheeling away, delicate touches from Mellotron and sleigh tambourine being perfect accents.

It's the block of vocal that most obviously stands out, but even then there are contrasts within that across the song, moving between four voices, then to Gabriel and Collins, to Gabriel alone singing 'Harlequin, Harlequin' or Collins singing the gorgeous top line 'All is not lost' above a bed of voices in the final verse, all of those changes hugely effective. Singles were not an essential part of the scene for a band like Genesis in those days, but why 'Harlequin' was never considered for release in the days when the singles chart could handle things that were rather more adventurous is mystifying.

Ending the album on a crescendo is 'The Fountain of Salmacis', like 'The Musical Box', a piece that had endured from the *Genesis Plays Jackson* sessions. Initially clocking in at nearly 15 minutes, it was hacked down by half by the time they came to put it on *Nursery Cryme*, but the editing lost none of the song's power nor scope. When critics talk of 'symphonic rock', there is no better example of the form than this, a fusion of orchestral approaches and rock music, genuinely progressive in every way. Moving on from the D'Oyly Carte of 'Harold the Barrel', this was the stuff of La Scala in Milan.

Banks had taken that initial organ introduction and had mixed it with Mellotron, the rising and falling of its sound like waves crashing off a beach. But throughout the song, it's the sound of the five-piece taking flight as an ensemble that is especially thrilling, a potent glimpse of what they could go on to create. Collins really comes to the fore, the step-up in quality that Genesis have finally found on the drum stool lifting everything, the music swinging far more than it had in the past, for all that John Mayhew was no slouch. Casting a glance at the First Division of the time, it was the difference between playing George Best instead of Clyde Best in your team. Collins' contribution in turn, was pulling Rutherford along with him, his bass playing on this by far the best he had offered Genesis thus far, his melodic sensibility that was so evident on 12-string now finding its way into the approach he brought to the bass. Gabriel seeks out the opportunity to add some lovely flute lines midway, giving a fresh texture. That they were now recording on 16-track rather than eight-track equipment was particularly helpful in adding these extra colours and giving them an opportunity to shine rather than having to have to fight to be heard.

Of course, it's Banks' work that underpins the song throughout on organ and Mellotron, both in solo flourishes and as an ensemble player. He and Hackett had already produced some fine moments playing in tandem on the album, but it's on 'The Fountain of Salmacis' that they are in excelsis, most notably at the end as Hackett unfurls a beautiful guitar solo across the final minute of the song, a wholly characteristic example of the liquid nature of so many of his solos, the river finally dissolving in the crashing sea of Banks' returning Mellotron at the end.

It's a formidable piece of work that should have been a stage favourite for years, but it never quite connected with audiences as it might have done – Italian crowds, who lapped up its operatic virtues, aside – perhaps because of its lyric. Gabriel wanted to use this a setting for a retelling of the Greek myth of Salmacis and Hermaphroditus, anything but standard fare in the year of 'Brown Sugar' by the Stones and 'Gimme Some Truth' by John Lennon. But for those willing to dig into something off the beaten track, Gabriel and Banks concocted a strong lyric, one that was perhaps a little more knowing and self-aware than it was given credit for. The waters of Salmacis, according to myth, would make men who drank from it effeminate and soft. Those had been some of the descriptions aimed at *Trespass* in particular and Genesis in general, so perhaps taking on such a subject amid music that was much more fiery, was a playful way of underlining that there was more going on under the surface of this group than might be obvious on first encounter.

And so *Nursery Cryme* reached its conclusion, a third version of Genesis having recorded their third album under the name. From gauche songwriting schoolboys on *From Genesis to Revelation*, to exploring what they might become as a working band on *Trespass*, to now assimilating two key new members on *Nursery Cryme*, to have created such strong work amid so many changes and with four of the members still only 21, Collins a year younger still, was a quite remarkable achievement. That the process had been successful was seen in the continuing decision to credit all five members on each of the songs, whatever their contribution, as Hackett explained:

> All titles by all? The idea was that early on, we considered the arrangement was as important as the song. Just because someone came up with the framework, it doesn't mean the spaces in between aren't important. We all had a crack at filling in the spaces, we were racking our brains to come up with original bits of detail. I guess at its best, the group mind was in force.

Nursery Cryme may not have been as consistent across its two sides as they might have wished, but in the circumstances of having to weather the storm of losing Anthony Phillips, it was a solid statement of intent. It's been overlooked a little across the years, the focus always on 'The Musical Box' and perhaps 'The Fountain of Salmacis' rather than the album as a whole, but there are little gems throughout the grooves and it deserves reassessment.

There was no pre-album single to give the profile a boost, but when the album did see the light of day on 12 November 1971, Charisma called on one of their former artists, Keith Emerson, now riding high with Emerson, Lake & Palmer, for an endorsement. As part of a full-page ad for the album, Emerson was quoted at some length:

These days it's hard for a new band to step over the line and gain recognition and be listened to, especially if their music contains hidden subtleties. In the light of such hardship it is important that the original conception should be carried through, worked on, and improved on, and to hope that sooner or later someone's going to 'dig' you. If nobody does, so what! You are a musician and that's what matters. There are a lot of people 'digging' Genesis but not enough; sooner or later, they are going to make it and you'll have wished you had been in on it at the start. This is not the start for Genesis, neither is it the end. No bullshit: Their new album really is incredible.

Emerson's enthusiasm might have been good for morale, but *Nursery Cryme* did not reach the charts – at least, not until May 1974 when it spent a week at number 39. Nonetheless, it marked a step forward, the reviews largely positive if a little bemused, Chris Charlesworth's in *Melody Maker* typical of the time: 'Genesis try a little harder than most. They don't so much lay down tracks as tell imaginative stories based on characters more suited to nursery rhymes than songs by a contemporary group. Theirs is an acquired taste. 'Harold the Barrel' is a lesson in fertile imagination to less original bands.'

Noting that fertile imagination was a fair comment, but it became something of a backhanded compliment over the years, suggesting that Genesis had their collective head in the clouds and were a bit too clever for their own good. There was an element of that perhaps, but this was a far more grounded group than most gave credit for, whatever their eccentricities. On the surface, *Nursery Cryme* is mostly rooted in Victoriana, but it uses 1871 as a prism through which to view 1971 and the way the modern-day had been shaped by the past. It distils that Victorian mood in a very subversive fashion, exposing the dark corners of the Empire and of the British way of life, poking at the underbelly in its different ways, questioning the unquestionable, wondering if the glorious tales of Empire that they were told – and this must be especially true of Charterhouse pupils, educated to feed and run the British Establishment machine – were really true after all, and if there wasn't maybe another perspective, another interpretation.

Viewed like that, 'Nursery Cryme' is rather more dark and unsettling than any of those contemporary political songs, dripping in slogans, empty in their fullness. Power to the people indeed.

1972: Better Not Compromise

The release of *Nursery Cryme* into the pre-Christmas market in November '71 might not have been the best timing to give it a real chance, swamped as it was in the rush of seasonal sales, but its failure to improve significantly on the sales of *Trespass* in the UK was a concern. Mike Rutherford recalled in *The Book of Genesis*, 'There was a very strong feeling towards Strat from the others at Charisma to give us the boot – or rather, just to stop worrying about us. 'Let them sort of drift out quietly' seemed to be the way they were thinking.'

Tony Stratton Smith was not one to be easily distracted, though, and in response, he redoubled his efforts across the next 12 months, starting with that Keith Emerson endorsement of the band in the press ads through to financing an American debut for them in December 1972. Such glamour as that was well in the future, though, as Genesis got back to the daily grind of slogging up and down the country in rented vans to play the club and college circuit. Phil Collins remembered one especially dispiriting occasion in Hugh Fielder's book, a show in Aberystwyth in February '72 when the van broke down three times on the way to the gig, the band arriving too late to play:

> So we thought, 'Well, we might just as well go home now.' We had a drink, went home and broke down four times on the way back. Peter was learning the oboe at the time and every time we stopped, he would practice in an AA box. We were all waiting for the breakdown man and trying to get to sleep while he played his oboe in the AA box with a towel round him to keep warm.

The band maintained an exhausting pace in trying to boost the profile of *Nursery Cryme*, playing around 60 shows inside the first four months of 1972. Significantly though, that included another visit to Belgium, as well as France and Germany and then a brief Italian tour in April. It was these countries that were going to give the band succour – and Stratton Smith reinforcement – in the early years when growth in support in the UK was stubbornly gradual. In historical terms, the trip to Belgium in March was especially important, for it provided the earliest recorded footage of Genesis in action – the brief snippets thus far released from the Roundhouse in 1970 aside. They spent a couple of days filming for *Pop Shop*, a TV show also known as *Rock of the '70s* and which featured

Family, Van der Graaf Generator, Atomic Rooster, Emerson, Lake & Palmer and Curved Air among others. It became a staple of late-night TV in the UK in the late '80s, generally screened at about three in the morning and later passed around on VHS at record fairs the length and breadth of the land. It eventually got an official release as part of the 2007 box sets and offers a fascinating snapshot of the time, for all the restrictions imposed by a sterile TV studio. It certainly underlined an interview Steve Hackett gave in *Disc* later in the year when he said, 'If we appear more like an orchestra than a band, then it's because we've got classical overtones and that doesn't worry me'.

Even so, that performance does underscore some of the problems they had early on in their career. If you're a Genesis nut, it's enthralling. The music is thrilling and seeing them perform it up close underlines its complexity, but visually, that display of technique aside, it's not especially arresting. The Belgian TV company desperately tried to liven it up by applying the techniques of the day, such as clunky photo montages, but it's a hard sell to the neutral. Tony Banks and Hackett were seated throughout, Rutherford standing stock still at the back when playing bass or joining them in the seated position for the 12-string sections. Collins offered a little more for the viewer, not least because he was wearing a vest with an embroidered Genesis logo that looked as if it might have come from one of those knitting patterns he used to model for. It's like watching an octopus; his ability to be all over the kit and the accompanying coordination required quite extraordinary, but really, it's left to the lead singer to try and generate some excitement. It's clear Peter Gabriel is a powerful performer even so early in their career, working the camera to demonic effect in 'The Musical Box', throwing a few Jagger-esque shapes at the end of 'The Return of the Giant Hogweed', but for those who weren't converted, there was nothing much to write home about. Nor write in the music press about, which was more to the point for a band looking for an audience. That was a problem that Gabriel would fix (or fox) later in the year.

Italian audiences were less concerned with the show but transfixed by the music, particularly the increasingly classical overtones that had come to the fore on *Nursery Cryme*. It reached number five in the album charts there and they played a well-received and attended, if chaotic, series of shows that persuaded Tony Tyler to give them a glowing review in *New Musical Express*: 'It's incredible how clever this band is. Not only in lyrics – which are quite excellent – and in presentation, which is simultaneously dramatic and pensive – but in sheer instrumental ability.' Watching them in front of a rapt audience clearly offered a different perspective to the hurly-burly of a college gig. They had tailored their set accordingly, too. The acoustic introduction was limited to just the one song in Italy, 'Happy the Man', and then, depending on the length of the set – they generally played two sets at each venue – it was straight into the crowd-pleasing 'The Fountain of Salmacis', a song beloved of Italian audiences, though longer sets allowed for 'Stagnation' as the acoustic to electric bridge in between. There was no let-up to the end from there, though they were experimenting with a new song called variously 'Rock Me Baby' or 'Bye Bye Johnny', which eventually developed into 'Can-Utility and the Coastliners'.

'Happy the Man' had been around for some time and was finally committed to tape in March 1972, just prior to that Italian tour. Recorded at Richard Branson's residential Manor Studio in Oxford as a tryout for the next album sessions, it was released as a single at the end of May. A piece that began with Rutherford, it's a characteristic 12-string sunny sounding strum and has some lovely flute lines from Gabriel. It gives some sense of what *Trespass* might have sounded like had Collins already been in the group and they had begun to employ his backing vocals in unison with Gabriel, rather than those thicker blocks of sound they went for then. Lyrically, it's typically sardonic Gabriel in lines such as, 'Like a nun with a gun, I'm wonderful fun', the bigger picture seemingly inspired by John Dryden's poem of the same name, about enjoying the day, not giving yourself up to regrets of the past. Regrettably, it did not chart.

By now, Gabriel had also begun to take on additional elements of theatricality, shaving the front of his head, using heavy black eye make up and wearing a heavily jewelled collar, photographer and early biographer Armando Gallo referring to this look as the 'ageless Egyptian prince', first unveiled at the Great Western Express Festival in Lincoln at the end of May. But with the singer's ankle steadfastly refusing to break for a second year running, there was no lengthy dedicated writing period available to the band this year, days grabbed here and there in and around a punishing touring schedule, and all of this with recording dates looming at the beginning of August 1972. After the failure of 'Happy the Man', both Manor Studios and producer John Anthony were jettisoned, the dissenting voices at Charisma getting louder and louder. Genesis checked into Island Records' Basing Street Studio, now Sarm West, in Ladbroke Grove in London to make what was going to be a critically important album.

Foxtrot

Personnel: Tony Banks, Phil Collins, Peter Gabriel, Steve Hackett, Mike Rutherford
Producer: David Hitchcock
Engineer: John Burns
Cover art: Paul Whitehead
Recorded at Basing Street Studios, London, August 1972.
Released: 6 October 1972
Label: Charisma Records
Running time: 51:08
Tracklisting: 1. Watcher of the Skies 2. Time Table 3. Get 'Em Out by Friday
4. Can-Utility and the Coastliners 5. Horizons 6. Supper's Ready
All songs by Banks/Collins/Gabriel/Hackett/Rutherford.

For a group as notoriously self-deprecating as Genesis, there was a palpable sense of confidence going into the recording of what would become *Foxtrot*. Interviewed in *New Musical Express* during the course of recording, Gabriel said that he felt the band was on the verge of a breakthrough in popularity in the UK, adding, 'It's really just the result of having worked things out on the road over the past two years and finally evolved with the right combination as a result'.

Gabriel was clearly sensitive to the groundswell of interest they were experiencing at gigs in the UK, the venues where they played generally getting fuller, audiences more enthusiastic as word spread about the band. Although it meant taking a longer route to acceptance than one that might have been engendered by press hype, it was ultimately to prove a more enduring one. Certainly, in and around London, as well as other pockets across the country, their power was growing. 'Home Counties Genesis Freaks Unite' was the slogan for a show at Watford Town Hall on 28 June, the thousand attendees all being given a Genesis '72 rosette to mark the show. Further evidence of their growing popularity came with their slot on the Friday night of the Reading Festival on 11 August when they were given a standing ovation, the crowd still baying for more a full five minutes after they'd left the stage.

The Reading Festival appearance came midway through recording and they used the opportunity to showcase one of their new songs, album opener 'Watcher of the Skies'; the title, if not the lyrical idea, lifted from Keats' poem *On First Looking Into Chapman's Homer*. They had played the song live as far back as June, albeit with a different vocal delivery from Gabriel on the verse lines. But it was the introduction that stopped people dead in their tracks. This time, it was Banks at the forefront, the monolithic sound of the Mellotron immediately indicating that Genesis had moved on again, the claustrophobic Victoriana of *Nursery Cryme* supplanted by something from science fiction.

Not only did it shift the musical terrain, but it also ushered their new producer out of the equation too. Bob Potter had been put forward by Charisma as a replacement for John Anthony, but right from the outset, the atmosphere between him and the band was frosty. Having worked with Lindisfarne in the past, Potter's remit was to give Genesis more of a commercial edge, a greater sense of immediacy that might cut through to the record-buying public. Immediacy was not really on the band's agenda, either in terms of their music or the pace at which they wanted to work. Methodical to a fault and determined to achieve something as close to perfection as they could, Genesis would not be hurried and nor would they compromise on their songs. When Potter was adamant that 'Watcher of the Skies' needed to lose its introduction if it was going to get anywhere near being on the album, the die was cast and Potter was well on his way. Island engineer Tony Platt was the next possibility, but he and the band couldn't see eye to eye – Platt went on to engineer for Mutt Lange on AC/DC's *Back in Black*, as well as producing Iron Maiden, Gary Moore and Cheap Trick among others – and so he was moved swiftly along too. Eventually, they settled on David Hitchcock, who had produced Caravan and East of Eden and was rather more sympathetic to what Genesis were looking to do. He was ably assisted by engineer John Burns who would himself go on to produce the band's next two albums. They were both more than happy to kick things off with 'Watcher of the Skies'.

The Mellotron introduction illustrates Banks' approach to the instrument, using it as a sound in its own right rather than simply a replacement for strings, choir or flutes as it was initially intended. Instead, he coaxed from it an unearthly lament for a barren landscape, all life snuffed out, be it by some apocalyptic disaster or a planned abandonment of the planet for pastures new. The lyric was initially inspired by the view from the roof of their hotel in Naples while the band were on that April tour of Italy, Banks and Rutherford colouring it with little pieces of inspiration from Arthur C. Clarke's *Childhood's End* and the Watchers characters from Marvel Comics.

'It was intentionally melodramatic to conjure up an impression of incredible size,' said Banks in *The Genesis Songbook*. 'On the old Mellotron Mk 2, there were these two chords that sounded really good.

There are some chords you can't play on that instrument because they'd be so out of tune, but those chords created an incredible atmosphere.' Hackett later likened it 'to the sound of a spaceship coming in to land' and played live, particularly in the Palasports of Italy, it made the foundations shake as the band came to open their set with it for the following couple of years after *Foxtrot* was released.

Musically, this is a band at the top of its game, long gone the diffidence of *Trespass*. Following on from Banks' majestic introduction, the polyrhythmic interplay between him, Rutherford – offering melodic, driving bass – and Collins – battering out a Morse code message to the disinterested universe – is like nothing the band had served up hitherto. 'Watcher of the Skies' also hints at a sense of melancholy that would pervade the record, Hackett's weeping guitar in the coda powerfully emotional. There's something deeply mournful and achingly lonely about the song, setting the tone for what was to come on an album that saw Genesis at both their most cynical and their most hopeful – contrasts that would colour music, lyrics and album sleeve. These were young men who had taken a look at the world around them and had concluded that while the possibilities were endless, the reality was galling.

That fed into the lyric of 'Time Table', the punning title misleading, for this was a song written in its entirety by Banks rather than Gabriel. Drawing on the old cliché that has become the staple of a hundred antiques shows on TV in recent years, it asks the question, 'If only that ancient table could talk, what would it tell us?' The carved oak table in question dated back to medieval times, so just what had it seen in the intervening few hundred years? Banks' answer seemed to be the more that things change, the more they stay the same. Reflecting on the perpetual state of hubris by which humankind is governed, the lyric argued that every generation, every hierarchy is convinced that they are the greatest to have ever roamed the earth, oblivious to their failings and to how little they have really learnt from the past. Each talks of honour and integrity, of fresh enlightenment, but in the end, every disagreement gets settled the same way – sacrificing the weak so that their overlords might continue to thrive. Be it 1572 or 1972, 'Time Table' argued that human nature had shown little evolution, an idea that Gabriel would pick up on the following year in the denouement of 'The Battle of Epping Forest', when, with their henchmen all dead, the 'Black cap barons toss a coin to settle the score'. Not unlike 'Dancing With the Moonlit Knight' on that next album, 'Time Table' has that 'Greensleeves' feel to it, not least in the tinkling music box sound in the middle eight – that was achieved by picking the piano strings inside the lid with a plectrum, creating a sound that is midway between piano and guitar, something that Genesis were especially good at, Banks and Hackett combining to create hybrid, composite sounds.

'Get 'Em Out by Friday' was very much in the vein of 'Harold the Barrel', both in terms of its mini-operatic construction and its social commentary, though this was rather more pointed. Rather than a general sideswipe at a repressive British culture, Gabriel was inspired this time by a TV programme about rogue landlords in Islington. Property speculation, substandard housing, crumbling tower blocks and a dollop of corruption on top was a feature of early '70s Britain, Monty Python having produced their famous 'Architect's Sketch' in late 1970, featuring one housing development that transports the tenants on a conveyor belt into a slaughterhouse. Following the Grenfell Tower disaster in London in 2017, you could well ask, has anything changed since? Gabriel's lyric made it clear that the housing market is one where profit comes before people, 'The Winkler' being sent along to persuade people to give up their existing homes and move into a block of flats instead where, lo and behold, the rent has gone up again before they've even had time to move in.

He wasn't finished there, though, for he transports us into what was then the future, 2012, where all the TV channels are taken over for a special announcement that there will be an immediate restriction on human height – four feet, and that's your lot. The announcement is made on the Dial-A-Program cable service, the name of a cable TV system that the singer's father had pioneered some years previously. Gabriel has subsequently suggested that the idea of restricting people to four feet in height was an early bit of green advocacy, smaller people requiring fewer resources. But while he was already interested in the environment as an early adopter of green issues in the 1970s – he is the wobbly cyclist on the back of the *Foxtrot* sleeve, a nod to the fact he would cycle everywhere back home in London – the lyric was surely written from a more cynical position at the time given that the poor old tenants of Harlow New Town were once again going to be the guinea pigs, this time for fitting twice as many people onto the same plot of land. He then skewers the inherent hypocrisy in the final couplet, 'With land in your hand you'll be happy on earth / Then invest in the church for your heaven.' It's a neat reminder that amongst those with the biggest property portfolio in the land were the Church of England, with businessmen like the song's villain, John Pebble of Styx Enterprises, happy to show their faces in the congregation every Sunday to prop up their positions as pillars of the community. That disenchantment with the Establishment and with 'high society' was especially barbed on the *Foxtrot* cover. From the aristocratic croquet lawns of *Nursery Cryme*, this time, the focus was on the fox hunt, the fox having escaped their clutches by heading into the sea and jumping on an ice floe, a pun on Fox's Glacier Mints that were particularly popular at the time. The red dress is both a disguise, to show how cunning the fox is, and a nod to Hendrix's 'Foxy Lady'.

It's the foxing of the Establishment that is central, though, the four huntsmen doubtless the riders from the apocalypse, though whether famine really was a cross dresser remains a matter for conjecture. What is in no doubt is that war's horse is displaying what Gabriel later described as a 'high degree of sexual excitation', the crusty old colonel on top oblivious to his steed's erection – all this was long before David Bowie's *Diamond Dogs* sleeve. The horsemen's appearance obviously feeds on the lyric from 'Supper's Ready', as do the shrouded men, but at a wider level, the horsemen represent the evil that men do, evidenced by the nuclear submarine – there was a great deal of controversy at the time over US submarines being based off the coast of Scotland – and the ailing whale, victims of overfishing, these being the early days of the 'save the whale' campaigns. It's a very angry cover masquerading as something humorous, right down to the man burying his head in the sand, a rather more personal jibe at the music business that was doing its best to ignore Genesis.

The surprising thing was that although the cover was set on the shoreline, King Canute – or Cnut the Great – wasn't there, given that the story of him proving that he could not hold back the sea was the source material for 'Can-Utility and the Coastliners'. Hackett's telling of his story had something of 'Time Table' about it but was, if anything, more despondent about the way the world had moved – the more things change, the worse they get in this instance. For Canute was that most unusual of things, a monarch who had tired of the masses blowing smoke up his fundament and claiming for him Godly powers that he did not possess. What is now largely forgotten is that the story of Canute trying to hold back the waves was not one of deluded self-aggrandisement but was instead the King trying to prove to his people that he was a mere mortal, no more nor less, with no greater control over the elements than any other. 'We heed not flatterers' was a line that had particular resonance in 1972 with the likes of Richard Nixon and Idi Amin stalking the world stage and demanding just that, but it's no less relevant today either.

In classic Genesis style, it went through distinct sections, from a lilting, largely acoustic opening that essentially came from Hackett, before going into a glorious instrumental break built around Rutherford's 12-string, with Banks using the Mellotron strings to do more than just mimic an orchestra, playing a meandering pattern that has the flavour of one of Hackett's guitar parts, illustrative of how the band were influencing each other. Banks later told *Electronics & Music Maker*, 'Steve and I would play games, one inventing a new sound and the other trying to imitate it. By combining the two, we got another sound and went on from there.' The end section sees Banks and Hackett soloing in turn before Gabriel returns with a vocal melody written by the guitarist, straining at the edge of his range. Reflecting later on Genesis at that stage of their evolution, Hackett noted:

Phil Collins had a love of big bands, the rest of us shared a love of classical music; I think we were influenced by everything from blues to pantomime to humour, a number of things that might be outside the typical progressive area. People think of progressive rock as being characterised by Mellotron, Hammond organ, tricky time signatures, everything impenetrable, a bit like a mathematical task, but I think in actuality while that was a part of what intrigued us, the power of a good song, a good lyric, a good line, a good riff, a good hook, something that refuses to go away, that was what drove us because those are the things that drive a song forward.

If Hackett had played a large part in writing 'Can-Utility and the Coastliners', then 'Horizons', which opened side two, was all his. A classical guitar piece, it was the only survivor from Bob Potter's few days at the helm, recorded when he was getting exasperated with the length of time it was taking Rutherford to restring his guitar. Trying to fill the time productively, he asked if anything else was ready and Hackett obliged with this solo piece which he had based on a Bach piece, *Prelude From Suite No. 1 in G Major for Cello*, evidence again of how Hackett saw the guitar as a synthesiser in its own right, able to take on different tones and roles. It's a beautiful, intricate little piece, a pause for breath before what was to come, and further evidence of how important Hackett was becoming to the band. Not that he was aware of it, for prior to recording the album, he was preparing to leave until Banks and Rutherford took him to one side and explained how much they liked his playing and what a big role it had in their overall sound.

That the most English of bands should have the most English of temperaments – no need for compliments and the assumption that people should be able to work out for themselves what everyone else was thinking – didn't always make life easy, as Hackett explained to me later:

> I've come to the conclusion that most people improve immensely with praise rather than criticism. I think praise from someone that you respect can work miracles. I've had my own heroes and if occasionally they've said nice things about stuff I've done, then you take that literally, wonderful, praise from Caesar! That is invaluable. So I don't say to people that they should give music up as a bad job; I'll more likely say 'well done'. And invariably, people tend to come up with something better next time. I listened to a lot of people growing up, I had people who I thought were inspiring. Ian McDonald was very encouraging to me in my early days, just a year or so before I met Genesis. I'd seen him with King Crimson and he was a multi-instrumentalist at that time and they were a band that seemed to play and sing flawlessly as far as I was concerned, I was mightily impressed. Ian happened to have been in the Army with a friend of mine, Phil Henderson, who was with Quiet World, the band I joined before Genesis. He came to a rehearsal one day and he was very helpful, tried to put us in touch with EG management, came to one of our recording sessions and told me he liked my guitar playing. Of course, when I heard that, I was in heaven! 'He liked my guitar playing?' The Gods have come down from Olympus to see what the rest of us mere mortals are doing! Sometimes people make a quantum leap forward; I think that comes from praise, from encouragement.

Temperamentally, there was a real dichotomy in Genesis. While they were dismissed by some critics as being rather soft having come via Charterhouse rather than the mean streets of the working class, the truth was that Banks, Gabriel and Rutherford had been schooled for a certain kind of future and, however much they rebelled against it, just a few years out of Charterhouse, it was still very much part of their make-up. They'd been brought up to be self-reliant, to be the governing class at a time when that had very specific connotations. The legacy of that was, if you survived it, you were likely to be ambitious, competitive and hard as nails, however personable and charming on the surface. Those three definitely had those steely qualities, as well as being the founder members with the extra authority which that inevitably carried with it. Hackett was naturally less competitive and less self-confident, certainly in those early days, nor did he necessarily have the political skills (or will) to manoeuvre his material through the democratic process and onto vinyl. A perfect example of that was the song that ultimately became 'Shadow of the Hierophant' on his debut solo album, *Voyage of the Acolyte*. A version of that had come to the fore during the *Foxtrot* sessions but wasn't included on that, nor the two subsequent albums. As he said years later in the *Chapter and Verse* book:

> I felt that the others were so much more accomplished than me in terms of writing. I always expected someone was going to put a line through it: 'Must try harder. Must come up with proper verse and chorus.' It was probably a product of the overbearing English school system: 'Knock them down and they'll get a very pleasant surprise by the time the exams come around.' But then chaps like me need encouragement. I need to be told that I'm better than I am. Flattery goes a long way with me.

For the more gregarious Collins, that was all less of an issue, especially given that at that time, he didn't really see himself as a writer in the same way, his input coming more in the arrangement of the music. That wasn't to say that he was entirely happy, Hackett recalling that he was approached to join Lindisfarne at one point. Apparently, he gave the matter serious consideration, though it's hard to see how he would have fitted in there given that his gripes with Genesis were largely musical, telling *New Musical Express* that he'd like to see the band being 'more Mahavishnu'. Given the way Collins became seen as the great simplifier both inside the band and solo in the 1980s, his yearning for Genesis to become more technically complex is intriguing. Indeed, the push and the pull in the band was illustrated when, at roughly the same time, Hackett was quoted in *Disc*: 'There aren't many melodic bands about. I think everyone's trying very hard in the wrong directions – that's where we win out because we tend to go for melodies whatever we try to do.'

Either way, both ends of the spectrum were more than satisfied by the album's closer, for on *Foxtrot*, all roads led to 'Supper's Ready'. Perhaps the most striking thing about the 23-minute piece is that prior to playing it back in the studio once it was completed, they'd never actually heard the full thing. In that, it is the embodiment of F. Scott Fitzgerald's famous quote that 'the test of a first-rate intelligence is the ability to hold two opposed ideas in mind at the same time and still retain the ability to function', defining cognitive dissonance. It's the stress and the tension of carrying what are in fact, seven very separate ideas in mind all at once that gives 'Supper's Ready' its unique character and the emotional heft of the final pay off when the song reaches the 'New Jerusalem' climax. The idea that the band could keep all those different musical ideas in the air and finally mould them together into one is testimony to their skills as writers, as musicians, and as conceptualisers, for all five had real input in making 'Supper's Ready' what it became – not just Genesis' masterwork but perhaps the pinnacle of prog. You'd think that almost by definition, a song that lasts 23 minutes would have to topple over beneath the weight of its own self-indulgence – and progressive rock did give us plenty of examples of that, the dust that surrounded the odd diamond such as 'Close to the Edge', 'Flight' or 'The Underfall Yard' – but there's no sense of that at all in 'Supper's Ready'. For all the incredible playing, the sense of experimentation, the classical overtones, the moments that are simply surreal, it never loses sight of the melodic imperative that Hackett spoke of, it didn't drift into obscurity, swings like Sinatra and crescendos on a vocal as soulful as Marvin Gaye on 'What's Going On?'.

Having given themselves permission to go further than 'The Musical Box' and give over virtually an entire side of vinyl to one song, David Hitchcock's first contribution was simple but crucial. There was no need to try to record the whole song in one go, do it in discrete sections instead, concentrate on getting those three or four minutes right, then move to the next part and then join up the dots at the end of the process. From there, things gradually began to come into focus. 'Lover's Leap' became the jumping-off point, a guitar piece that Banks had initially written at university, around the same time as the organ intro to 'The Fountain of Salmacis'. With Banks joining Rutherford and Hackett on guitar, it's when Banks takes up the melody on the pianet that the character begins to shift. There's a duality to the music already introduced by Gabriel's vocal, not just lyrically, but the fact that at times he's singing two distinct lines, the one mixed slightly lower in the background a strangulated octave higher. That was the original vocal, but on Hackett's suggestion, he took the voice down an octave, far better suited to the melody. The two together hint at the dual nature of the song, the theme, to boil it down to its simplest form, being the fight between good and evil.

'The Guaranteed Eternal Sanctuary Man' picks up the tempo, the drums now kicking in, Banks playing an organ piece that's a little reminiscent of 'Stagnation'. It culminates in the parody of the 'Rocking Carol', Gabriel hauling eight schoolkids into the studio to sing the 'We will rock you little snake' refrain. They were paid the princely sum of 50p each. It's a little more subtle than Pink Floyd's children's choir singing 'We don't need no education' and leads into 'Ikhnaton and Itsacon and Their Band of Merry Men', the song's battle scene, heralded by a keyboard fanfare from Banks, set against Rutherford's 12-string strum, Hackett soloing over the top of that to bring in the necessary sense of chaos. Genesis' innate sense of dynamics then kicks in; the volume turned right down so that you can barely hear the beginning of 'How Dare I Be So Beautiful' – a title stolen from Jonathan King's habit of asking himself that very question whenever he caught sight of his reflection. At the end of this section, it's Narcissus who falls in love with his own reflection, at which point all hell breaks loose.

Genesis' grasp of the power of contrasts has already been well noted, but the sudden change heralded by the arrival of 'Willow Farm', a self-contained stomp of Gabriel's, is taking the sublime all the way to the ridiculous and back again. The shift came at Banks' suggestion, concerned that what they had so far was meandering towards being a simple rehash of 'Stagnation'. By heading into 'Willow Farm', what looks on paper as though it should be a car crash works to perfection, everything that came before suddenly seeming even more beautiful and romantic, everything that follows increasingly dramatic. The pastoral passage, featuring Gabriel's flute melody that follows, gradually builds the tension as the song moves into 'Apocalypse In 9/8 (Co-Starring the Delicious Talents of Gabble Ratchet)', the jewel in the crown of Genesis music. Even at the time, they realised they had struck something very special, Collins telling *New Musical Express*, 'It's the best thing we've done. It started off as a jam. Steve and Peter were away for some reason and Mike started playing this movement on bass pedals – totally abstract with no time signature at all. Then we tied it down and worked it out to a two-bar riff. I just knocked a beat out and it became a bar of nine. That's the way things are often done in the band and that's the sort of thing I'd like to work more to because I like playing in time signatures.'

Over the top of the complex rhythmic pattern held down by Collins and Rutherford, Banks plays a flowing solo that eclipses anything he'd recorded to that point. That it was written as a trio signposted the way that a lot of Genesis music would evolve in the future, from the second part of 'The Cinema Show' on *Selling England by the Pound* all the way through to songs like 'Second Home by the Sea' and 'Fading Lights' in later incarnations. It's a lengthy section, which is then topped by Gabriel's glorious 'Six, six, six' vocal, the cherry on the top in much the same way as on the closing section of 'The Musical Box'. But this time, there's still more to come, the celebratory coda of 'As Sure as Eggs Is Eggs (Aching Men's Feet)' ushered in by a drum roll and pealing bells before the melodic reprise of 'The Guaranteed Eternal Sanctuary Man' to bring the song to its close, Gabriel's vocal – 'I felt as if I was singing from my soul – almost like I was singing for my life' – the eventual climax after the previous twenty minutes of foreplay as Banks later referred to it. Musically, 'Supper's Ready' is magnificent, but it goes beyond that. It's an emotional tour-de-force – and isn't that what music is really all about in the end?

But what's it all about, Peter? The singer took charge of the lyric from beginning to end, a precursor to the way he would assume control on *The Lamb Lies Down on Broadway*. It was derived from experiences he and his wife had gone through, making this his most personal lyric to date. He and Jill had been staying at her parents' flat in the Old Barracks in Kensington, along with John Anthony. Anthony had been talking about his interest in spiritualism when there was a sudden change in the room's atmosphere. 'It was like a Hammer horror film, except it was for real,' said Gabriel. 'We saw other faces in each other. It was almost as if something else had come into us and was using us as a meeting point.' He chose to exorcise some of his fears by writing of the battle between the forces of light and those of darkness, undercutting it with the theatre of the absurd that was 'Willow Farm', before building to the eventual victory, the 'New Jerusalem', a reading of a new heaven on earth from the Book of Revelations in the New Testament. There really was no escaping the influence of the name Jonathan King had bestowed upon them.

At the time, there was some uncertainty within the band about the lyric, Collins telling *New Musical Express*, 'Peter was rushing through the lyrics while we were putting down the backing tracks. Perhaps more time would have made it better.' Nearly half a century on though, it's a brave man or woman who would now suggest that there was a single word in 'Supper's Ready' that was out of place.

The record-buying public seemed to agree, for *Foxtrot* became Genesis' first album to chart, going straight in at number 12 before tumbling down the following week. It was evidence that their policy of sticking to their guns and refusing to compromise had been worth persevering with and that all the hard work on the road, gradually building a live following, had begun to reap some dividends. The response in the music press was positive too, Jerry Gilbert positively gushing in his *Sounds* review of the record: 'Must surely become one of the major works of the year. *Foxtrot* shows us the Genesis that we've seen all too often on stage and been longing for on record … a showcase for the genius of this young, experimental band.' Tony Tyler, writing in *New Musical Express* noted that this was, 'A brilliantly broadened instrumental Genesis with vaulting arrangements', while Chris Welch's *Melody Maker* review claimed that, 'Genesis have reached a creative peak'.

Which was all very well, but as the release of the album approached, Charisma were thinking of ways to sell some more records and move Genesis up the league table. Amongst the ideas being kicked around in the press office was the thought of paying somebody to dress up in red dress and fox head to mimic the character on the album cover and generate some publicity that way. This caught the attention of Gabriel, who thought, 'If anybody was going to do that, it was going to be me!' And so, on 28 September 1972, just before the release of the album, something remarkable happened during Genesis' show at the Dublin National Stadium, an old boxing ring. During the instrumental section of 'The Musical Box', Gabriel disappeared off stage, only to return for the closing section clad in a red dress of his wife's and a fox's head. This not only surprised the crowd but the other four members of Genesis who had not been privy to the singer's intentions. In a band that prided itself on being a democratic unit, this met with a predictable frostiness, but as Gabriel pointed out, had he put the idea to the vote, it would almost certainly have lost. It's not hard to see the band's point of view at that stage, not least because the fox's head was just a gimmick – where did it play into the story of 'The Musical Box'? But when pictures of Gabriel wearing it started appearing regularly in the music press, with interest in the band increasing every time, they began to see its value, not least when it meant they were able to book a proper theatre tour under their own steam early the following year.

Before that, though, there was a first trip to the United States to make a spectacular debut at New York's Philharmonic Hall as headliners at radio station WNEW's annual Christmas concert. Playing a show in Boston the day before, the group were dismayed to find that because of differences between power supplies on either side of the Atlantic, Banks' keyboard rig, in particular, was beset by problems. When they were unable to get into the Philharmonic Hall in time for a soundcheck, it meant they were facing an uphill battle at that night's show. All kinds of technical problems assailed them through the set and they came offstage convinced they had been a failure, Rutherford hurling his bass across the dressing room and Gabriel demanding an immediate flight home. Out in the audience, though, Genesis had gone down a storm, Tony Stratton Smith telling *Sounds*, 'What impressed me most was that in spite of the technical hang-ups, they got 100 per cent reaction'. The $16,000 that Charisma and Buddah, Genesis' American label, had ploughed into the concert was to prove a very wise investment.

1973: The River of Constant Change

It's a rare thing that a single gig marks a turning point in an artist's career. For the most part, they're all part of the continuum, one long slog to gradually build an audience and then capitalise upon it. Within a tour, one show is much like another, some better, some worse, but few are especially significant beyond the possibility of breaking a box office record here, opening a new venue there. But for Genesis, there's little question that the show they played at the Rainbow Theatre in London on 9 February 1973 was truly groundbreaking. That was the night where they moved into the big league, going from club band to the kind that could fill theatres across the UK. It was the night when the artistic growth of the band, particularly across their three Charisma releases, was finally and rightly acclaimed by an adoring audience. It was also the night when Peter Gabriel went from being seen as an engaging, if eccentric singer with some interesting ideas on presentation, to becoming a fully-fledged rock star and so, in some respects, it was also the night that set Genesis on the path towards their next line-up change. Swings and roundabouts…

Even prior to the Rainbow show, there had been some disquiet in the ranks, Steve Hackett saying to *Disc*, 'Obviously, Peter gets singled out and I think people are trying to make him into a cult – there are obvious comparisons with your present stars. I think it's a shame that people can only see as far as the superficial thing. When people write about Genesis, they tend to write about the way Peter Gabriel is dressed.' Tony Banks agreed in a feature in *New Musical Express*: 'Peter's emergence as a spokesman and focal point is something that we only came to terms with recently when we realised it was essential to get some sort of attention for the group by pushing in one direction. It was necessary in order to make the transition from just being another band to something different – but I think we all regret having to do it.'

After the Rainbow show, there would be no going back, although, at first sight, it was the stage itself that had undergone the greatest transformation. The early '70s was the era of gear, where each band seemed to be involved in a competition to see who could fill the stage with the most hardware, have the biggest speaker stacks, the arms race escalating to the point where more than one band resorted to piling up empty cabinets on stage. Genesis were keen on tidying things up a little, as Mike Rutherford explained during the box set interviews. 'We had this idea of hiding all the gear, having spent the last five years with big stacks of equipment behind us. We just went out and bought a white gauze curtain, which cost us £50, and six ultraviolet tubes and put the curtain in front of the gear. It worked, it was so simple and easy, yet it gave the stage a very special atmosphere.' Certainly, the new staging was effective, but it was Gabriel's armoury of new costumes that made the biggest splash. As the set opened with 'Watcher of the Skies', Gabriel was silhouetted against the backdrop, a pair of batwings around his shoulders, UV-sensitive make-up around the eyes picked out as the only lit point on the stage. From there, he ran through the gamut of masks and costumes, including a variety of hats to denote his different roles in 'Get 'Em Out by Friday' and the crown of thorns, flower head and box mask for 'Supper's Ready', which climaxed in a blinding magnesium flash that gave him the split second he needed to lose the menacing black cape and appear dressed all in white, representing good's final triumph. It was a theatrical tour de force, quite unlike anything that anyone had put on to that point, including the more obvious candidates such as David Bowie or Alice Cooper.

Things were building very nicely for the band by now. *Foxtrot* continued to perform well in the UK and there were a dozen dates to play in North America, including a couple of support slots with Lou Reed, as the band briefly followed up on their first visit the previous December. There were hopes of playing a celebratory UK show at Wembley's Empire Pool on 25 May, but that was scuppered when, for some reason, tickets couldn't be printed on time. Tentative plans for a UK tour in the summer were also shelved as time came around for the writing of the next album. That meant that following a couple of European dates at the beginning of May, Genesis were off the road until September, a headline appearance at the Reading Festival aside, an evening when Gabriel appeared inside a pyramid, head poking out of the top. If that wasn't enough, he was about twenty feet in the air at the time, atop a hydraulic platform.

The idea had been that they would have the summer to get a new album ready and in the shops in and around that Reading Festival appearance, on the bank holiday weekend in late August, capitalising on that new momentum with a relatively quick follow up to *Foxtrot*. There were some clear ideas as to what shape this new record – and the one after that – should take, Gabriel telling *Sounds*, 'I hope the next album will be a mixture of shorter compositions with a possible single and also a long composition if one evolves naturally. There will be some concise numbers, though, in fact, there's more likely to be a big concept thing on the album after.' But the open-ended sessions meant that the band struggled to find a focus. Writing and rehearsing in a house in Chessington – much to the annoyance of the neighbours who, in time-honoured fashion, were banging on the walls and shouting, 'It's not even proper music!' – and then in the Una Billings Dance Studio in London, where they'd written a lot of *Foxtrot*, they found that fresh inspiration was in short supply beyond working on a couple of pieces that they had already been kicking around for a while.

Hackett admitted that he was coming at the new record much more as a player and arranger than as a writer, which may have accounted for some of the dearth of material, but generally, it was something of a struggle and it became clear quite quickly that they would not be hitting that initial deadline. With no concerts booked until the autumn, Charisma were concerned that they might lose a lot of the impetus that they had built up in the previous year and so in order to plug the gap, a decision was taken to release a live album.

Live

Personnel: Tony Banks, Phil Collins, Peter Gabriel, Steve Hackett, Mike Rutherford
Producer: John Burns & Genesis
Engineer: Alan Perkins
Recorded at Manchester Free Trade Hall, 24 February 1973 and Leicester De Montfort Hall, 25 February 1973.
Released: 20 July 1973
Label: Charisma Records
Running time: 46:44
Tracklisting: 1. Watcher of the Skies 2. Get 'Em Out by Friday 3. The Return of the Giant Hogweed 4. Musical Box 5. The Knife
All songs by Banks/Collins/Gabriel/Hackett/Rutherford except 'The Knife' by Banks/ Gabriel/ Mayhew/Phillips/Rutherford.

The album was concocted from tapes recorded for the American radio show *King Biscuit Flower Hour*, meant to help promote the band on FM radio in the States. Needing some fresh stop-gap product, Tony Stratton Smith essentially commandeered those tapes and persuaded a fairly reluctant band into releasing them. The clincher was that the live album would come out at a budget price of £1.99 rather than standard album price of around £2.99, and that would allow them to get it into general shops rather than specialist record stores, the likes of W.H. Smith and Woolworth giving them exposure to new record buyers. That meant it had to be a single album, which in turn meant there would be no place for 'Supper's Ready' on there. That emasculated the album somewhat, removing the outstanding track from the set, but to have included it on successive albums was asking too much, not least because it would have meant losing two or three of the songs that did make it onto *Live*.

That would have been a shame, especially in terms of the older pieces, all of which were spruced up from the studio versions, displaying a harder edge in different ways. 'The Return of the Giant Hogweed' was yet more aggressive than on *Nursery Cryme*, the closing section of 'The Musical Box' taking on a more sinister edge as Gabriel squeezed every ounce of the drama from the lyric. It was 'The Knife' which was the most changed, though, naturally enough given that Collins and Hackett had not played on *Trespass*. Collins switched feels deftly across the song's near ten minutes, injecting his personality into the music, Hackett providing a fine interpretation of Anthony Phillips' work on the original. Yet it was Gabriel's contribution that was the most marked, the singer having substantially changed the song's lyric from the original, the only time that he did that across his time with the band.

These were the moments that made the release of *Live* worthwhile artistically as much as commercially but looked at from this distance, it is an album that largely treads water, waiting for the next release. Had it been a double – and a test pressing of a double album was produced in the Netherlands, and some were circulated as promos among radio stations – then it would have perhaps been more satisfactory. That would have given scope for the inclusion of 'Supper's Ready', but just as important in a way, it would have also allowed for the inclusion of Gabriel's pre-song monologues, giving those who hadn't seen the band live more of an idea of just what an engagingly eccentric live proposition they were. As a sop to that, they did include one of his stories on the chaotically designed back cover, the tale of the girl in the green trouser suit. That was to have significant repercussions the following year.

The album did what Charisma had hoped for on its 20 July release, charting at number nine and widening the fanbase once again while the band continued to toil over the new studio album, which now had a definite completion deadline of the end of August, ahead of an October release – by which time they would have been back on the road for the best part of a month.

Selling England by the Pound

Personnel: Tony Banks, Phil Collins, Peter Gabriel, Steve Hackett, Mike Rutherford
Producer: John Burns & Genesis
Assistant engineer: Rhett Davies
Cover art: Betty Swanwick ARA
Recorded at Basing Street Studios, London, August 1973.
Released: 13 October 1973
Label: Charisma Records
Running time: 53:44
Tracklisting: 1. Dancing With the Moonlit Knight 2. I Know What I Like (In Your Wardrobe) 3. Firth of Fifth 4. More Fool Me 5. The Battle of Epping Forest 6. After the Ordeal 7. The Cinema Show 8. Aisle of Plenty
All songs by Banks/Collins/Gabriel/Hackett/Rutherford.

Much was familiar about the sessions for *Selling England by the Pound*. Recording took place at Basing Street Studios again, John Burns, the engineer on *Foxtrot*, now at the helm as co-producer alongside the band themselves. But beyond the confines of the Ladbroke Grove studio, it was a different landscape from the previous summer. Progressive rock had grown in popularity to the point where it was perhaps the dominant force in album sales across the world. *The Dark Side of the Moon*, *Close to the Edge*, *Brain Salad Surgery* and *A Passion Play* were all released inside the same twelve months as *Selling England by the Pound* and all enjoyed massive sales. That very success formed a central part of the album's contradictions. This most English of music was tearing up the charts in the US as well as the UK at the very moment when rampant Americanisation – Wimpy bars, Coca-Cola and huge supermarkets – was swamping the English way of life.

These disparate elements, focused around the album's title, itself taken from a Labour Party pamphlet bemoaning the loss of English autonomy following the joining of the Common Market at the start of 1973, were deep in the grooves of this record, Banks acknowledging in *Sounds*, 'The main concept is an English feel running right through it, but there are a lot of different sides to it.' Steve Hackett agreed, noting, 'Genesis was very European sounding. There was an American influence, of course, the rock drums, the beat, the sound of the voice and sometimes the accent, but there was something essentially British that the band had. I think its Englishness and the very naming of the album *Selling England by the Pound*, had a lot to do with the selling of the band to the Americans, appealing directly to the Anglophile market over there. The Brits did hold sway for quite some time over there in the wake of The Beatles.'

That was where the irony and the tension existed as Genesis were writing and recording in 1973. Their two brief visits to the United States had given them a view of some very different possibilities, while the financial imperatives were also underlining just how important the 'new world' was likely to be to their future. Hackett sketched out the dilemma in a *Sounds* interview: 'It's a dreadful thing to say, but I really see our future as lying more in the States ... we can't survive financially without America.' These were the realities, but for a band with such an avowedly English sensibility, they brought real concerns with them.

So, the USA. The EEC. The IRA. OPEC. The TUC. 1973. A year of acronyms cutting through the cosiness of the post-war consensus, sculpting a new UK in their wake. And then there was Watergate. *The Exorcist*. The arrival of Pizza Hut. The spread of McDonalds. *Kojak*. Americana colonising ye olde Albion. No wonder Gabriel's plaintive opening to the album was 'Can you tell me where my country lies?' Did it lie in Brussels? On Madison Avenue? In Saudi Arabia? On the Greenwich meridian? Did it exist at all any longer and if it did, what vestiges remained and could they be preserved?

In a world where change was the currency of the day, 'Dancing With the Moonlit Knight' was questioning the pace and the validity of much of it. 'For her merchandise, he traded in his prize', 'Chewing through your Wimpey dreams', 'Knights of the Green Shield stamp and shout' (Green Shield stamps were an early form of supermarket loyalty stamps that could be collected and exchanged for heady consumer durables, a Nectar card for the analogue years, but it doubled as a reference to the legend of Sir Gawain and the Green Knight); these were not lines that spoke of a nation at ease with itself, but one that was losing its identity and its sense of self in its headlong dash after the greenbacks. The sense of questioning extended to the band itself, perhaps to Gabriel in particular, Hackett's admission of their forthcoming American dependence not sitting well with them.

This wasn't mere flag-waving for little England, though, Gabriel explaining in *Melody Maker* that, 'I hate patriotism, but we try to be English.' That Englishness was found in a respect for folk traditions that could be heard in his acapella delivery of the opening lines – Hackett was to pick up on this years later when on his *Genesis Revisited II* album, he prefaced his new version of the song with a brief snatch from the

Tudor piece 'Greensleeves', long attributed to Henry VIII. But those folk associations were peppered throughout the song in such references as the 'hobby horse', a regular motif in mummers' plays, Morris dancing and May Day celebrations. Elgar's *Land of Hope and Glory* was invoked too, as was Old Father Thames in a heady mix of folklore and finance. Gabriel continued to play with idea of the past and the present, as well as what the nation was told and whether it was true in the live presentation of the song, when he donned one of his more elaborate consumes to portray himself as Britannia, the embodiment of imperial Britain, and 'the voice of Britain before the *Daily Express*' as he pointed out in his introduction. (As an aside, it's a nice consequence that the 'Paper late!' line in the song eventually begat a new one, *Paperlate*, coming from Collins repeatedly singing that line in a soundcheck, creating the groove that they used on the lead track on 1982's *3x3* EP.)

That Gabriel proclaimed Britannia was ill and was speaking from the English Channel – or, depending on the venue, the Atlantic Ocean – 'where it is cold and wet' – spoke again of a country caught between two stools, one that didn't know where it's future lay. Was it as part of a new post-war Europe or as a satellite of the USA? In either direction lay the dilution of Englishness. Was that worth the price? These were complex questions that, had they come from the pen of Lennon or Dylan, would have been lauded as the new voice of a generation. Genesis were not that obvious and the message tended to get missed.

Musically, 'Dancing With the Moonlit Knight' went through distinct sections again, the initial melody having been written by Gabriel on piano, Hackett picking it up and reinterpreting it on guitar with a riff that has since become something of a signature of his. From there, it moves into an electric section that came from improvisation in rehearsals. From the outset, Hackett lays down a marker that electric guitar is going to play its biggest role yet on a Genesis record with the fastest playing of his career, using the tapping technique, all leading into the massed Mellotron choir, an emotionally powerful section before Gabriel returns. Meanwhile, not for the last time on the album, Collins produces impossible drumming that's beamed in from another planet.

It ends in a more pastoral section that had the working title 'Disney', the band seeing it as something suitable for a cartoon soundtrack. In concert, it became an eerie proposition, Hackett playing some jagged lines across what was essentially a fade out. At the writing stage, there was talk of joining the song with 'The Cinema Show' to create another side-long epic, but conscious of not repeating themselves in the wake of 'Supper's Ready', that idea was discarded.

'I Know What I Like (In Your Wardrobe)' opened with Gabriel sounding like the white rabbit from *Alice In Wonderland*, fittingly enough now that the Charisma logo was Tenniel's illustration of the Mad Hatter's tea party. A chunk of the song had been around for a while, dating back to previous album sessions, before the band finally came together to turn it into a song, as Hackett recalls:

> I really wasn't worried about operating as a writer on this album, and yet I ended up kicking off a couple of key things for the band – the guitar riff on 'I Know What I Like' had been around since *Foxtrot,* but everyone thought it sounded too much like The Beatles and so they didn't want to do it. But I kept playing it, Phil got interested in it, and finally, everyone else joined in. It became our first hit – and no one else has ever said to me that it sounds like The Beatles!

That's very true, but it is Collins' Ringo-esque roll into 'There's always been Ethel' that's the kicker that turns this into a potential single, and it's a nice piece of conceptual continuity that their first hit contains mention of Banks and Gabriel's school band, the Garden Wall. Lyrically, it has the same preoccupations as 'Harold the Barrel', the disapproving face of English propriety looking down on those who do not conform to the norm, and it's those little eccentricities which pepper the song that perhaps prevented it from being a bigger hit. After all, how many hit records concern themselves with wardrobes, keeping your mowing blades sharp or feature the lead singer blowing a raspberry and then scatting? All of which was to the good, keeping the song very rooted in Genesis country.

The single also became inextricably linked to the album cover, a figure lying on a park bench, looking for a bit of peace and quiet while being badgered by all kinds of critical figures, all wanting him to do something or be someone. The painting in question was the work of Betty Swanwick, the band having deliberately chosen to move away from Paul Whitehead after he'd been at the helm for the previous three albums. Where Whitehead had illustrated the covers after hearing the songs in the past, this time it was a chance viewing of Swanwick's pencil sketch, *The Dream*, at the Royal Academy that had inspired the lyric. Gabriel immediately wrote down the names of a number of characters in the exhibition catalogue, Jacob at that point being called 'The Fool', and from there created the lyrics. Art historian Beth Williamson has noted that a 'Juxtaposition of tradition and the modern was at the heart of Swanwick's concerns', which aligned perfectly with the themes of *Selling England by the Pound*. It's surprising that the band initially asked her to come up with a new work for the cover, but in the end, time was against them on that front. As a compromise, they asked her to reprise *The Dream*, bring it to life in watercolour and to add the lawnmower, which was now a part of the lyric, as well as a garden fork. The pastel colours only add to the piece's Englishness, making for one of Genesis' most satisfying album sleeves. The association with the group didn't do Swanwick any harm either. In 1974, she found her work on the cover of the Royal Academy's catalogue for their Summer Exhibition – in the foreground, the ghosts of Sir Joshua Reynolds and Angelica Kauffman are enthralled by some abstract art while in the background, a very contemporary crowd that could have come straight from a Genesis gig are staring at an old fashioned portrait of the Queen on horseback.

Perhaps the most enduring song on the album is 'Firth of Fifth', certainly instrumentally. Banks brought it to the writing sessions as three distinct pieces, but ultimately they were combined into one song at Rutherford's suggestion, Rutherford also helping out on the lyrics. Both have been dismissive of them, but in the context of the record, they work. It's a different facet of Englishness this time, almost like the words of a hymn, something of William Blake about it, if not at that heady level. If anything, it suffers from starting and finishing on two brilliant couplets, the rest of it not quite living up to the rest.

The song opens in suitably majestic form, a Banks piano solo that is akin to Hackett's 'Horizons' on the previous record, this one having a hymnal quality to it. Like 'I Know What I Like', part of this had been around a year earlier, Banks recalling in *The Genesis Songbook*, 'Phil found it very difficult to play on this one part of it, so we dropped the idea. I'm glad we did 'cause I developed it a lot better. I think it was great to be told 'no' at that point and produce something a lot better as a result.' For all that it's a Banks song, it's in the rehearsal room that it really took flight, the contributions of the others to the arrangement making absolute sense of the 'all songs by all' approach to the credits. Following the initial lyric, there's a lovely flute melody that leads into a piano solo that then shifts onto synthesizer, Rutherford and Collins underpinning it all masterfully – this is surely the pinnacle of Collins' complexity as a drummer, certainly inside the band, and it works superbly. As the synth solo goes on, Hackett begins to coast over the top of it before leaning into the melody and producing the finest guitar solo in the Genesis repertoire, bending the notes to add a new flavour to it, the song eventually fading out on a reprise of the piano introduction. In one form or another, the song has been a hardy perennial in the repertoire, either in full or instrumental form.

The next song was something of a departure, 'A little love song, which is quite a breakthrough', as Gabriel told *Sounds*. 'More Fool Me' was a collaboration between Collins, who got another crack at a lead vocal after writing the lyrics, and Rutherford who produced the music, a sparkling acoustic accompaniment. The words are classically Collins, highlighting the simpler, more direct style that would win him legions of followers on *Face Value* in due course, and it was a distinct departure for the band. That said, while the vocal has a certain winsome charm, there's nothing that really marks it out as the voice of a coming global superstar. It lacks real conviction in the delivery and you can see why, on the strength of that, he wasn't immediately considered for filling Gabriel's shoes full-time in due course. The performance of this is light years away from the brilliant way he took on the material on *A Trick of the Tail*, indicating what strides he made once he got the bit between his teeth.

The song actually works better on the CD, coming as a pretty interlude between the meat of 'Firth of Fifth' and 'The Battle of Epping Forest', but on the original vinyl, it feels slightly odd as the end of side one. Perhaps it should have traded places with 'After the Ordeal', but on such a long album – 53 minutes – timing concerns were paramount to get the best sound they could after abusing the limitations of the vinyl so much, and so the end of a side was the only place for it. Perhaps its inclusion had political overtones, too, for the drummer wasn't entirely happy with his situation in the group and Rutherford revealed later on that the band thought he was about to leave. Speaking at the time, Collins told *Sounds*, 'My song came about because we were all going to do feature spots, but I was the only one who actually got it together. There's a lot in each of us that doesn't come out in the band. Steve and Tony should do instrumental things.' That sounds not unlike the way Yes had set things up on *Fragile*, but Genesis weren't really that kind of band, full of hotshot soloists. Collins aside, the best technical player in the group, they were still very much driven by songwriting and the desire to deliver the best possible version of the song, utilising the ensemble rather than blazing away individually.

Perhaps because he sat slightly outside the group of songwriters at that stage, it was Collins who had the itchiest feet. He was already involved in session work and had created a pick-up band, Zocks and the Radar Boys, who played pub gigs in and around London, often involving former Yes guitarist Peter Banks among others – essentially a forerunner of Brand X. There was also talk of a solo release too, as he told *Sounds* in November '73: 'I'm cutting a single which came about when I demoed some songs for Mike and Anthony Phillips, who used to be in the band. Strat liked what he heard and decided to put it out as a single, although I don't know yet what name it'll go out under.'

This was the legendary 'Silver Song', penned by Phillips and Rutherford on the departure of Jonathan Silver from the band and destined to become a millstone around Phillips' neck for years:

I'd worked with Phil before because he'd come down with some friends to help sing on the demo of the hymn that Mike and I did for *Beyond an Empty Dream*. I got to know him pretty well. He lived in Epsom, my parents were in Send, near Woking, and Phil didn't drive in those days, so I'd drive him to and from there when we were working on things. I got to know him pretty well, he played in our football team once as well, I think, so we got on very well. 'Silver Song' was an odd one, in that it was designed as a single but was never released. It suffered from being a good demo and a slightly stiff master, but all my friends loved it, it was commercial and although it was set to be a single, it never got released and I had people always asking me, 'Why hasn't it come out?' I think the record company were a little disappointed because it lacked the country looseness of the demo. Subsequently, I was plagued by it, it followed me around, people asking about it, trying to wedge it into every other project I did! There was a stage where they were trying to get other artists to cover it, but nobody would, possibly because Phil had made it so much his own. I remember he took a rough mix of it into a radio station to play, possibly Nicky Horne at Capital, and that got heavily bootlegged. It would have made a lovely single, but it's one that got away, and nobody quite knew the reason why.

It eventually showed up on the reissues of Phillips' *The Geese and the Ghost* and on hearing it, he was right – it should have been a single, although perhaps for Genesis' longevity, it was maybe a good thing it wasn't at the time.

Released or not, it was indicative of some growing unease inside the group, Gabriel having already floated one bizarre idea in *New Musical Express*: 'Phil and I are considering getting together an album of completely banal pop tunes absolutely riddled with clichés so that he can sing and I can play drums.' Hackett indicated that the frustration was, in part, because of the public perception of the band. 'More solo work will be creeping in because it's difficult to get individual identities across when the band is personified as a whole by Peter. This does create a problem in the band – no bitterness towards Peter, but there are some terrible misconceptions and it becomes frustrating when people are wrongly credited with doing certain things.'

Nobody could mistake the lyricist on 'The Battle of Epping Forest' though, for that had Gabriel's fingerprints all over it. Another of his comic operettas, this was sourced from a newspaper clipping that detailed a meeting of two rival gangs in Epping Forest, out to settle the rights to run a protection racket in a small area of east London. Although Gabriel had long lost the clipping by the time it came to write the words, the general idea proved fertile ground and he pieced together an incredible cast of characters across the song's twelve minutes. The lyric is full of epic Gabriel wordplay, vocal characterisations, all delivered at 100mph. It's genuinely funny, another slice of English life that fits into the general theme of the record, but initially, at least, it was perhaps too much for listeners to take in, especially with so much going on musically too. For Genesis fans, though, that's a part of its charm because it doesn't matter how often you listen to it, there's always some new piece of detail that grabs the attention. The band generally look askance at it, largely because it is so busy, but there are so many ideas in it, and they come at you so thick and fast – Hackett playing reggae guitar in time with an echo, Harold Demure nipping up a tree, the arrival of the crooked vicar – that if you don't like one, there'll be another along in a minute.

The calm after the storm, 'After the Ordeal' has a similar feel to 'Dancing With the Moonlit Knight', rooted in earlier English music. Hackett's guitar parts, first on nylon on his own composition and then on electric playing a melody written by Rutherford, are things of beauty and the song is also another nice reminder of Gabriel's worth as a flautist in a glorious flourish at the end of the track. Personally, the biggest drawback is that I can never hear the opening strains without thinking of Tony Hatch's theme to the soap opera *Crossroads* – but that's probably just me. There's some lovely, restrained playing throughout on what is predominantly Hackett's composition, though it has the sense of being one of those famous Genesis bits that perhaps was better suited to being amalgamated within a longer song. There were arguments as to whether this should have made it to the final album – and over whether 'The Cinema Show' should have been edited down – but in the end, the compromise was to put everything on the record. That compromise was the right way to go.

'The Cinema Show' kicks off in classic Genesis vein, building around a glorious 12-string piece from Rutherford, written in a tuning he has long since forgotten. It's perhaps the prettiest of all of those guitar pieces, dating all the way back to *Trespass,* and it's a pity that the front section of the song was later jettisoned in live performance. There's much to enjoy in there, including some lovely lead lines from Hackett and the chance to bask in some warming harmonies, straight from the Crosby, Stills & Nash playbook. The bone of contention came in the second half of the song, where there were complaints from Gabriel and Hackett that the instrumental section, particularly the keyboard solo, went on for too long, but frankly, that's nonsense. It's the same as 'Supper's Ready' in that you need the prolonged build-up in order to get the real payoff. What's different here is that payoff is instrumental rather than vocal, perhaps because Gabriel didn't write the lyric, which was the work of Banks and Rutherford? As it is, the improvised instrumental section written by the Banks, Collins and Rutherford trio was a big part of the live set for years after and rightly so.

All it lacks is that big vocal finish because instead, it fades out so that it can run into the album closer, 'Aisle of Plenty'. That acts as a nice bookend to the album, reprising the melody from 'Dancing With the Moonlit Knight' as they'd done within the one song in 'Supper's Ready', but it also crystallises that theme of an England – perhaps one that never really existed – being under attack, notably from naked commercialism, advertising, selling English biscuits by the pound. Gabriel's subtext is that this is now a country that knows the price of everything and the value of nothing. As an aside, it's this album that underscores the fact that of any of the later progressive bands, it's Big Big Train who are the true inheritors of the early Genesis mantle, not as copyists but because they embody similar concerns for the country and what we have lost as a culture by the never-ending rush for profit.

The reaction to the new record was positive, reaching a new chart high of number three. The review in *Sounds* argued that 'the composition of the album as a whole is such that it remains fluid and carefully wrought for the best possible impact'. In *New Musical Express*, Barbara Charone was effusive: 'The band's best, most adventurous album to date ... Genesis stand head and shoulders above all those so-called progressive groups.' There was plenty to agree with in the reviews for on a playing level, the band had continued to come on in leaps and bounds and there are sections of material that are up there among the very best things Genesis have ever done – the end section of 'The Cinema Show', the piano introduction and the instrumental section of 'Firth of Fifth', the first half in particular of 'Dancing With the Moonlit Knight'. If it had a fault, it was that this was a great record that felt as if it should have been even better.

It's an album where the instrumental sections are more memorable than the vocal parts, the start of 'Dancing With the Moonlit Knight' excepted, and that was telling, suggesting a fresh fracture coming within the band. Gabriel was less than enamoured with the lyrics to 'The Cinema Show' and 'Firth of Fifth and it seems that in one respect, *Selling England by the Pound* was the Rubicon – other than cover versions, he was very rarely going to be happy to sing anyone else's words again.

These were considerations for the future, however, for by the time the album was out, Genesis were touring again. The journey back to the road had not been an easy one, for their staging plans were scuppered by tragedy elsewhere, Gabriel explaining in the press, 'The idea was to have an inflatable set onto which one could project, but since Summerland, everything has gone to pieces because although it's fireproofed by the old regulations, the new ones rule inflatables out.' (The Summerland leisure centre disaster happened on the Isle of Man on 2 August 1973 when a fire spread through the building after a cigarette or match was dropped on the floor. Some 50 people were killed, 80 seriously injured.)

As a consequence, Genesis retained much of the staging they'd used earlier in the year, plus a sprinkling of new costumes for Gabriel. They played a series of three triumphant shows at London's Rainbow Theatre in October, Jerry Gilbert's *Sounds* review catching the general mood: 'What I particularly enjoyed about Friday's show was the spiritual and emotional content of the show which came flooding across. The ten-minute standing ovation at the end of it all was in no way exaggerated.' There were dissenting voices, however, the coming direction of travel of the *New Musical Express* hinted at in Andrew Tyler's piece on the same show: 'Maybe they'll eventually decide you don't need to throw everything you know into every song to make things work.'

Following fifteen sold out shows in the UK and two days in Shepperton Studios to produce an 'In Concert' film that only got an official release in the 2007 box sets, it was off to North America again for a tour that would take them through to Christmas. By now, they had engaged the services of Tony Smith as full-time manager, and their financial position was very much on their minds, as Collins told *Sounds*:

> We had to put our ticket prices up this time which is a sad thing to do, but it's a vicious circle, because we can't go on playing for nothing and getting ourselves into more debt, but at the same time, we can't stop doing what we are doing because that's what the band's all about. The financial situation is something we never think about because if we did, it would depress us. We're taking all our own stuff across to America, so we'll lose money out there too.

Those shows did begin to create a following for the band, though, notably on the two coasts. On Thanksgiving Day, they played an incredible show at the Felt Forum, one that found release as one of the very best Genesis bootlegs, *A Death in Anytown*, which is highly recommended as a snapshot of the band at perhaps the peak of their time as a five-piece. While in New York, they received an endorsement that they would always cherish, as Hackett recalled:

> I remember Peter Gabriel was very excited that he'd heard John Lennon had given us the thumbs up on a radio station, WNEW, probably interviewed by Scott Muni. This was when we were in New York and barely able to get a gig in the rest of the States at that point. He said we were one of the bands he was listening to, just as *Selling England by the Pound* was coming out, and that was a great lift. Maybe he was just thinking he should say something nice about some contemporary band and he picked us out of the air, I don't know, but we took it quite literally that he was listening to us at home. 'Lennon likes what we do? That's good!' I don't think we capitalised on it enough at the time actually, we should have had press handouts reminding all the American folks at home that we'd arrived! It took a lot longer to become known in those days, you didn't have Twitter, Facebook, websites, so news travelled at the speed of one telephone at a time! It was word of mouth and that meant slow growth for Genesis in America. We relied on college radio; that was what broke us in the early days, long before MTV. Things did work at

a different speed, but it probably helped the band not to get too big-headed too quickly. Made us try harder probably.

1974: I'd Give You All of My Dreams

Another year, another tour. Genesis kicked off 1974 with a show in Bristol, followed by a five-date residency at the Theatre Royal, Drury Lane, during which they made use of the theatre's *Peter Pan* wire to fly Peter Gabriel above the stage during the final section of 'Supper's Ready', the singer ascending to the heavens as he sang of the New Jerusalem. More dates followed in Europe ahead of another lengthy jaunt in the States that started at the beginning of March and lasted just over two months, the band having six guitars stolen ahead of the final night of the tour in New York.

1974 was to see the band hit another milestone in their career – their first hit single, 'I Know What I Like (In Your Wardrobe)', spending seven weeks in the chart and peaking at number 21 for two weeks. It might have gone higher yet, but the band refused to appear on the BBC's *Top of the Pops* show, and nor would they allow a clip from the *In Concert* film to be screened in their place either. Tony Banks explained the reasoning to *Disc*. 'We made an excuse to the BBC. We told them all our equipment had been flown to the States. That's true, actually, but it isn't the real reason we backed out. It was a question of managerial policy. We work best in a live atmosphere and we don't like the way groups are staged on *Top of the Pops*. The lighting's too harsh – the whole thing turns out too plastic. I'm the only member of the group who wouldn't have minded performing the single on the show. I think that if you're going to the bother of releasing one, you might as well go the whole hog and promote it. But I know what the others mean.'

'Twilight Alehouse' was finally given a release as the B-side to the single, snatches of the song going all the way back to *From Genesis to Revelation* when it appeared as a link piece at the start of 'The Serpent'. One of those typical early Genesis songs that went from acoustic to electric, it was regularly played live across 1970 and '71, and had been a contender for a place on *Nursery Cryme* and *Foxtrot*. It had been released as a free flexidisc with *ZigZag* magazine in October 1973, but this offered a more permanent method of keeping hold of a fine example of a style that the band were about to move away from forever.

Thoughts were turning towards the new record, Gabriel promising that, 'We're going into the new album with a strong feeling that change is about to take place … we really want a radical change'. After the difficulties they'd faced in finding a location to write *Selling England by the Pound*, for the new one, they were going to go back to the idea of cutting themselves off from everything, as Phil Collins told *Melody Maker*: 'We're all going to live in a house in Surrey to work. They're going to bring down the Island mobile studio to try and capture more of the excitement and feeling we put into our playing. Whenever I tape a rehearsal, it always seems to have more feeling than when the final LP comes out after it's been mixed and remixed in the studio.'

The Lamb Lies Down on Broadway

Personnel: Tony Banks, Phil Collins, Peter Gabriel, Steve Hackett, Mike Rutherford
Guest musician: Brian Eno
Producer: John Burns & Genesis
Assistant engineer: David Hutchins
Cover art: Hipgnosis
Recorded at Glaspant Manor, Capel Iwan, and Basing Street Studios, London, August – October 1974.
Released: 22 November 1974
Label: Charisma Records
Running time: 94:12
Tracklisting: 1. The Lamb Lies Down on Broadway 2. Fly on a Windshield 3. Broadway Melody of 1974 4. Cuckoo Cocoon 5. In the Cage 6. The Grand Parade of Lifeless Packaging 7. Back in NYC 8. Hairless Heart 9. Counting Out Time 10. Carpet Crawl 11. The Chamber of 32 Doors 12. Lilywhite Lilith 13. The Waiting Room 14. Anyway 15. Here Comes the Supernatural Anaesthetist 16. The Lamia 17. Silent Sorrow in Empty Boats 18. The Colony of Slippermen 19. Ravine 20. The Light Dies Down on Broadway 21. Riding the Scree 22. In the Rapids 23. It
All songs by Banks/Collins/Gabriel/Hackett/Rutherford.

The 'house in Surrey' in question was Headley Grange, made famous by Led Zeppelin during the recording of their fourth album, later playing host to Bad Company and the Pretty Things. It's fair to say that none of these bands were conscientious housekeepers, and when Genesis arrived to set up, bringing their families with them in some cases, they found it infested with rats and knee-deep in filth. Unsurprisingly, they were less than thrilled, Steve Hackett summing things up: 'We used this derelict house in the country and I like to be comfortable! Maybe it was a 'back to the dorm' philosophy, mattresses on floors, it was pretty spartan, which got me down. I didn't really relax into the feel of the album which, having come from an album I was really happy with, was hard.'

Hackett, of course, was not in the band when they decamped to Christmas Cottage back in 1969 to really form the idea of Genesis and write, and their writing stint in 1971 at Tony Stratton Smith's rather better-appointed country house came at a point when he had newly joined his first professional band. Fast forward three years, and for him – and the rest of the group – life was different. At 18, 19, 20, it's very easy to become dedicated to something to the point of obsession because, by and large, everything else can wait. Further down the line, as you head into your mid-20s, life begins to become more complicated, and that was exactly what faced some members of Genesis as they headed for Headley Grange. In Hackett's case, his marriage was breaking up; a situation made all the more difficult by the fact that he had a son, Oliver, born in February 1974. Gabriel's situation was, if anything, even more complex. His wife Jill was heavily pregnant, with the baby due in July, but all had not been well between them, Jill having had a brief affair with Genesis tour manager Regis Boff late the previous year, 'My pathetic little bid for attention', as she later told Spencer Bright for his biography of Gabriel. Genesis' punishing working schedule, allied to their lack of financial success with the band still heavily in debt to Charisma, was beginning to cause personal issues and to fracture the 'one for all' ethos of the early days.

Beyond that, there was still a certain itchiness of feet – Collins was playing with his pub pick-up group Zocks & the Radar Boys and was looking to do more sessions, Gabriel regularly expressed an interest in writing songs with Martin Hall, Hackett was building up an increasing stockpile of material that wasn't making it through the selection process, and Rutherford was working on an album with Anthony Phillips. In short, they were growing up and confronting the kind of everyday problems that hit us all when we do that and find ourselves having to juggle fresh and increasing responsibilities while our ambitions, tastes and ideas are still developing and changing. Holding everything together in such circumstances, particularly in an artistic situation where the protagonists all have strong opinions, is never easy. Those opinions were beginning to become increasingly divergent, and that was to create some musical tension which, while not making life easy, did perhaps make for a fertile writing environment – great art doesn't always come out of serenity after all.

Going into the record, the band decided that the time was right to take on that project which confronted all serious rock bands of the age eventually – the concept album. Various ideas were kicked around,

Rutherford's suggestion that they base it on Antoine de Saint-Exupery's book *The Little Prince* getting the most serious consideration alongside Gabriel's preferred idea, which, at that time, didn't have a central character. He later admitted to Armando Gallo that going through the usual democratic process was 'bullshit on my part, as there was only one story which I was going to develop'. Given he was the singer and perhaps the principal lyricist, it made some sense that it should be his story that was developed, but this time, that alone wasn't enough. Noting that few books were written by committee, he insisted on writing all the lyrics himself, a suggestion that was rather less well-received within the band, particularly by Banks and Rutherford, who between them had contributed somewhere close to half the lyrics in the past. There was concern that having just one writer would mean the words all being similar in character, a reasonable criticism, as was the worry that the notorious snail's pace at which Gabriel worked would mean he wouldn't get the lyrics ready on time. Yet Gabriel's reasoning was equally sound. Irresistible force met immovable object, the singer getting his way in the end, though that then meant that during the writing process, the group was essentially divided between lyricist and musicians, Gabriel working on the words separately from the rest of the band, who were jamming away to produce the music. It was perhaps the best compromise, but good as the finished product was, it meant that both words and music were lacking key contributors.

Hindsight does show that Gabriel's ear was closer to the ground than his colleagues and that he was right in his desire to take Genesis in an earthier direction. Although punk was still a couple of years away when work started on the album, he could feel the winds of change, that patience was beginning to grow thin with the bands that had dominated the first half of the '70s. An inveterate reader of the music press, he understood its power, underlining his unease with it in a spectacular stand-off with Neil Spencer in a *New Musical Express* interview just prior to the album's release. 'We wanted [Rael] to be this earthy and aggressive sort of person, but instead of making him a British earthy person, whom almost the entire staff of the *NME* would knock us for writing about because we know nothing about earthy British people, or so it goes … we've chosen an American person, who clearly we can't even pretend to know anything about. So there is that separation, partly resulting from our, er, being subjected to the rights and wrongs of the class struggle.' For all that withering fire though, he knew that Genesis needed to wriggle

free of the trap that was beginning to get them in its grasp, telling Daryl
Easlea later: 'We were beginning to get into the era of big fat supergroups
of the seventies and I thought, 'I don't want to go down with this Titanic'.'

Work carried on apace at Headley Grange, so much so that it became
evident that there were enough musical ideas around to push for a
double album, thereby increasing Gabriel's workload – though how he
would have got all the ideas inherent in the lyrics across in anything
but a double is a moot point. Having reluctantly acquiesced to Gabriel's
demands regarding the lyrics, it was a bombshell when, in June, he
called the band together to ask them to put things on hold for six
weeks. You'll recall that the story of the girl in the green trouser suit,
one of Gabriel's onstage monologues, was printed on the back of the
Live album. That had come to the attention of William Friedkin, then
the hottest new director in Hollywood on the back of the success of
The Exorcist and *The French Connection*. He had checked Genesis out
when they played a residency of six shows at Los Angeles' Roxy just
before Christmas 1973 and had been further intrigued by Gabriel's
stories. Looking to bring some new ways of thinking to bear on the film
industry, Friedkin contacted Gabriel and asked if he was interested in
working on some story ideas and perhaps a script.

He probably caught the singer – who had turned down a place at film
school in order to persevere with Genesis back in 1969 – at precisely
the right moment. He and Jill had repaired their relationship, but she
was nearing the end of her pregnancy and the idea of taking a month
or so to leave Headley Grange, work at home on some film ideas, and
be there with his wife as the birth approached was obviously seductive.
Attacking a fresh medium, and without the need to deal with the band's
quasi-democratic approach to everything, was exciting too, offering a
better way of tapping into the visual sides of his interest than a concert
situation, with its limited budgets and scope, ever could. Gabriel was
sold on the idea.

Life, however, is never quite that simple, for it was equally
understandable that the rest of the band, having given Gabriel his head
with the lyrics, were pretty hacked off at the thought that their somewhat
tardy singer, already behind on the work, was now looking at taking six
weeks off to pursue something that was of no value to the collective.
The timing was certainly off. Had Friedkin approached Gabriel earlier in
the year, it might have been something he could have slotted into their
downtime before they started writing again. But now, with everything

in full swing, the idea that they should sit twiddling their thumbs while Gabriel went off and enjoyed himself went down like the proverbial lead balloon. Band politics played a part here, of course. As noted, there was general frustration that Gabriel was seen as the star of the show and this could only exacerbate matters, while the others would not have been human if they'd not experienced a pang of jealousy at their singer getting an opportunity that was not extended to the rest of them – the fact that Friedkin was talking of using Tangerine Dream for the prospective soundtrack can't have helped either. It was also true that, at that point, only Gabriel looked to have any kind of viable career away from the group because he had been the focal point and so had a name that resonated beyond the Genesis umbrella. The others? They would have soldiered on as Genesis with the music they were making, but what if it didn't sell?

The issue went beyond politics and on to practicalities and financial realities. Their debt to Charisma Records was substantial, said to be in the region of £150,000, roughly £1.6million in today's money. While that was not recoupable from the individuals if the band folded, all future record sales of the back catalogue would go to pay that off if they quit – and had Genesis called it a day at that point, without having achieved a breakthrough in America, that back catalogue would have been largely worthless. Recognising their problems, they'd taken on Tony Smith to manage them and to sort out their business headaches – on one US tour, their road manager had contrived to throw away all the receipts from the entire tour, news of which left the taxman entirely unsympathetic. But engaging Smith meant they had to become more businesslike. Having someone on board who understood the figures also meant having somebody who saw what they needed to do in order to improve those figures, to pay off those debts and to gradually start earning some money in return for all their hard work. If they weren't going to compromise on the show – and they weren't – then they had to make those shows pay, which meant doing more of them in a concentrated timeframe, thereby employing crew, tour buses, articulated lorries for the gear, for a shorter period, thereby saving money. It also meant playing the biggest places you could hope to fill and at a higher ticket price. That's economics. It's also the end of the hippie dream, and Gabriel, in particular, found that he didn't enjoy being part of the machinery. Unfortunately, at that point in Genesis' evolution, there was little option, for they simply weren't big enough to enjoy the luxury of taking a year out. Moreover, there was a tour booked to start in the UK in October, then running across Europe and North America through to the following March, hefty deposits paid everywhere in order to secure the halls. Missing those dates was not an option if the band was to have a future.

As is always the way in such situations, personal or professional, heels were dug in and it eventually came down to an ultimatum – was Gabriel with Genesis or Friedkin? Backed into a corner, he chose Friedkin and left the group. The band hunkered down and carried on writing, thinking they would then write lyrics to fit the music themselves later on. Tony Stratton Smith was rather less sanguine about the collapse of his investment of so much time and money and Friedkin, on hearing that Gabriel had quit the group, was equally horrified, insisting that he had never intended it to be such a firm commitment. He began to backtrack on things. Stratton Smith was able to suggest a compromise and it was left to Rutherford to call Gabriel to make peace. According to *The Book of Genesis*, the singer said, 'If you're not going to allow me to do anything else, I'm not going to stay.' And Mike had replied, 'If you delay the project, we can reach an agreement.' Gabriel was back in the fold, for the time being, at least.

The problems were not over, though. Gabriel's first child was due at the end of July, just as the band were to start recording, using the Island mobile at Glaspant Manor in Carmarthenshire, southwest Wales. When Anna-Marie was born on 26 July, the birth was fraught with complications for mother and child and it was thought that the baby would not survive. There were several weeks where it was touch and go as to whether she would pull through – thankfully, she did – and understandably, Gabriel wanted to be with his family during the crisis. The problem was that they were in St Mary's hospital in Paddington while recording sessions were underway – mostly for songs that were still missing lyrics and often melodies too – 230 miles away. Gabriel recalled in *Chapter and Verse*, 'The roads were terrible, it was like an eight-hour journey … and the band were really unsympathetic. They knew it was serious, but in my mind, there was absolutely no question that on one side was life and death and on the other, an album, and I knew where they go in my priorities.' It was another, much more serious example of how Gabriel found himself being boxed in by being in the band and it was starting to come to a breaking point. 'No-one seems to care, they carry on as if nothing was there' indeed… Rutherford was gracious enough to admit in the video that accompanied the *1970-75* box set that, 'We were so unsupportive. We were young and very into the album and what we were doing, while poor old Pete was having to deal with the terribly traumatic touch-and-go birth of his daughter. We gave him no help at all, actually. I'm sure it must have been very hard.'

Work carried on and eventually, the double album *The Lamb Lies Down on Broadway* was delivered, though not without some feverish late activity back in Basing Street Studios where a lot of the vocals were put down, and where Brian Eno's assistance came in handy to add some 'Enossification' to Gabriel's voice. The band were working in shifts at the end to try and get the mixes finished, though, by this time, Hackett was out of action. At a party backstage at a Sensational Alex Harvey Band gig in mid-October, he'd overheard somebody say, 'They're good, but they'd be nothing without Alex'. It's an indication of just how fraught everything had become by that time, personally and professionally, that he transposed that to being the same as saying Genesis would be nothing without Gabriel. He crushed the wineglass he was holding, severing a tendon and nerve in his thumb, necessitating several days in hospital and a month of convalescence. It meant that all the UK dates and some in Europe had to be postponed, at not inconsiderable cost. The irony of the band now having to take a month off was not lost on Gabriel. 'It was an incredibly stupid thing, and it happened at the most important time,' he told *Melody Maker*. 'We've lost all the money deposited on the halls. I think the rest of us will have to go and busk outside other people's concerts ... We're not a group that goes around smashing up hotel rooms, Rolls Royces and TV sets. But Steve goes out for a little tentative raving, and this happens.' Hackett pointed out to Armando Gallo in *I Know What I Like* that, 'I think I had just had an argument with Peter about the album, telling him that I didn't like the way he was working on it. Peter was very late with the lyrics and we went ahead and recorded all the instrumental parts, and he would come in after, singing over everything ... over passages that I thought were instrumental. To me, it was like taking a painting that I had done and painting red all over it.' That had long been a Gabriel trait, the end sections of 'The Musical Box' and 'Supper's Ready' the obvious examples, but it's indicative of Hackett's state of mind that he reacted so extremely to it on this occasion.

The smallest consolation in it all was it meant that by the time those dates were eventually played, at least the album would be out because after all manner of delays, it finally hit the shops on 22 November. And of all their albums, it was the one that needed the most digesting, not least in terms of the story. Gabriel had provided lengthy sleeve notes inside the gatefold of the Hipgnosis cover, though whether they made the storyline clearer or not was a moot point, the singer all too often giving into the temptation to obfuscate things further with a pun or a clever rhyme. On the subject of temptations, looking at *The Lamb Lies Down on Broadway* as some kind of autobiography is an irresistible one. Gabriel argued that his inspirations had been *Pilgrim's Progress*, *West Side Story* and Jodorowsky's movie *El Topo*. The latter, a 'cowboy spiritual film', was clearly a big influence, Gabriel saying, 'The main character has to learn lessons from a series of teachers, and once he does, he has to kill them to find himself'. That concept – in a metaphorical, not literal state – has been a Gabriel obsession for years, something he returned to in the '80s when he wanted to create a theme park of sorts where the visitors had to confront their fears to move onto the next ride, but it was plain that a lot of his current preoccupations seeped into the lyrics too. How could that be otherwise when much of the material was about the role of the subconscious? The album had been set in New York not merely to give a concrete – in every sense – frame of reference, but because on their trips to the city, all the band were amazed to see steam seeping through the gratings on the street and rising into the air – 'something moving in the sidewalk steam'. As Gabriel explained in *Beat Instrumental* in April 1977, that was a perfect metaphor for an underworld of the mind, so much bubbling away beneath the surface that the rest of the world would only see occasionally. 'One of the first things you notice when you go to New York is the steam rising from out of the manhole covers in the streets. It's a very strange sight and it gave me the idea of a vast underground world going on which we are not aware of as we walk on the surface. It all ties in with the conscious and the subconscious mind.'

The character of Rael, the Puerto Rican punk – before that had any Sex Pistols connotations – was not the beginning of the story apparently, but arrived in order to give it shape. When Gabriel spoke of him in interviews, it was clear that he identified with his creation, who he saw more as an Everyman. 'It's the idea of him being an outcast in a totally alien situation. I identify with him to a certain extent. This guy is slotless, his name is supposed to be raceless. He feels as if he's a waste of material, part of the machinery. All he can do is escape or give up.' With the gift of hindsight, you don't need to be a psychiatrist to see what the underlying meaning of all of that was, particularly since the sleeve notes contained the line, 'I'm putting [a character] down to watch him break up, decompose and feed another sort of life'. Short of wearing a giant hat that opened up to reveal a neon sign blaring, 'Help, get me out of here!', it's hard to see how Gabriel could have made his feelings any clearer, and it's extraordinary that none of his colleagues noticed – though Collins says he still hasn't read the notes to this day – nor that any journalists came to the obvious conclusions at the time.

The story included a healthy dose of moral fable too – that a casual sexual dalliance brought with it hideous disfigurement only resolved by castration was a punishment that might have caused even Mary Whitehouse, keeper of the nation's morals at the time, to wince, while given his domestic situation, you could read a hint of hostility, even blame, there. To balance that up, there's a hefty dose of Kafka-esque self-loathing, in part because of his role as a star, in part his failings as a husband, in part his guilt at the prospect of walking out on Genesis – 'the cushioned straitjacket' – which would jeopardise the financial position of both his family and his friends. In opposition to that, there's an incurable optimism that flies in the face of the reality of everything that happens to him, perpetually betrayed by brother John, yet always going back for more.

Having said all that – and it's easy to forget this about a record that has for so long revolved around Gabriel – *The Lamb Lies Down on Broadway* features some of the very best music Genesis ever made. The title track was the last song that the original writing team of Banks and Gabriel wrote together and it's one of their very best, establishing a more direct edge to the band from the outset. It's a telling evocation of the city that never sleeps, setting the Manhattan scene perfectly as well as introducing us to the street kid Rael, the incessant keyboard line summing up the non-stop energy of the place, Hackett's buzzing guitar conjuring up the fly that's about to meet its maker.

'Fly on a Windshield' is a song of two halves, an atmospheric opening as Rael is taken beneath the cloud of dust settling on Times Square – a quarter of a century later, the image of the 'wall of death', and a crust of dust settling on the skin were redolent of the horrors of 9/11. That contemplative opening, acoustic strum with a muted Mellotron in the background, is suddenly replaced by the instrumental crunch as the fly hits the windshield, Banks' favourite moment in the Genesis canon. Indicative of the way they worked at Headley Grange, conjuring moods with their music, this was originally called 'Pharaohs on the Nile', and features some of Hackett's most thrilling playing on the record swooping in and out of focus. It ebbs into 'Broadway Melody of 1974', from the title to the lyric, an evocation of all things American, the good, the bad and the ugly. It underscores that this is a harsher Genesis with a punching bass riff on top of the Mellotron, again buried much lower in the mix than on previous records, an accompaniment more than a lead instrument this time.

Having established the new terrain, there's room for something a little more romantic in Hackett's fluid guitar melody on 'Cuckoo Cocoon', a song where Collins comes to the fore again as a backing vocalist, though he's almost taking a lead role here, singing alongside Gabriel. The singer adds some lovely flute to the song, Banks' rhapsodic accompaniment shining through much more strongly on the 2007 box set remix.

The heartbeat bass that opens 'In the Cage' finds Rael gradually coming to his senses again after being enveloped by the cloud, the pulse gradually quickening as he starts to realise he's not in Manhattan anymore but trapped. A song written by Banks and brought to the sessions, it's the organ part that propels the song along through to a magnificent synth solo, more in the mould of what we'd come to think of as classic Genesis, but with an updated, metallic edge to it. That leads into the 'Outside the cage' section, long since a tour de force in the Genesis live set, as is the keyboard solo that plays under the 'Raindrops keep falling on my head' vocal. It's hard not to read plenty of Gabriel's situation into the lyric, trapped inside the cage, which along with others 'forms a star', but it's the introduction of brother John that's most interesting, refusing to help Rael, leaving him in a violent rage. Is John the rest of the band, is he the music industry or is he another side of Gabriel himself, his alter ego, the part that enjoys playing the rock star, who enjoys the trappings, who won't let him escape, forcing him into submission?

When you consider that Banks, Collins, Hackett and Rutherford were in large part completing music for lyrics they hadn't seen nor had any real idea about, it's astonishing that *The Lamb* is as cohesive as it is, the moods of the different elements so sympathetic with one another. But come the end of the process, there were holes that needed filling, Gabriel needing some music to go with 'The Grand Parade of Lifeless Packaging', the piece put together in Basing Street. It's a bizarre marching song of sorts, the tone set by Banks, some of Gabriel's vocals further processed by Eno. It's both comment on the rat race in general, the demands of society that force people to squeeze themselves into pre-packaged roles, and on the music industry in particular, this week's trend, costume, even face mask, hanging up ready to be filled by one band or another, fooled into thinking they have artistic freedom when they're really little more than 'sales representatives'. Within the story on the sleeve, the line 'individuals may move off the path if their diversions are counter-balanced by others' leaps out, speaking to an industry trying to play both sides of the street. From that perspective, it's a song heavy on self-loathing for the lyricist who finds his ideals being crushed by the wheels of the industry.

Rutherford was the main instigator of 'Back in NYC', which starts side two, a very atypical Genesis song for the time, heavier than anything they'd done to that point, built around a six-string bass riff. Gabriel picked that up with a powerfully aggressive vocal that indicated the real difference between his voice and that of Collins, melodically so similar, perhaps explaining why Genesis played this song so rarely after Gabriel's departure, despite it being a perfect live song. At this stage, Collins didn't have that gravel in the voice – that only came later, largely through years of having to sing over the top of the band in concert, often in a key too high for him, and for Gabriel for that matter. The unremitting synth line from Banks echoes the ideas on the opening track, rooting Rael back in Manhattan again – though this time according to the story, it's merely a perfect reconstruction of the city of his childhood, 'faces and traces of home'. Gabriel gives us a bit of his back story in revealing that his hero had previously spent time in juvenile detention in Pontiac. Shaming those 'sitting in your comfort' is Gabriel's attack on the 'bleeding hearts and the artistcs' that Roger Waters would later take to task on *The Wall*, making the point again that on Rael's mean streets, there aren't too many options.

For all that, he tries to make a clean start, metaphorically shaving the hair from his heart. 'Hairless Heart' is a glorious piece from Hackett's wing of the band, the interplay between his beautiful, weeping guitar and Banks' Mellotron and synth work always such a highlight of the band's output, this one prefiguring the sounds they would create together on 'Entangled' a year later. Had *The Lamb* not been a double, perhaps instrumental ideas like this would not have seen the light of day which would have been sad, but even so, Hackett admits to struggling with the sheer scale of the project: 'It was becoming a monster – double album, concept, which I was rather anti at that time. We were getting so bogged down with the bulk of the stuff that any spontaneous ideas I had couldn't fit, so I put them to one side.'

Where much of *The Lamb* saw a division between Gabriel on words and the rest on music, it wasn't quite as clear cut as that. 'Counting Out Time' was obviously written entirely by Gabriel, albeit that it's really brought to life by Hackett's jerky, guitar synth solo. Collins' voice is prominent again in support, sometimes louder than Gabriel's and it's clear that the arrangement and production on this were very influenced by 'I Know What I Like (In Your Wardrobe)' and the possibilities of getting another hit single. The hook isn't as strong this time though, while the slightly risqué lyrics – Rael, with his newly virginal heart was now on a quest to lose his physical virginity, joining the sexual dots courtesy of a self-help manual, *Erogenous Zones and Difficulties in Overcoming Five of Them* – might have been too far out there for the more prudish radio DJs.

'Carpet Crawl' is undeniably the loveliest track on the album. It was another latecomer, Gabriel toiling long and hard over the melody, Banks and Rutherford developing the music, starting with a reprise of 'The lamb seems right out of place' section of the title track. It's a deceptively simple song, one which has endured to become a Genesis standard, unusually for them at just five minutes long. Gabriel's voice is gorgeous, warm, full, and when Collins joins him on the choruses along with Hackett's ghostly guitar, it's emotionally very powerful. Never mind the fame and the potential for fortune; walking away from a band where you could create something like this must have been the real heartbreak for Gabriel. Cloaked in sensuality – the lambswool carpet, red ochre corridor – the 'you've got to get in to get out' phrase, as well as explaining the figures trapped in this underworld and their attempts to escape, may be a sexual metaphor too, not least because Gabriel returned to it in 'Humdrum' on his first solo album – 'Out of woman come the man / Spend the rest of his life gettin' back where he can.'

The singer's contribution to the second side is especially strong, for 'The Chamber of 32 Doors' was mostly his composition too. Those carpet crawlers from the previous song find themselves finally confronted by 32 doors, 31 of which lead back to where they started, like being stuck in a giant Escher drawing – and maybe that's what the music business had become to Gabriel. The final lines of the song, 'I'd give you all of my dreams, if you'd help me / Find a door / That doesn't lead me back again, take me away,' are not that far detached from 'Solsbury Hill' on his first solo release, famously about his departure from the band. *The Lamb* was all about Gabriel writing about the subconscious, but his own subconscious was busily writing about him. Banks and Hackett are again imperious, Banks creating a churchlike atmosphere, Hackett's yearning guitar figure that opens the song setting the scene. Collins' lovely, loose drumming going into the country and western feel of the 'I'd rather trust a countryman' section, along with the tubular bells, are crucial components, as are the little piano accents added by Banks both there and at the final summing up of the song.

That having a full four sides of material was a challenge begins to become clearer on side three as they dig into the vaults to rescue some unused bits. 'Lilywhite Lilith' is a case in point, cannibalising a riff and melody from 'The Light', a song they played live around 1970 and into early '71, something that Collins had brought in right at the beginning of his tenure with the group – the band tried to resuscitate it as a live tune at the start of the *Wind and Wuthering* tour in 1977, but jettisoned it after one night. Opening with more distorted bass and guitar from Rutherford and Hackett, it starts off the new side with a bang, very much as 'Back in NYC' had the previous one. Lilywhite Lilith becomes Rael's spirit guide despite her blindness, navigating by the way the breezes blow, maybe another admonishment to self not to plan too far ahead but to simply go with the flow and trust to instinct, while having to 'face my fear' is another example of that burgeoning Gabriel obsession.

'The Waiting Room' is another beneficiary of the space Genesis had given themselves on the double album, what we would now term a soundscape, all atmospheres and sounds that are deeply eerie initially. Banks noted that, 'Steve and I are sort of talking to each other', while Collins is getting full value out of his huge percussion rig. The well-worn story is of the writing session at Headley Grange, when they switched the lights out and agreed to play a section that went from dark to light, a storm suddenly whipping up outside until the mood of the music hit that change and the sun began to come out. There is what sounds like a thunderclap three minutes in to cover the shift in gear and from there, Rutherford comes into his own with a bass pulse that brings the piece home, Hackett adding some distinctive lines.

'Anyway' is another triumph of recycling, the piano introduction first used on *Genesis Plays Jackson*. With Rael preparing to meet his hero – Death – at the heart of chaos comes a ferocious Hackett solo that neatly sums up Rael's mental state. It's Hackett who picks up the story on 'Here Comes the Supernatural Anaesthetist', a finished piece that he brought into the rehearsals. Opening on Rutherford's gentle acoustic strum, with Gabriel and Collins singing in unison the brief lyric detailing Death's modus operandi, lead guitar then takes over with perhaps Hackett's best, certainly most extended playing on the record.

As it turns out, Death's aim is not infallible, and Rael finds that he has survived their encounter, finding his way down a long passageway to an ornate pool where he meets 'The Lamia', three snakes with female faces, a tale from Greek mythology. The tale evolved over time, from a character who stole the children of others after her own were taken away to a vampiric creature who preyed on younger lovers; this being the version of the story that Keats used in his poem *Lamia* and which Gabriel seized on. Able to resist anything but temptation, Rael jumps into the water with them. Sinking their teeth into him, Rael clearly disagrees with them and the Lamia are soon dead, Rael absorbing them into himself by eating what remains.

Musically, it's a much more traditional sounding Genesis track than many on the album, more romantic, brought into the group wholesale by Banks who was then able to write the melody to fit Gabriel's lyrics. There's a blistering, melancholic solo from Hackett at the song's conclusion before it slips into the next track, another ambient piece, this time based around a riff of Rutherford's. 'Silent Sorrow in Empty Boats' does exactly what the title suggests, illustrating a grey, brooding, fog-laden landscape as Rael travels on to his next adventure in 'The Colony of Slippermen' on side four. That too opens with another instrumental section that really is entirely separate. The working title was 'Chinese Jam', a sound collage of sorts mainly of Hackett's composing, then awkwardly segueing into the main track, another Banks composition. It comes in on a burst of organ playing that's not unlike the intro to 'The Knife' and goes through a series of changes as Gabriel gabbles through the lyric. In that sense, it's a more refined version of 'The Battle of Epping Forest', words and music not in quite such a fight this time, but there's certainly plenty going on. Again, its longevity has suffered given it's not a lyric that's easily lifted from the album and dropped into the concert situation or played on radio, working only within the context and confines of the story, but for all that, there are significant moments that have endured, notably the keyboard solo from the 'Raven' section. It was initially the bridge that got them from 'In the Cage' to 'Afterglow' on the 1980 tour and then became absorbed within the longer medley that included the instrumental section of 'The Cinema Show' on later tours. Most significant of all though, are a couple of lines of lead vocal from Collins in the role of brother John. After the slight hesitancy of 'More Fool Me', the confidence and power of this delivery is quite startling and really does give a sense that Collins could step out and sing in his own right. That would prove to be quite handy.

Lyrically, 'The Colony of Slippermen' moves the story along further in one song than most of side three did. Finding himself surrounded by a host of 'slubberdegullions' – there's a term that wasn't a staple of rock lyrics – covered in slimy lumps, Rael discovers that these horrific deformities are the consequence of each one of them enjoying some intimate moments with the Lamia and that he too now shares their appearance. I feel an idea for a costume coming on… Not only that, they are now enslaved by their need to satisfy an unquenchable hunger of the senses, inherited from the Lamia. Were this to be released now, you can't help but imagine that Gabriel would have found himself at the centre of a social media storm about the misogynistic bent to some of the lyrics, and it's doubtful that it would have been headed off by the rather drastic method of restoring Rael's youthful complexion – castration. Rael and John volunteer to meet Doktor Dyper who, post-operation, proudly hands them their dismembered members in a plastic tube, which he advises them to wear around their necks, for they can use them again, on occasion, providing they provide plenty of notice – a bit like getting a prescription for Viagra. Probably. In Gabriel's case, perhaps it refers to cutting himself off from the rock star part of his life and personality. Cock rock, anyone?

Not content with emasculating his character, Gabriel pours further misery on poor Rael, for as they are leaving the colony, down swoops a raven and steals the 'tube right out of my hands'. Chasing after it, he calls on John for his help but, once again, John's having nothing to do with helping his brother. 'Even though I never learn, I'd hoped he'd show just some concern' is a line with multiple readings for Gabriel's own predicament. Happy to see somebody else suffer for a change, just as Rael looks set to catch up with the raven, the bird drops the tube into a ravine. Ever had one of those days? 'Ravine' itself is another atmospheric interlude to give everyone a moment to catch their breath again and to consider Rael's latest disaster. It showcases Hackett's incredible ability to conjure sounds that have seemingly nothing to do with the guitar from out of six strings and an armoury of pedals, the wind whipping through the ravine this time. Meanwhile, Rutherford's 12-string contributes to the atmosphere, a piece not unlike one of the main themes from *The Shout* film soundtrack that he worked on with Banks in 1979.

With the deadline pressing, Gabriel finally had to admit he wasn't going to get all the lyrics done on time. Briefing Banks and Rutherford on the gap that needed filling, they produced the words for 'The Light Dies Down on Broadway'. As the title suggests, the song contains a reprise of the title track, albeit slowed down, but it also uses 'The Lamia' in the verses, more conceptual continuity. It's quite a pivotal song lyrically, for from out of nowhere, Rael is given a glimpse of home and a route back to Broadway, an opening in the bank through which he can perhaps get out of this nightmare. Or will it just take him to another dream? As he tries to decide, he hears a familiar voice, his brother John calling for help from the water down below. 'All he can do is escape or give up,' remember? Despite the constant rejections, Rael decides to go and save his brother, the window into his own world closing as he does so. He's stuck there for good.

'Riding the Scree' shows the compositional strength of the trio of Banks, Collins and Rutherford, this piece evolving from jamming together as they had done on 'The Cinema Show' in the past, Collins and Rutherford essentially holding things together while Banks solos away on top. The fanfare section from this song was another that was bolted onto the instrumental section from the earlier piece when they played it as part of a medley. The lyrical action sees Rael burying his fears once again and launching himself down the treacherous slope – 'a bank too steep to climb' moments earlier – and into the water to try and save his brother. A late reminder to Gabriel himself that however steep the mountain, however great the fears, you have to confront them and punch your way out?

Given that the two are now in the raging water, 'In the Rapids' is a remarkably gentle song that doesn't quite fit the action. Musically, it's a very pretty piece of Rutherford's that would have worked as the beginning of something grander and perhaps more stately, but as it is, it feels unrealised. That's a pity because lyrically, this is another cornerstone song as Gabriel rushes headlong towards the finish line, scrambling to squeeze everything in. Plunging into the water, Rael grabs hold of his brother and hauls him to dry land, but when he comes to look at his brother's face, he sees only his own. Has he sacrificed everything to save the other? Must he submerge his own needs, his own ego, to help those who rely on him to survive? At this point, the sleeve notes read remarkably like the girl in the green trouser suit story from *Live* again: 'In this fluid state, he observes both bodies outlined in yellow and the surrounding scenery melting into a purple haze. With a sudden rush of energy up both spinal columns, their bodies, as well, finally dissolve into the haze.' Has Rael achieved spiritual fulfilment? Does he now have all the answers? Was it all worth it? 'It's over to you', is the final, perhaps inevitable, but still slightly unsatisfying, conclusion on the graphic novel of a sleeve.

'It' on the other hand, is a nice finale, guitars to the fore on a piece written by Hackett and Banks, a driving rhythm from Rutherford giving those two the opportunity to run lines in and out of one another in a manner they would return to again on the fast section of 'Inside and Out' from the *Spot the Pigeon* EP. Gabriel meanwhile indulges his love of a good pun to the max in his final vocal with the band. 'It's only knock and know all, but I like it.'

It's a good song, musically excellent, but it's not the powerful climax that we'd been waiting 95 minutes for. It wasn't 'The New Jerusalem', it wasn't 'Why don't you touch me?', it wasn't 'Martyrs, of course, to the freedom that I shall provide.' The emotional pay-off wasn't there to the same degree, compounding the issues that the album had overall, especially in the hands of the critics, who had to make a judgement call on it after maybe three or four plays in total, if that. The reality is that it's a lopsided record because the first two sides are full of great songs, where the last two are full of great ideas. Over time and endless plays, that doesn't matter so much because fans will take the album in the round, live with it and come to an understanding of it, have their own relationship with it. But on playing it for the first time, being unfamiliar with it, it feels as if it starts to meander too much and peters out a bit on side three, then is in too much of a rush to get everything over and done with on side four.

Those drawbacks were very much part of the critical response to the album. Writing in *New Musical Express*, the digestively troubled Pete Erskine opined, 'I suppose listening to this is a bit like busting for a crap and having to wade across a ploughed field in wellies to reach the hedge on the other side'. Stalwart Genesis supporter Chris Welch wasn't a lot more encouraging in *Melody Maker*: 'I wish that rock musicians would learn the importance of self-editing. A few golden miraculous notes and some choice pithy words are worth all the clutter and verbiage in the world … It is lacking in character as they plod through arrangements with little fire or purpose. I have the feeling it is a white elephant.' There was some respite from Barbara Charone in *Sounds* however: 'Stop bitching about the demise of rock'n'roll and the dire lack of anything new. *The Lamb Lies Down on Broadway* sticks out of the present vinyl rubble like a polished diamond.'

Hindsight suggests that Charone knew her onions for *The Lamb* has endured far better than the other reviews suggested it might, though at least Welch's critique was understandable on the basis of a short acquaintanceship with the album before filing his copy. It is adventurous and it is, in parts, unfocused. Some of the pieces that promised least on initial encounter are ones that have endured best of all, especially the instrumental sections on sides three and four. Above all else, above any other record in the Genesis discography, and in most other artists' too for that matter, *The Lamb* repays every listen, for every time I play it, there's always some new detail that comes to the fore, something that I'd not previously heard, however many hundreds of times I've heard it now. A diamond indeed, even if the public wasn't quite so certain at first – *The Lamb* only reached number ten, in part because a double album was so much more expensive, especially in the financially straitened run-up to Christmas as it was on its 22 November release.

With Hackett restored to health, next up was the tour. The band had decided on a brand new show that would see them play the album from start to finish with one, maybe two encores afterwards. No 'Supper's Ready', no 'The Knife', no 'Firth of Fifth'. It was brave, bordering on suicidal, but it represented their complete commitment to the project and perhaps their willingness to bend over backwards to keep Gabriel in the fold. He said at the time, 'What would really excite me is to see the album as a film. The film would make the story more comprehensible, but we're working towards that for in concert presentation.' That staging included Gabriel taking the part of Rael, clad in jeans and leather jacket, the Slipperman his only real costume change, one that was quite dramatic enough for anyone, though he did find himself trapped within a swirling cone for 'The Lamia' and appearing in silhouette as a devilish figure while the band played 'The Waiting Room'. This time around, the real attraction was three film screens at the back of the stage on which played out much of the story through around 1,450 slides that changed in time with the music. Or at least they were supposed to, Collins calculating that the whole thing worked no more than four times on the whole tour.

America would see the first shows, Chicago getting the premiere on 20 November, the album still not even in the shops. That must have been some night. Even so, things were going surprisingly well. That is until they reached Cleveland at the end of November, just half a dozen gigs into a 100 date tour. After the first of their two shows there, Peter Gabriel knocked on the door of Tony Smith's hotel room, went in, and told him that he was leaving Genesis.

Imagine the emotions that Smith, who had just left a highly successful concert promotion business in order to manage Genesis, must have gone through at that moment. He asked Gabriel to take a few days to reconsider, but Gabriel was not going to change his mind this time.

The rest of the band were informed a couple of weeks later as the tour reached Canada and they flew back home for the Christmas break after a show in Buffalo, New York, on 18 December. It's unlikely to have been an especially festive season.

Right: 'More is more.' 'No, less is more.' Steve Hackett and Peter Gabriel in hair-related disagreement, January 1973.

Left and below: Tony Banks, Phil Collins and Mike Rutherford in fetching 'new wave' purple check jackets, three years ahead of their time, January 1973.

Left: The artwork for *Trespass*, the first Genesis album on Charisma, leaned heavily on the Biblical connotations of their name. (*Charisma*)

Right: Artist Paul Whitehead took his lead from Peter Gabriel's macabre lyrics for 'The Musical Box' when painting the *Nursery Cryme* sleeve. (*Charisma*)

Right: The band were less happy with Whitehead's *Foxtrot* cover, his third for them, but the fox in the red dress was to provide inspiration for their theatrical breakthrough. (*Charisma*)

Left: The budget *Live* album from early 1973 illustrated Gabriel's early use of masks on stage, the cover capturing the '666' section of 'Supper's Ready'. (*Charisma*).

Left: Phil Collins in those far off days in 1973 when he was 'only' the drummer, January 1973.

Right: The first mask that Peter Gabriel used with the band was the fox head, cribbed from the *Foxtrot* cover, accompanied by a red dress he stole from his wife's wardrobe. It was used, rather incongruously, at the end of 'The Musical Box' in early 1973.

Left: By the end of 1973, the fox head had been replaced by the old man mask. That made much more sense as Gabriel acted out the frustrations of wizened little Henry on the opening of his musical box.

Right: Not all (keyboard) heroes wear capes – the forever understated Tony Banks in January 1973.

Left: The flawless flautist Peter Gabriel enjoys a rare moment in the instrumental spotlight in France in early 1973.

Right: From black to white, Gabriel's change of clothing emphasised the eventual triumph of good over evil at the conclusion of 'Supper's Ready'.

GENESIS

SELLING ENGLAND BY THE POUND

Left: Betty Swanwick's sketch 'The Dream', reprised for the *Selling England By The Pound* cover, inspired the lyrics for 'I Know What I Like (In Your Wardrobe)'. (*Charisma*)

Above: Promotional pound notes, Gabriel in full bloom replacing the Queen, were issued to support sales of *Selling England By The Pound*. (*Charisma*)

Right: *The Lamb Lies Down On Broadway* was a marked change for Genesis, not just musically but visually too, with this graphic novel-style cover. (*Charisma*)

Left: Colin Elgie's depiction of lyrics from *A Trick Of The Tail* underlined the fact that the first post-Gabriel album was still rich in Genesis' characteristic storytelling. (*Charisma*)

Left and below: Genesis would go on to become video stars in the MTV age, but back in 1976, they were just finding their way with this promo for 'A Trick Of The Tail'.

Left: The *In Concert* film shot at Stafford Bingley Hall in July 1976, captured Genesis' first tour with Phil Collins behind the microphone.

Right: Mike Rutherford and Phil Collins duet on the chorus of 'I Know What I Like (In Your Wardrobe)' from the *In Concert* film. Note how carefully Collins has positioned the microphone ...

Above and right: Collins at the microphone and Banks at the controls of his battery of keyboards for the 'Many Too Many' promo shoot at Knebworth, June 1978.

Left: Colin Elgie's majestic, autumnal artwork and richly textured sleeve perfectly captured the essence of the music on 1976's *Wind & Wuthering*. (*Charisma*)

Right: 'Spot the ball', the perennial newspaper competition, provided the inspiration for the sleeve to the 1977 *Spot The Pigeon* EP, combining the themes of the first two tracks. (*Charisma*)

GENESIS
Spot The
Pigeon

Match Of The Day
Pigeons
Inside And Out

Right: Steve Hackett's last hurrah, *Seconds Out,* remains the best live album in the Genesis canon, a superb summary of the four and five-piece years. (*Charisma*)

Left: The new, slimmed-down Genesis produced a commercial breakthrough with 1978's *...And Then There Were Three...* album which featured the UK hit single 'Follow You Follow Me'. (*Charisma*)

Left and below: Peter Gabriel embarked on a typically idiosyncratic solo career in 1977, giving his albums no title, leaving them to be identified only by the cover. These first two were later renamed *Car* and *Scratch*. (*Charisma*)

peter
gabriel

A CURIOUS FEELING
TONY BANKS

Left: Tony Banks released his first solo album, the concept *A Curious Feeling*, during Genesis' 1979 hiatus, Banks doing everything on it but sing and drum. This sleeve is from the 2009 reissue. (*Esoteric*)

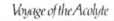

This page: Begun during his time within the band, by the end of the 1970s, Steve Hackett's solo career was in full bloom with three excellent, eclectic albums and two tours behind him. (*Charisma*)

This page: Aside from Genesis and a multitude of session work, the inexhaustible Phil Collins was also a driving force behind jazz-rockers extraordinaire Brand X. (*Charisma*)

This page: Anthony Phillips' solo career got underway with a sequence of richly rewarding albums in the late 1970s that featured intricate sleeve design by Peter Cross. (*Esoteric*)

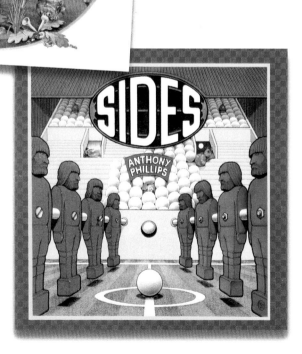

Left: When Genesis took *The Lamb Lies Down On Broadway* on tour across Europe in the spring of 1975, the lucky punter could buy this concert programme at the show. It'll cost a bit more on eBay now.

KNEBWORTH

A MIDSUMMER NIGHT'S DREAM

Saturday June 24th
Official Concert Programme
50p

Right: Genesis played the 1978 Knebworth Festival in front of a crowd of around 100,000 fans. The cover of the concert programme reminded everyone of the importance of keeping those mowing blades sharp…

1975: Leaving Your Cocoon

With gigs booked until the latter part of May, the first concern after Peter Gabriel's announcement was simply keeping the show on the road, for cancelling more than 75 concerts would have been financially ruinous, while finishing the tour would at least see Genesis coming nearer towards breaking even. Gabriel was doubtless already handling a healthy dollop of guilt at leaving the band to fend for themselves, having been built up as the star of the show and, after some discussion, he was persuaded to not only complete the tour but in its aftermath to keep his silence until the rest of the group, who were ready to carry on, had found themselves a new singer. It wasn't an entirely frictionless decision, and Phil Collins recalled in *The Book of Genesis* that, 'I remember he was being offered money just to finish the tour. I remember £3,000 being mentioned. And we all said, 'Well if he's having it, we want it – £3,000 each'.'

The show carried on through the USA and on into Europe, garnering better and better reviews as it went. A Paris show on 3 March 1975 became something of a press junket to help boost ticket sales for the additional UK shows that had been tacked on the April/May tour. Max Bell told *New Musical Express* readers, 'Never have I seen or heard any group get the reception Genesis got that night. The sustained concentration needed by everyone to fulfil the show's maximum potential makes the performance even more remarkable … an hour and a half of inimitably impressive brilliance from the best stage band we've got.' Chris Welch, now over his initial distaste for the album, was equally fulsome in *Melody Maker*: 'Genesis are now at a peak of their creative and performative powers. It has taken them years of work to reach their present pitch and it's exciting to realise that their full potential has yet to be tapped.' Oh.

That everyone was sworn to secrecy did, inevitably, make life tough on the road. Press interviews were kept to a minimum for obvious reasons and Gabriel avoided most of the ones that were done, though he did speak to Max Bell in March and said, 'I'll tell you something. We're not going to be a band to sit still. We'll self-destruct before we stop running.' Was that a coded message that the band had self-destructed or, in the afterglow of some successful shows in Europe, was he simply caught up in the enthusiasm for what Genesis had done? At the same time, Collins addressed *Melody Maker* and made it clear that after the tour, the various members of the band were going to take some time out to do other things: 'Steve's started doing a solo LP. Mike is doing his own

LP with Anthony Phillips. Tony has been approached by Strat to do an orchestrated LP of Genesis songs. Hopefully, all the solo LPs will surface at the same time, and people will be very surprised at what comes out.'

There had been some hopes within the camp that perhaps Gabriel could be dissuaded again, just as he had been the previous summer, but this time nothing was going to change his mind, so unhappy was he with the music industry, with what it was doing to him, to the strains it was placing on his family. Equally, it was plain to him – and perhaps the other members too – that he had painted himself into a corner with *The Lamb*. If anything, it had made him even more the star in the public perception, so totally identified was he with the album and the concept. Having written 95% of the lyrics, there was also little chance of him going back to singing words penned by the others and there was equally little chance of the others accepting that.

In essence, Genesis' concept of being a democratic band, lopsided though that democracy might have been, was always a self-limiting concept with an inherent sell-by date. It's far easier to keep a band going when it has a defined hierarchy, especially in terms of the writing. In The Who, Pete Townshend was the chief writer and gave the band its direction. Led Zeppelin was Jimmy Page's band first and foremost. In the Stones, Jagger and Richards were the songwriters and prime movers. Ups and downs they may have had in those bands, but everyone knew their place. But in a group like 10cc, there were four songwriters, all eager to put their ideas forward, all wanting to get their songs on the next record. Eventually, they imploded under the weight of it all. That was part of the problem with Genesis. They had five musicians, three of whom were prolific writers, with another who was catching up quickly. There was less and less space available on one album a year for each of them to be heard. A group must also always be a compromise from everyone's point of view if it is to continue. Everyone has to feel they are being appreciated, but everyone also has to be making sacrifices, otherwise, resentment festers. When someone is no longer able to make those sacrifices – and artists are notoriously incapable of making creative sacrifices for long – it's time to get out while you can.

All of that said, it's amazing that young bands stick together at all, particularly when you look back to those who operated in the '70s and how hard they had to work in an era before MTV, then the internet, downloading and streaming could spread the word for you. You had to pay your dues, play the gigs, build the audience, first in the UK, then Europe, then the US, and you had to do it in person, in concert, getting in the van and on the bus and taking the music to the people. While you were doing that, you still had to be writing, recording and delivering a new album every year as well, on top of playing 100, 150 gigs, rehearsing new material and putting it into the show. These bands were predominantly young men, starting out at 19, 20, full of ambition and the musketeer spirit. But get to 24, 25 and they were starting to get married, to have children, facing all those other responsibilities that start pulling all of us in different directions. And this, at a time when you've not really matured as a person, when you can't compartmentalise things so easily, when everything seems a big deal. There's huge financial pressure to make the band work, to make the show exciting, you're still building that audience, probably not making much, if any, money, but now you're wanting to buy a house to make family life work, though you probably need to be away from home longer in order to make the money to pay for it. And if that's an impossible thing to do, if you have success, all the trappings that come with that are things that serve to pull a band apart too – not always money, but ego, credits, parties, models, drugs, drink, the hangers-on, the need to build an organisation, fund the crew. Life comes at you fast.

Whether money changed hands or not, the magnanimity of Gabriel's gesture in playing out the tour and, particularly, in not doing a Bowie and announcing the death of Ziggy Stardust at the last show in Besançon, should not be underestimated. Equally, the rest of the band did well in an unenviable situation when it's only human nature to be looking at Gabriel as a traitor to the team – he admitted he'd felt the same about Anthony Phillips back in 1970. It was to everyone's relief when the tour was finally concluded on 22 May 1975, the remaining four-piece agreeing to take a couple of months out and then reconvene with fresh ideas and see what shape the new Genesis would take.

The first visible signs of it all, however atypical, came with the release of *Beyond an Empty Dream* on Charisma in April 1975, including 'Take This Heart', the modern hymn that Mike Rutherford had written with Phillips. This was a live recording featuring the Charterhouse Choral Society, though a beautiful piano demo from 1972 featuring Phillips alone was later released on his *The Archive Collection Volume One* and the original re-released on *Seventh Heaven*, his collaboration with Andrew Skeet. Rutherford continued doing some work with Phillips but was also soon involved along with Collins on Steve Hackett's first solo record – the first Genesis solo album, as it turned out.

Steve Hackett – Voyage of the Acolyte

Personnel:

Steve Hackett: guitars, Mellotron, harmonium, bells, autoharp, vocal, effects

John Hackett: flute, ARP synthesiser, bells

Mike Rutherford: bass, bass pedals, fuzz 12-string

Phil Collins: drums, vibes, percussion, vocals

John Acock: Elka Rhapsody, Mellotron, harmonium, piano

Sally Oldfield: vocal

Robin Miller: oboe, cor anglais

Nigel Warren-Green: solo cello

Percy Jones: bass on 'A Tower Struck Down'

Johnny Gustafson: bass on 'Star of Sirius'

Steve Tobin: Parrot and cough

Producer: Steve Hackett & John Acock

Engineer: John Acock

Assistant engineers: Paul Watkins, Rob Broglia

Engineering help: Louie Austin on 'Shadow of the Hierophant'

Cover art: Kim Poor

Recorded at Kingsway Recorders, June – July 1975.

Released: October 1975

Label: Charisma Records

Running time: 40:52

Tracklisting: 1. Ace of Wands 2. Hands of the Priestess (Part 1) 3. A Tower Struck Down (Steve Hackett / John Hackett) 4. Hands of the Priestess (Part 2) 5. The Hermit 6. Star of Sirius 7. The Lovers 8. Shadow of the Hierophant (Hackett / Rutherford)

All songs written by Steve Hackett unless otherwise stated.

Voyage of the Acolyte had hatched partly because of the amount of material Hackett had stockpiled and which hadn't yet been used by Genesis and partly, as he admitted during a Californian radio interview in April 1976, out of a sense of self-preservation that had been brought home to him by Gabriel jumping ship. 'Music is a precarious business and if someone doesn't establish themselves as an individual entity, if the ship goes down, perhaps they're going to sink with it. Genesis may last another ten years, it may fold tomorrow.'

In the circumstances, this was perfectly understandable, but it was that collection of material still on the shelf that was the prime mover, especially coming out of *The Lamb*, a project that he hadn't especially enjoyed and where he'd found it difficult to come up with music that suited the band. Certainly, he had contributed to the material that had been improvised at Headley Grange, but the pieces that he had written prior to that and were more fully formed were not necessarily finding favour at that stage. In addition, he found that he had some downtime at the end of the project when Gabriel was taking an age in completing his lyrics, and this again provided an opportunity for him to do some writing at home, prior to the accident with the wineglass.

> I thought that the future was uncertain. Pete had already threatened to leave once and it felt as if that might happen for real at some stage soon. I really built up my first album there. Largely it was material that didn't fit in with Genesis and it became *Voyage of the Acolyte*, the title suggested by Tony Stratton Smith. When Peter actually did leave, the band wasn't entirely sure it would continue and we had a couple of months break after the tour before coming back together again. Mike got involved in recording with Anthony Phillips, which was originally their record but ended up as Ant's *The Geese & the Ghost*. Phil was starting the Brand X thing, so we were off in different directions at the time. The problem with creative ideas is that you start on a project and it has to finish by a certain date and then on the very last day, all these ideas suddenly come along, they're part of the subconscious incubation period. If your schedule is flexible, that's ok and that was how *Voyage* came together over the months leading up to it.

Recording was to take place at Kingsway Recorders, in the basement of what was essentially an office block in Holborn, which meant that recording couldn't start until 6pm. That meant that, according to an interview on the Hackettsongs YouTube page, the album was:

> Done with no sleep, lots of cigarettes, cups of soup. I was very hyped up for it, but I was worried too. When I was going in to do the album, I'd never done a single, let alone a whole album on my own, so I didn't know if I could carry it off. I really didn't know if I'd come out with a bunch of outtakes or a full album. I had this air of trepidation, but on the first day, we did the first part of 'Hands of the Priestess', and it was a breath of fresh air to me; I felt it was going to work. I gradually gathered strength each day. I felt that I didn't have a duff track on it, so the whole thing took off and I was on a high.

That track is split into two distinct parts, lovely 12-string playing alongside a flute melody, very much about mood and atmosphere, leading into that liquid electric guitar playing that had long been a Hackett trademark. It was a much-needed change of pace after album opener 'Ace of Wands', still a favourite among Hackett fans today, but an absolute whirlwind with enough ideas inside its five minutes to fill five different tracks. Collins and Rutherford formed an extraordinary rhythm section on this, Rutherford really cutting loose in a way he hadn't on Genesis material which was generally more tightly arranged. Hackett's 12-string playing is exceptional, and having brother John on flute shows the value of a trained musician. In parts, it's very much in that Mahavishnu Orchestra mould, a much jazzier feel, before there's a pastoral section, not unlike Rutherford's later composition, 'Your Own Special Way'. It then flies off into another frenetic section notable for a singular backwards guitar solo and then some lovely lead playing, more in the Genesis mould. With Collins, you can see where his playing is heading into Brand X territory, and it's also a piece that must have been an influence on 'Los Endos' later the same year. Hackett later said on Hackettsongs, 'Mike and Phil were an incredible rhythm section and here they were doing my bidding. It kept changing, every few bars, there were maybe probably too many ideas on that piece, masses of hooks, but I wanted to hold the attention. Tony complimented me on the bassline, I was thrilled with that. We recorded it at three in the morning – where did all that energy come from?'

A largely instrumental album, it covered plenty of bases, 'A Tower Struck Down' something heavier, quite keyboard-heavy and intriguing in its liberal use of found sound, from a cough to a Nuremberg rally, before the tower comes crashing down, Mellotron emerging from the rubble. Percy Jones added a squelchy bass part to the song, Jones a key member of the Brand X project. We were five songs in before we had a song, 'The Hermit', featuring a lead vocal from Hackett, well down in the mix. There's a certain shyness and uncertainty about it, singing to an acoustic guitar accompaniment, some lovely arpeggio playing. The oboe melody had been written back in 1970, something he had played together with his brother John when he auditioned for Genesis. Ever willing to showcase the talents of his brother, the concluding part of the song relies heavily again on the flute melody, guitar no more than a supporting player.

The second side of the album featured two epic pieces, split up by 'The Lovers', initially a classical guitar piece, prefiguring the kind of material Hackett would produce on later albums such as *Bay of Kings* and

Momentum. 'Star of Sirius' precedes it, starting as a gentle acoustic piece with a Collins vocal before heading into a faster section. That was a new setting for Collins' voice, but he handled it nicely, the song then spinning out into more impressive keyboard contributions from John Hackett and a range of different guitar sounds at the conclusion, some nice solo riffs. The co-write with Rutherford, 'Shadow of the Hierophant' ends the album in the grand manner. Sally Oldfield provides a pure, operatic vocal before the song gradually builds to a crescendo, relentlessly churning like the sea, a piece with real grandeur to it, one that certainly had Genesis potential. The package was completed by Kim Poor's artwork, capturing the feel of the music and the Tarot card inspiration that had been behind much of it, though personally, the gatefold illustration seems much superior to the front cover itself.

By the time *Voyage of the Acolyte* was released in late October, news of Gabriel's departure had already leaked out, but with Genesis' return to the studio well publicised by then, critics fell on the new record with real interest, looking to divine what clues they could for how the band might survive without their singer. Barbara Charone was bullish in her Sounds review: 'The similarity [with Genesis] will surprise a lot of people who assumed the band to be at the mercy of Peter Gabriel's artistic wrath. All the songs here add substance to the notion that Genesis write songs as a group … *Voyage of the Acolyte* confirms the talent Steve Hackett displays through his work with Genesis while promising good things for their next album.'

The public were suitably impressed, the album reaching number 26 in the charts and offering something of a bridge towards the future. Certainly, Hackett was very happy with the album, telling *Sounds*, 'I'm definitely more confident about submitting ideas to the band now. The album showed me that once I was happy with an idea, there was no reason why it shouldn't work. I wasn't particularly confident about my abilities as a writer and arranger before I did the album. I couldn't come up with a solo album of quality every year. This was just something I've wanted to do for a long, long time.'

Completing work on the album meant that he was late in reconvening with Genesis in their rehearsal space in Acton – in his autobiography, Hackett says he missed a single day, other accounts put it at three – and this perhaps had greater long-term significance than might initially have appeared. By the time he arrived, Collins, Rutherford and Tony Banks had already sketched out most of 'Dance on a Volcano' as a trio and had begun work on 'Squonk'. With Banks bringing in 'Mad Man Moon' and 'A Trick of the Tail' and much of 'Robbery, Assault & Battery', and Rutherford having composed a significant chunk of 'Ripples', which Banks then helped him finish, there was already a lot of material in the air. Hackett conceded later that after doing *Voyage of the Acolyte*, he was inevitably light on music to contribute and was trying to come up with ideas on the spot.

Perhaps if he had taken the material he used on that back into the group, some of that might have found its way into the album and he would have immediately made his play for taking a bigger role in the post-Gabriel world. Or perhaps that material might not have made it through the committee and would have been shelved again, only adding to his frustrations. Equally, the other three had grounds for concern in that having lost their singer, rather than concentrating exclusively on the band in the attempt to weather the storm, their guitarist was out there releasing his own record before Genesis had been able to respond. Banks admitted to the *World of Genesis* website in a 2009 interview, 'The first time I ever thought of doing a solo project was after Peter left the band … then I thought, if Genesis is going to carry on, we really need to put all of our best ideas into that next album. Obviously, Steve did go off and do a solo album at that point, which was kind of difficult for us in a way, because we felt we needed all hands on deck at this particular time.' At the same time, from Hackett's perspective, having tasted the freedom of having complete control over his music and the opportunity to get it all out there, the temptation to join Gabriel in leaving the group was a strong one and the fact that he decided he should return to the mothership says much about his dedication to the band and its music too.

The reality of groups is that, like it or not – and they generally don't – they all need somebody who will drive them, who will channel all their energies into it, will prioritise it and will drag the others with them from project to project. This isn't always so in the early years when everyone understands that they all need to be heading in the same direction if they are going to achieve a breakthrough. But somewhere along the way, be it a bump in the road, be it the achievement of success, that unity of purpose tends to get fractured and somebody tends to take the responsibility of keeping the show on the road, either by volition or because nobody else will do it. It's not a post that makes anybody popular, and it isn't necessarily a permanent role, but it is crucial in ensuring a band continues to exist, particularly in trying times. Roger Waters took charge of things with Pink Floyd after Syd Barrett left and then especially after the post-*Dark Side of the Moon* malaise set in. Paul McCartney was the Beatle who tried to step into the void and keep the band active after Brian Epstein died. Mick Jagger became the business head of the Rolling Stones, to the clear contempt of Keith Richards, but without that, the Stones would have likely ceased to exist 30 years or more ago. Somebody in a band generally has to dedicate themself to it and, while not denigrating the commitment of the others, it was Banks, above all, who was wholly determined that Genesis were going to survive the loss of Gabriel. Perhaps that was to be expected, for Banks and Gabriel had long been the dominant personalities. David Hentschel, drafted in as co-producer for the new record, recalled that when he was an engineer on *Nursery Cryme*, 'There was a degree of friction, between Peter and Tony predominantly because they are both very strong characters. As much as Genesis prided themselves in being a democratic outfit, there were definitely two people in charge at that point.'

There's no right or wrong answer in such situations, just as there was no right or wrong way for any of the four to react to Gabriel's departure and their prospects for the future, but it seems the seeds for future discontent were already being sown, even as a new Genesis was emerging. What would that Genesis look like, though? Logically enough, having satisfied themselves that they had some excellent new material to work with, next on the agenda was finding a new singer. There was an intention that Collins would take a bigger role, singing lead on the softer songs such as 'Ripples', but with Collins very definitely seeing himself as the drummer – 'a respectable gig!' as he termed it – there was no real thought that he might take over as the frontman. Instead, an advert was placed in *Melody Maker* for a singer for a 'Yes/Genesis type group', which elicited a weird and wonderful mix of around 400 applicants, some sending tapes of them singing over the top of Genesis albums, others dressed in a variety of capes and costumes. But if *The Lamb Lies Down on Broadway* had taught the band anything, it was that they wanted to produce a stage show where the focus was once again on the music. Certainly, there would be great lighting effects, perhaps backdrop films, but Genesis were going to be presented as a band once again, back to the way it had been before Gabriel donned a fox's head. 'We had one from a guy called the Red Hooker,' Rutherford told *Sounds*. 'He sang a song called 'I Got The Sex Blues Baby', and sent us a picture of him wearing what we assume was a red dress.' For some reason, he wasn't invited to audition.

The applicants were whittled down to around twenty possibles, and the band got into a routine whereby once a week, they would take a break from working on the new material and test out two or three singers, the audition pieces including 'Cuckoo Cocoon', 'Firth of Fifth' and 'Squonk'. But as the weeks went by, nobody was coming up to scratch, none of them sounding as good as Collins had done when he had run through the songs for them first. They were still resolutely a four-piece when, on 16 August, a copy of *Melody Maker* arrived in the studio with a picture of Gabriel in his batwings on the front page and the headline 'Gabriel Out of Genesis?' It wasn't the first sighting of the rumour, *New Musical Express* having run stern denials about his departure a month earlier, but this time, there seemed to be some substance to it – given that they'd been in the studio as a four-piece for a month already and were auditioning singers, it's surprising they had been able to keep things quiet for so long. A week later, *Melody Maker* confirmed the split and Chris Welch then penned a piece in which he 'Recalls a Great British Band', essentially an obituary.

In damage limitation mode, the band did the press rounds, Collins indicating that by mid-September, finding a new singer was no longer quite such a pressing matter. 'I do most of the singing actually – there's just the four of us. We start recording soon … and we may feature one or two singers as guest vocalists sort of, on a few tracks.' Banks added, 'The music won't change that much at all. You've got to remember that in the past, everything Genesis has written has been created by the five of us. One person leaving will change that one fifth. The songs will carry on the same.' Having interviewed them for *Sounds*, Barbara Charone gave them a ringing endorsement: 'As much as I liked them before, I am just as willing to like them now. The band will undoubtedly be different, but they will undoubtedly be as good.'

Recording began at Trident Studios in October. Backing tracks were duly recorded, and singers continued to audition. They arrived at one individual, Mick Strickland, who they thought might fit the bill and he joined them in Trident to try to record 'Squonk', only to find that the key was completely wrong for him and he couldn't sing it – such was the peril of having already recorded the backing track. As Collins laughed later, 'There was never any thought of changing the key, such was our contempt for the vocals!' This was the lowest point in the whole process, for it was beginning to look as if they'd never find a new singer until Collins piped up with, 'Can I have a go at 'Squonk' tomorrow when we come in?' It's revealing that in subsequent years, David Hentschel told the *Rock History Music* website that, 'The story is often that Phil needed to be coaxed into doing it, but in fact, Phil didn't need any persuading at all. He really wanted to do it but he didn't want to be seen as being too pushy!'

His pass at 'Squonk' was suitably impressive, and from there, he took on the other songs that had been earmarked for the 'new singer', knocking them off one by one. 'It seems so obvious with hindsight,' Banks told the BBC later. 'But we had no idea how he'd cope with the hard songs and it wasn't until he'd tried 'Squonk' that we realised he was good at it.' And then there were four...

1976: A Living Story

A Trick of the Tail

Personnel: Tony Banks, Phil Collins, Steve Hackett, Mike Rutherford
Producer: David Hentschel & Genesis
Engineered by: David Hentschel and Nick 'Haddock' Bradford
Cover art: Colin Elgie at Hipgnosis
Recorded at Trident Studios, London, October – November 1975.
Released: 2 February 1976
Label: Charisma Records
Running time: 51:08
Tracklisting: 1. Dance on a Volcano (Rutherford/Banks/Hackett/Collins) 2. Entangled (Hackett/Banks) 3. Squonk (Rutherford/Banks) 4. Mad Man Moon (Banks) 5. Robbery, Assault And Battery (Banks/Collins) 6. Ripples (Rutherford/Banks) 7. A Trick of the Tail (Banks) 8. Los Endos (Collins/Hackett/Rutherford/Banks)

Having learnt some of the error of their ways with *Selling England by the Pound* and *The Lamb Lies Down on Broadway*, the scheduling around *A Trick of the Tail* was much better worked out. Time to write, time to record, time for the fans to digest the new album before playing live, without everything overlapping and with deadlines looming as it had done across the previous records. They were all well aware just how important this one was, and nothing was going to be left to chance.

The decision over the lead singer role finally made and communicated to the outside world, the fact that Phil Collins had sounded so good on 'Star of Sirius' on Steve Hackett's *Voyage of the Acolyte* brought a welcome boost in confidence to proceedings, so there was real expectation – and some nervousness – amongst fans when *A Trick of the Tail* hit the record shops at the beginning of February 1976.

For the vast majority, those nerves were settled almost the moment the stylus hit the vinyl. 'Dance on a Volcano' was both identifiably Genesis and yet a cleaner, more focused sound. It was certainly in the great tradition of Genesis album openers that pulled you in from the outset, Mike Rutherford's 12-string riff with the answering drum break and punchy bass pedals supremely powerful. Collins had the idea of 'using accents to interrupt the arpeggiated 12-string, and we all hit them together,' recalled Hackett later, 'It was like the band working on telepathy … There aren't many tracks in 7/8 that swing like this.' Much of that was down to Collins' feel on the drums, but then everyone already knew he was a great drummer. But how was the singing? The answer came a minute and two seconds in. As soon as 'Holy mother of God' had passed his lips, the massed ranks of Genesis fans breathed a sigh of relief. That part of the new equation was going to be alright. This song was immediately new territory for him vocally, requiring him to sing harder and faster than anything he'd tried before, certainly as a lead singer, and he passed the test with flying colours. While not denigrating his predecessor, he was perhaps technically better than Gabriel, whose great strength had been his ability as an interpreter of the lyrics, a key reason why he had grown unhappy in singing other people's words. Gabriel inhabited a lyric in a way that Collins did not, not yet anyway, but Collins presented a lyric in a way that was more easily processed. Collins' voice was certainly not lacking in character, but it was not dripping in the idiosyncrasies and eccentricities that made Gabriel so unique. While hardcore Genesis fans might have mourned the loss of that, they – and a wider audience, previously put off by Gabriel's strangeness perhaps – could comfortably embrace Collins' approach.

In purely sonic terms, Genesis had never sounded better than they did right from the outset on the new album. Much of the praise for that could be laid at co-producer Hentschel's door, for his work was technically brilliant. Equally, though, the changeover from Gabriel to Collins was important in that regard. For all that the two of them had similar sounding voices – heightened by the fact that Collins had so often sung in unison with Gabriel and so was a part of that composite voice – Gabriel's vocals contained more low notes and was thicker in texture, eating up the sound frequencies. Collins' voice was lighter giving the instrumentation more room to breathe within the spectrum. Similarly, Tony Banks was no longer relying quite so heavily on the thicker sounds of Mellotron and organ, which again ate up the frequencies, his use of piano and synthesiser instead again making space.

It really shouldn't be underestimated just how good Genesis sounded just one song in, and just how important that was. All these years later, after CDs, remasters and remixes, we've come to take a certain level of sound quality for granted on their recordings, but back in the 1970s, it wasn't necessarily that way. In part, they were victims of their own ambition, trying to cram so much music onto the vinyl that the medium simply couldn't cope with the dynamic range, muddying the sound on occasion. On top of that, they'd had their issues with producers too, but with the arrival of Hentschel, they found a wholly sympathetic pair of ears who had the ability to translate what he was hearing onto tape. Where at times in the past, the songs had limped out of the speakers, 'Dance on a Volcano' jumped out and grabbed you by the throat. This was a crucial advance at the most important moment. It was a fine song to open with too, everyone contributing as player and writer, Hackett coming into the song a little late when the first section was already written, but adding the frenetic 'Let the dance begin' section at the end, in the vein of 'Ace of Wands' from his own album, making explicit the jazzier end of the band's tastes.

Hackett made another telling contribution as a writer on 'Entangled', a song inspired by one of Kim Poor's paintings. 'I was thinking about a psychiatrist at the time, hypnotising a patient, taking him back into a world of troubling dreams,' Hackett explained as part of a series of *Hackettsongs* videos that he produced early in 2020, putting the spotlight on some of the songs he'd been involved in during his career. 'The lyric is basically mine; what sounds like the chorus is from Tony.' In that sense, it has a very Lennon & McCartney feel to it, the two styles rubbing up against each other, one being more wide-eyed, the other cutting it down with a hefty dose of cynicism, as The Beatles did on 'We Can Work It Out' or 'Getting Better' – 'Got to admit it's getting better / Couldn't get much worse.' While the patient on the couch is putting his faith in the doctor, the doctor is busily calculating the bill.

The guitar intro was played at half speed and then sped up, before Rutherford and Banks came in on chiming 12-strings to create an atmosphere that harked all the way back to *Trespass*. It's a beguiling sound that sucks the listener in, somewhere between a waltz and a lullaby, building to a lovely chorus, the vocal much more what we'd been accustomed to from Collins. It ends on a lengthy instrumental section of layered guitars, and what Hackett referred to, when introducing the song on stage during the subsequent tour, as 'The Maria Callas school of synthesiser playing from Mr Tony Banks'. The song swells into a huge blanket of sound, combining synthesiser and Mellotron, but the separation of the instruments is another stride forward, each available to hear separately rather than the less distinct slabs of sound that had sometimes been found on earlier recordings. It's such a good song, and such a great collaboration across the group, that you can't help but feel saddened that Hackett was never quite secure enough at that time to understand just how important he was to Genesis and that founding members Banks and Rutherford were never sufficiently aware nor understanding of those insecurities to make it crystal clear to him that he was a vital component of the band. If only they'd talked about it … but then we English didn't do that kind of thing, certainly not in the 1970s.

'Squonk' was another real test of Collins' vocal dexterity, Genesis at their heaviest. A clanging Rutherford riff and those brutal bass pedals again, augmented by Collins working according to the John Bonham playbook, it had the same sort of attack as 'Back in NYC'. Collins handled it well, though if there was a track where Gabriel was missed in purely vocal terms, it was perhaps this one. Collins grew into it in concert over the years as his voice got roughened up by the sheer volume of work it was put through in the studio and on stage, but even here, it's a sound performance, though he performed it better on *Seconds Out*. Musically, it's still very much in the same area as *The Lamb* had been, but lyrically it harks back to earlier Genesis tales of myth and fable, this one featuring the squonk, a creature that was so ugly, it spent most of its time weeping and, if caught, dissolved into tears. Chris Welch suggested in his album review that this might be a less than generous reflection on their erstwhile singer – perhaps the ugliness of the squonk reminding him of the Slipperman – but the band were at pains to deny it.

There was another change in pace with Banks' gorgeous 'Mad Man Moon', a horribly overlooked Genesis classic down the years, perhaps because, like the album's title track, it was never performed live. Based initially on a grand piano part with a restrained, ghostly guitar in the background, Collins handles the rise and fall of the lyric beautifully. In typical Genesis fashion, following a lovely solo section from Banks that culminates in a cascading piano section, it segues into a new 'I'm the sandman' section that introduces fresh momentum. Banks has long complained that that section wasn't played as well as it might have been, but that's nit-picking from the viewpoint of the listener. Perhaps the writer had even higher hopes for it, but out in the audience, it rounds off the first side of the album on the highest possible note, the reprise of the opening figure bringing it to a lovely, melancholic conclusion. The lyric seemed in part inspired by the events of the summer of 1975, a long, baking heatwave across England causing all the usual chaos of water shortages and hosepipe bans, this in a year where famously, the cricket was held up in Buxton on 2 June by an inch of snowfall – that would truly have been a source of relief by late August.

Halfway through the album, and it could only be the most churlish Genesis fan, wholly wedded to the idea that there was no band without

Gabriel, that could have been disappointed with that first 26 minutes of music from this brave new world. Musically, they sounded better than ever, Collins had shown himself to be a fine singer, the songs were engaging. If anything was missing, it was the humour that Gabriel had generally brought to proceedings, either through his gymnastic wordplay – which they wisely didn't try to copy – or in his operettas such as 'Get 'Em Out by Friday'. Yet even that world had already been covered to some extent by the lovely, whimsical sleeve artwork that Colin Elgie produced. Illustrating the characters from the songs, it was a nod back to Paul Whitehead's interpretive sleeves from the earliest days, each of the songs featuring detail that followed through into the gatefold, the lyrics carefully inscribed as if on some Victorian parchment.

Darting out from that world came 'Robbery, Assault and Battery', a Dickensian tale that fit Collins like a glove, allowing him to roll back the years and plug into the role of the Artful Dodger from *Oliver!* A lyric that was written in the studio, telling the tale of a robbery gone wrong, this saw Collins adopting a role in much the way Gabriel had, and doing it just as convincingly, another box successfully ticked – it even allowed him to don a costume of sorts on stage, the burglar's hat and long coat, though no masks were involved. Musically, it feels a little bit ponderous through the vocal sections, propelled on a bouncy keyboard part that needs a shade more urgency, and it benefitted from being played faster in concert where the quality of the various contributions shine, notably Hackett's descending riffs. The instrumental break that represents the chase scene more than compensates though, Banks' solo in the vein of his *Selling England by the Pound* work, the rock steady Collins and Rutherford underpinning it as so often in the past, allowing him to work some magic on top.

'Ripples' begins with a chiming 12-string that would, in other days, have spun off into something like 'The Musical Box', but Rutherford and Banks had a different kind of drama in mind for this song as they fused two distinct sections together. There's a rather baroque quality to the first part before the tale of lost youth slides slightly awkwardly into an instrumental section, the 12-string fading out to be replaced by another lovely flowing Banks piano piece, this time decorated by a lyrical Hackett solo across the top, beautiful playing that marks a real highlight of the album. 'It sounds like backwards guitar, but actually, it's a Synthi Hi-Fli,' recalled Hackett for *Hackettsongs*. 'That lops off the beginning of the note, which makes it sound backwards. The real poignancy of the song comes from this section.' The final vocal section is powerful too, the interweaving of

Banks' piano and Hackett's guitar again the crowning glory, wringing the emotion from the song in a way that no other band of the period did. As Banks told the music press across several interviews at the time of the album's release:

> ...There's not that big a gap between what 10cc are doing and what we're doing. Much of our material is dependent on melody ... people who like mainstream pop, melody and songs will like us. That's what we've always been ... People like to think we're very complicated. That's why I'd like a hit. Genesis, as distinct from Yes and ELP, depend on the basic song rather than the fast playing and the fancy arrangements. It's closer to pop music really than heavy rock.

As if to underline that, Banks' song 'A Trick of the Tail' was clearly rooted in Beatles territory, albeit put through the Genesis filter in the same way that 'I Know What I Like (In Your Wardrobe)' had been. Another, and perhaps more successful attempt to lighten the mood in the way of 'Robbery Assault and Battery', there was a lovely, simple melody to it that should have given it a run at being a hit but, in keeping with most Genesis single releases to that point, it failed to trouble the scorers. This, in spite of the band recording a video that saw them gathered around the piano, a miniaturised Collins appearing on the keys and then on Hackett's guitar, Hackett donning a Godzilla-like glove to play the final refrain. Who could resist that? The British and American publics, for starters. Collins later called it the most embarrassing video he'd ever been involved in, though many of us might beg to differ.

Written around the time of *Foxtrot*, Banks went back to it, dusted it off and was pleased to put it forward for the new album because, as he said in *The Genesis Songbook* a year later, 'I like to get earlier things used because they're a bit simpler than how I write now. I got the idea for the lyric after reading William Holding's *The Inheritors*. It's about a race who were on earth before man and it's about the last survivor of the race. The very last chapter deals with our reaction to him, whereas the rest of the story is his reaction to us. It's about an alien with horns and a tail who appears in a modern city and how people react to him.'

The final track on the album, 'Los Endos' was possibly the biggest departure, very different to anything in the Gabriel era. It had actually begun as part of a different song, 'It's Yourself', which eventually saw a UK release as the B-side of 'Your Own Special Way' in February 1977.

Written by the group as a song, it wasn't up to the standard of the rest of the material on the album, and shelving it was the right decision, the initial song part thin on inspiration. But when the song dissolves into its instrumental section, the three chords that went on to become the opening to 'Los Endos' shine out. From there, there's a swirling, meandering instrumental section that has echoes of the third side of *The Lamb*, but not as atmospheric. They culled the right bit for 'Los Endos'.

It was the most obviously American influenced piece of music they'd ever produced and redolent of the tastes of Collins in particular, but also of some of the playing on Hackett's album. 'It was the first time I thought Genesis played the type of music they'd never played before – American music vaguely in the mould of Weather Report,' said Collins in *The Genesis Songbook*:

> It stemmed from this rhythmic idea I had. We also worked in some reprises because it was the end of the album, including the reprise of 'Squonk' at the end. It was the first time we hit on ... I say jazz, but I think we were playing a different kind of music on that track. It was still tight. It wasn't a blowing tune, but it was the first time we'd tried anything in that vein. To me, it was great to do that kind of thing with Genesis rather than playing it with Brand X.

The clarity that's a mark of *A Trick of the Tail* is especially notable on this tune which sounds huge and features all four of them playing at their peak, underscoring just how far they had all come as players from the early days. Hackett's languid guitar from 'It's Yourself' is the opening feature before Collins kicks things into gear and they're off into faster sections written by Hackett and Banks. It's a really up, optimistic piece that captures the essence of the album across its six minutes, as if the band, at the far end of perhaps the most important record they'd ever made, are collectively offering up a 'We told you we could do it!' to all those who had doubted their post-Gabriel future. It is a triumphant end and, as so often with Genesis records, it creates a satisfying conceptual conclusion with the reprises from earlier songs. Not only that, there's a genuine nod to their erstwhile frontman, a quote from 'Supper's Ready' that wishes him well: 'There's an angel standing in the sun / Free to get back home.' On first hearing at the time, it's the kind of moment when a listener finds he or she has something in their eye, for not only was it a touching tribute, it came at the end of 50 minutes where Genesis had answered every question that had been put to them. They had done more than survived. They were thriving.

What came next was the reviews, and they could hardly have been better. Chris Welch, writer of their obituary the previous summer, was forced to eat his words in *Melody Maker*:

> The results are at times breathtaking … there is an element of real mystery and magic about Genesis, of dark, brooding, mountainous forces, that the departure of Gabriel does not seem to have diminished … for every ethereal moment, there is a corresponding blitz of power. That has been the skill of Genesis past, and it is obviously going to serve them in good stead for the future.

Barbara Charone in *Sounds* was every bit as welcoming of the new album:

> 'Every single Genesis character trait abounds on this new album, healthy and well fed. It's all present in true glory; surrealistic fantasises, dreamy musical constructions, soundtracks for mind dreams, humorous anecdotes, beautiful melodies and haunting themes all charged with suitably aggressive dynamics. Gabriel's absence is not nearly as visible as one would imagine. Phil Collins handles the lead vocals with excellent panache and verve, fitting perfectly into the Genesis framework … This is commercial in the best sense of the word. Genesis have not sacrificed anything or cheated themselves to attain such successful results.

'The challenge has been good for us,' admitted Rutherford in *Sounds*. 'Bands do get stale. Suddenly it was fresh and pulled us together. You've got to work hard. It's good fun to push yourself harder. The first rehearsals all sounded so good we all got excited and haven't really looked back since.' All four members of the group had both written and performed at the top of their form but of course, it was Collins who had really come to the fore with a bravura contribution, and not just as the new singer. Clearly determined that nobody was going to forget that he was the drummer, he had pulled out all the stops and pulled Genesis into new areas, most notably in 'Los Endos'. For all that, it was as the singer that he was going to be judged this time around and, as Charone had noted in her review, his performance was overwhelmingly positive, be it on songs like 'Ripples' that played to the strengths everyone already understood, on 'Squonk' where he had to find something harder-edged, or on 'Robbery Assault and Battery' where he had to step into character and do so convincingly.

Having won over the doubters, Hackett told *Sounds*, 'It's quite ironic that Peter used to sometimes say none of us was irreplaceable. Those words have been borne out.' The further irony was that though Gabriel had been right, the four remaining members of Genesis had been amongst those who wondered if they could carry it off. Gabriel always believed that they would be fine in any combination simply because they were a group of excellent songwriters and that in the end, it was songs that really mattered, that conferred success and longevity on any artist. But it was Gabriel's very profile that had drained them of the belief that the public would be interested in them that made them question their viability. That uncertainty was understandable, especially in the UK where Gabriel had been very much the star of the show to the detriment of the others, the fact that all the songs in the past had been credited to Genesis as a whole leading many to believe that in reality, it was Gabriel who was doing the lion's share of it all. Individual crediting of the songs, plus a determination that the band would now do interviews as a group or at least in twos and threes, was an attempt to counter that, but it all came after the horse had bolted. Now, they were entirely dependent on the public – and the press – giving them a fair hearing.

In some senses, the stakes were higher because Collins had come out front. A new singer who failed could always be shunted out of the group for the next record, but if the audience hadn't taken to him, he could hardly be sent back to the drum stool with his tail between his legs, for all his protestations that drumming was his first love. This simply had to work. On the plus side, though, because he had been with the band for five years, he had won the respect and affection of the fans and so, right from the off, they were rooting for him. And when the music was so strong, when Gabriel's absence sounded like nothing more than a slight inconvenience rather than the disaster everyone had been worried about, Genesis were well on their way. Gabriel had suddenly gone from being Genesis' Svengali to people now wondering if all he'd really done was wear some funny hats. That was just as unfair as the articles writing off his bandmates the previous summer, but what his departure had illustrated was that a proper group with a strong chemistry is always greater than the sum of the parts. There were still four strong musicians and writers there, 80% of the collective remained intact, so of course, they should have been able to produce something that could live up to their high standards.

Equally though, this was now a slightly different group, for all that they had worked diligently to cover all the bases, including lyrically with a very song-heavy album at a time when they'd have been reasonably expected to rely on long instrumental passages. Lyrically, they weren't quite as incisive across the whole album as they might have been had Gabriel produced, say, three sets of words for the songs. Banks, Collins, Hackett and Rutherford were music men first and foremost, which isn't to say they couldn't write lyrics, but they viewed them as perhaps secondary. They had rowed back from the more contemporary slant that Gabriel had given to things on *The Lamb,* but even then, things were slimmed down from earlier albums, and that was ultimately perhaps the biggest legacy that Gabriel had bequeathed to them in that final album. They had become a sleeker, more streamlined force, and in another year or so's time, when the punk onslaught was at its height, that would be significant and would be a major reason why Genesis fared better than many of their contemporaries.

Having put the past behind them on record, could they do the same on stage, where perhaps his ghost loomed larger? There was a brief thought that they might avoid that question for a while, Rutherford explaining in *Sounds* just after *A Trick of the Tail* came out that, 'At one point we thought we wouldn't get back on the road this year because we're planning to record again this year. Then suddenly, I had the feeling that if we didn't go back on the road, it would become a very big thing to us. The best thing to do is to just get down and do it.' That's a measure of how nervous they were going into the new project that they might simply avoid playing live and try to build the band as a recording act first and foremost before hitting the road again. More surprisingly, though, there seems to have been a genuine thought that they would need to find a singer before playing live again. After Collins had made such a success of the job, it seems ludicrous that they would entertain the idea for a second and fairly swiftly, they saw sense. In his brilliant autobiography, Bill Bruford, erstwhile drummer with Yes and King Crimson, suggests that the clincher was a conversation he had with Collins when he was playing as an additional percussionist on some loose live shows with Brand X. 'Either he or I made the next step to the obvious solution: why didn't he become Genesis' singer and I play drums for a while behind him until he was settled in? Phil and I were admirers of each other's style and he knew enough about me to know that the nightmare scenario for a drummer-turned-singer – namely that the music might collapse around his ears like a house of cards – was unlikely to happen.' With Bruford aboard, it was full steam ahead and by the end of March 1976, Genesis were treading the boards again, starting with a show in London, Ontario.

Collins made it perfectly clear from the outset that he wasn't going to be a Gabriel clone, that he would not be donning a flower mask, or any other mask for that matter, and Genesis were better for it. That's no slight on Gabriel, for even if he had stayed in the band, by 1976 things were changing and the advance march of punk was in the wind. Almost overnight, the idea of costumes belonged to a different era and if Genesis only inadvertently moved on to a different kind of live presentation, it was to be to their long-term benefit. Everyone stepped up to the plate and Genesis became a more animated group, both Rutherford and Hackett doing song introductions as well as Collins, both also leaving their seats. Hackett explained, 'When Peter left, I felt we had to change – you couldn't just sit down on stage anymore. We were worried about the stage show so we all made a conscious decision to participate actively on stage.' Playing live was the acid test for a band with such a great reputation in concert and Collins admitted that he was nervous going into the tour, not so much because of the singing but because of the need to front things up and communicate with the audience. Again though, the fact that he had come from the band was his trump card because the fans were already on his side and were willing it to work. The contrast with Yes' fortunes a few years later when Jon Anderson left the band could hardly be more marked. They replaced him with Trevor Horn, singer of The Buggles who had recently had a number one hit with 'Video Killed the Radio Star', a slice of classic bubblegum pop that Jonathan King would have been proud to call his own. Fans were altogether less forgiving and had much less of a sense of humour about these things in the '70s than perhaps they have now and, in the UK in particular, Horn was given a torrid time as Yes toured – his colleague Geoff Downes, replacing Rick Wakeman, didn't have it any easier either. As the years have since shown, it meant that in *Drama*, Yes fans missed out on a fine album, but back then, Jon Anderson was Yes's singer and there was no replacing him, unless maybe Chris Squire had had a go. It was the same elsewhere – Ian Gillan was Deep Purple's singer, not David Coverdale, just as Ozzy Osbourne was Black Sabbath's frontman, not Ronnie James Dio, not Ian Gillan either. Rock fans of the time did not like change, but if Genesis had to lose Gabriel, replacing him with Collins meant the minimum of new information for them to take on board.

The concerts that took in North America and then the UK and mainland Europe were a triumph from the off, confirming that Genesis had prevailed on every level. So successful were they that shows were recorded for a potential live album in Paris, Glasgow and Stafford, the latter two shows also filmed for the *In Concert* movie that was released in January 1977, part of a double bill with *White Rock*, the official film of the 1976 Winter Olympics which boasted a Rick Wakeman soundtrack. Musically, the shows were outstanding, heavily featuring the new record but also harking back to some old Genesis favourites that were perhaps less closely linked with Gabriel's pyrotechnics, songs like 'The Knife' and 'The Musical Box' biting the dust. 'The Cinema Show', 'Firth of Fifth' and 'White Mountain' were all dusted off and 'Supper's Ready', thankfully, survived, each of them given a new lease of life by Collins' performance that was all about the music, little given over to theatrics beyond the lights and the slideshow behind the band. The addition of Bruford added an exhilarating twist to things too. The interplay between him and Collins on the instrumental sections was especially exciting, not just musically but visually too, something that Genesis were able to play on for many years thereafter. With Bruford, there was always a slight edge to the music as though it might topple over, the drummer often admitting over his career that he never played anything the same way once … It was only ever meant to be a short-term arrangement, and when Chester Thompson replaced him the following year, Genesis snapped back to a greater focus and solidity, often more powerful too, but it's a pity that a full live album has never emerged from that '76 tour, for it was a very special moment in time.

That tour wrapped up, there was a brief pause for a holiday and reflection, though not for Collins, who was busily overseeing the release of the first Brand X album as the tour was still drawing to its close.

Brand X – Unorthodox Behaviour

Personnel:
Phil Collins: drums, percussion, vibraphone.
John Goodsall: electric and acoustic guitars.
Percy Jones: electric and acoustic basses, marimba.
Robin Lumley: electric and acoustic pianos, Moog synthesizer, string synthesizer, echoplex.
Jack Lancaster: Soprano saxophone
Producer: Brand X and Dennis MacKay

Engineer: Dennis MacKay
Recorded at Trident Studios, September – October 1975.
Released: 18 June 1976
Label: Charisma Records
Running time: 41:07
Tracklisting: 1. Nuclear Burn 2. Euthanasia Waltz 3. Born Ugly 4. Smacks of Euphoric
Hysteria 5. Unorthodox Behaviour 6. Running on Three 7. Touch Wood
All songs written by Collins, Goodsall, Lumley, Jones.

Brand X had essentially formed from some of the session work that
Collins had been doing, working alongside John Goodsall, Percy Jones
and Robin Lumley, among others, on an album for Island Records that
was ultimately rejected by the company. That band had been a six-piece,
but on the album's failure, Phil Spinelli and Pete Bonas headed off to
do something else, leaving the other four as Brand X. Once Collins had
completed work on *A Trick of the Tail*, Brand X followed them into
Trident Studios to cut an altogether looser record.

Very much in the jazz-rock camp, the obvious influences being bands
like Weather Report, Return to Forever and the Mahavishnu Orchestra,
Collins was to the fore, forming a rhythm section with Percy Jones
that was compulsive listening. An all-instrumental album, *Unorthodox
Behaviour* opened with the impressive 'Nuclear Burn', in which everyone
was given the opportunity to shine, John Goodsall's guitar line giving
way to Robin Lumley and then taking charge again as this band clearly
determined that it was going to be fair shares for all right along the
way. It's interesting how high up Collins is in the mix throughout – not
least because he wasn't at any of the mixing sessions – but given his
burgeoning reputation in the musical world, it was a commercially savvy
decision.

The musicianship is of a remarkable quality and there are times when
that runs away with them and it becomes a record more for the players
than the listeners. Commendably though, they keep such interludes to
a minimum and 'Euthanasia Waltz', built around a languid guitar figure,
is something that had real commercial potential. 'Born Ugly' must have
been a favourite of Ian Dury & The Blockheads because a lot of their
sound is present in that tune, while 'Smacks of Europhic Hysteria' has a
funky, American feel to it. There's more than a hint of *Roxy & Elsewhere*
period Frank Zappa in there, ironic given that Chester Thompson, soon
to be Genesis' live drummer, was in that band. 'Unorthodox Behaviour' is

darker and more brooding, relying more on its atmosphere before taking a turn into 'Running on Three', altogether more frenetic initially before a lovely Goodsall guitar break takes centre stage, the album closing with the Latin-inflected 'Touch Wood'. It's a very good record on its own terms, Steve Clarke giving it a warm review in *New Musical Express*: 'Each of the musicians involved sound as if they're getting off on the whole shebang and in the process coming up with something wholly worthwhile.'

From Collins' perspective, as well as giving him the chance to fully reconnect with his role as 'just' the drummer, it was a musical safety valve of sorts, allowing him to explore sides of his interests and his playing abilities that weren't necessarily catered for in Genesis, 'Los Endos' notwithstanding. A selection of club dates and an appearance at the Reading Festival followed for Brand X, all of which allowed him to return to Genesis in the autumn of 1976 fully energised and ready to make their next record. While he had been playing, the other three members of the group had had a couple of writing periods since finishing *A Trick of the Tail*, both through the winter of 1975/76 before the tour got underway and then again since coming off the road in mid-July. Ahead of recording through September and October, they convened for rehearsals and, as Collins explained in *Sounds*, 'We thrash out the material that's around, pick the best things – what excites us all'. Rutherford echoed those remarks, noting, 'In Genesis, the influence of the other three is always strong on whoever's writing. It's a bit like quality control; everyone has to be really excited by something before we do it.' That was to have repercussions in the course of the next year.

Preparation was especially important this time, for Genesis were going to record abroad for the first time in their career. Having spent most of their time in debt, *A Trick of the Tail* had tipped them into the black at long last, but with that came a different problem – the taxman. Things hadn't changed a lot since George Harrison's bleak assessment of Mr. Wilson and Mr. Heath on The Beatles' *Revolver* in 1966, and for many bands, the moment they started making any money, the taxman came in and took most of it away. A loophole in the regulations meant that rather than going into exile abroad on a full-time basis, you could soften the taxpaying blow on your recording revenue by making the record outside the country, and so they were bound for Relight Studios in Hilvarenbeek in the Netherlands.

It was a return to the way in which they'd made *The Lamb Lies Down on Broadway* to a degree, albeit rather more intensely focused, as Collins explained to *Sounds* at the time. 'We were based in this little village, our own little world, miles from anywhere, and it enabled us to develop a schedule and stick to it. We'd get up in the morning and be in the studio by eleven and be out of it – literally – by three or four the next morning, every day for twelve days. We got so much done in that time. It's a nice way of working, but not for more than two weeks. It's so intense that you go a bit crazy after a while.'

Wind and Wuthering

Personnel: Tony Banks, Phil Collins, Steve Hackett, Mike Rutherford
Producer: David Hentschel & Genesis
Engineered by: David Hentschel
Cover art: Colin Elgie at Hipgnosis
Recorded at Relight Studios, Hilvarenbeek, September 1976.
Assistant engineer: Pierre Geofroy Chateau
Remixed at Trident Studios, London, October 1976.
Assistant engineer: Nick 'Cod' Bradford
Released: 17 December 1976
Label: Charisma Records
Running time: 50:54
Tracklisting: 1. Eleventh Earl of Mar (Banks/Hackett/Rutherford) 2. One for the Vine (Banks) 3. Your Own Special Way (Rutherford) 4. Wot Gorilla? (Collins/Banks) 5. All in a Mouse's Night (Banks) 6. Blood on the Rooftops (Hackett/Collins) 7, 'Unquiet Slumbers for the Sleepers… (Hackett/Rutherford) 8. …In That Quiet Earth' (Hackett/Rutherford/Banks/Collins) 9. Afterglow (Banks)

While the pace of work had been intense, the atmosphere around the new record was a little more relaxed than it had been going into *A Trick of the Tail*. They'd proved everything they needed to prove after the departure of Gabriel and were now going on to make a record that was to be judged on its merits. As a consequence, *Wind and Wuthering* is perhaps the greatest Genesis album of them all, though inevitably, there will be many who argue for others in the canon. The feel of the record is captured immediately by the title and by Colin Elgie's gorgeous watercolour sleeve, 'dark and grey' on the front with its skittering leaves and the lone tree on the landscape, with the hint of daybreak on the back cover to lift it. It's an autumnal album in its tone, in sound, in subject matter, the kind of record that demands the listener's attention, locked inside away from the worsening elements outside. Give it that degree of concentration and it repays you time and time again, for it has some of their finest songs, their best playing, their most unadulterated ambition, a complete lack of compromise, as well as that bittersweet knowledge when you play it now, that they would never sound like that again.

This is Genesis at their zenith, epic in scale, pointillist in detail, majestic and melodic, full of grandeur, humour, drama and, above all, the characteristic that few mention when discussing Genesis but which is in many ways their defining characteristic, real warmth and humanity. There is nothing cold about this record, nothing technocratic, nothing detached. From start to finish, it drips with genuine, unforced emotion. Perhaps that's why Genesis, more so than any of their contemporaries, survived the punk years unscathed?

'Eleventh Earl of Mar' is the customarily dramatic Genesis opener, the overture of guitar and keyboard line is, in its way, every bit as grand as the opening of 'Watcher of the Skies', but neatly trimmed back to around 40 seconds in a nod to the more concise times in which we now lived. Hackett's guitar, reminiscent of some of the playing on 'Supper's Ready', conjures up the idea of geese migrating for the winter, another tie in to the sleeve. The ensemble playing on the song is of the highest order, the energy never flagging, Rutherford producing a memorable bass part worthy of McCartney at his paperback writing best, Banks' organ playing a throwback to *Foxtrot*. It's a great vocal performance from Collins, relating Rutherford's lyric of a failed rebellion in Scotland in which he mixed and matched several different chunks of 18th-century history to come up with the whole story. It wouldn't be Genesis if there wasn't a twist and, after Hackett produces a guitar stomp that would have appealed to Mick Ronson at his most glam, the song drifts into a quieter section from the guitarist: 'There's another song in the middle of it which was intended to go somewhere completely different. I had a title 'The House and Four Winds', which I wanted to do as a whole kind of thing and that's what remains of it.' The whole song is archetypal Genesis, seamlessly welding all these different elements together in a group arrangement, even having time to create a synthesiser line that, in a piece of neat conceptual continuity, pops up again later on 'One for the Vine'.

Speaking of which, that is another example of the incredible ambition on show on *Wind and Wuthering*, a song containing enough different ideas and passages to power an entire album for most bands. Banks told *New Musical Express*, 'It's an idea I've wanted to do for a long time of using a lot of instrumental ideas which flow one from the other without repeating themselves.' The instrumental section in the middle, while different in tone and more idiosyncratic perhaps, is every bit the equal of the likes of 'The Cinema Show', and it's strange that it was never lifted for one of the live medleys that they played in later years. For all that it's a keyboard showcase in a lot of ways, Rutherford's point above about the others taking a vested interest in each song once it became a group tune was never better illustrated than here, for Collins makes it swing, Rutherford is again inventive on six-string bass and Hackett produces some soaring guitar. The group mind was clearly fully engaged.

Lyrically, Banks took the idea from Michael Moorcock's *Phoenix in Obsidian*. 'One for the Vine' is essentially the tale of a foot soldier who realises he no longer believes in the cause, and more particularly in the divine leader. On deserting, he finds himself stumbling into a wilderness, the tribe inhabiting it seeing him as 'God's chosen one', sent to save them and lead them to glory. Initially accepting the position until he can find his way home, he then tries to free himself before realising there's no way out and that he has to play the part and lead his believers into the kind of battle from which he had originally fled, whatever the consequences, only to see a distant figure disappearing into the ether, just as he had himself. 'Don't follow leaders, and watch the parking meters' as somebody else noted in song a decade earlier. 'It can have a very wide application to anyone who finds themselves doing something they didn't believe in before,' Banks said in *New Musical Express*.

Proof that Genesis still had an ear for a pop song, 'Your Own Special Way' was the choice for the album's single. Writing in *The Sunday Times*, Derek Jewell reckoned that 'Mike Rutherford's charming ballad could do as much for Genesis as did 'I'm Not in Love' for 10cc'. It wasn't a hit on anything like that scale, grazing the charts at number 43. But in America, it did begin to earn some radio play, crucial in taking the name into some of the nooks and crannies of the nation where Genesis had barely been heard, reaching number 62 over there. It has a nice, lilting chorus, but the real sparkle to the song comes from the 12-string guitar. The album version loses its way a little with an instrumental section that sounds like a musical box – not 'The Musical Box' you understand – but never really goes anywhere. The single edit is more successful.

'Wot Gorilla' is the album's 'Los Endos' and, in Collins' view, an upgrade, a view with which Hackett did not concur. He had brought 'Please Don't Touch' to the sessions, which was, in his view, superior, only to find that, 'One day when we were rehearsing, Phil said, 'I can't get behind this', and it was dropped'. Go back to those comments by Rutherford that 'everyone has to be really excited by something before we do it', and you can see the possibilities for friction even within an ostensibly democratic band. For what does democracy mean? Does it mean everyone having the vote and the majority then rules, or does it mean fair shares – 25% in this case – for all? Within Genesis, it meant the former, but like any band in the world, that was always influenced by internal politics and the ways in which one person could carry an argument or form alliances to push their material at the expense of others. Banks and Rutherford were founder members, their relationship going back five or six years before they'd met Hackett, they'd regularly been a writing pair right through Genesis' existence, it was perhaps inevitable that they would tend to side with each other, or certainly that things might feel that way to Hackett, trying to break through that power bloc and get more material through. These aren't rights and wrongs, nor a pointing of fingers, but merely a suggestion of the way life unfolds without us necessarily noticing it happen, nor the entrenched positions it cements us into. Certainly, Hackett was writing more and more after the confidence boost of *Voyage of the Acolyte,* but that was beginning to recreate the issues that had contributed to both Gabriel and Anthony Phillips leaving the band – too many strong individuals with too many strong ideas trying to get them all onto one record a year. Prophetically as it turned out, Rutherford told *Sounds* on the release of *Wind and Wuthering*, 'I think we all changed a bit [when Gabriel left]. Funnily enough, in a way it made us all more relaxed and calm with each other. It could just be numbers. I think four is easier than five, and three is probably easier than four. It gives people more room to breathe. Now there's more room for everyone to make their contribution felt more strongly, in terms of writing.'

'Wot Gorilla' divides opinions, Hackett calling it 'a very inferior instrumental' while for Collins, it was the kind of jazz-infused idea that he was encouraged to develop in Brand X and which he wanted to bring to Genesis. Rutherford noted that 'It's a reprise of a section out of 'One for the Vine'. It was Phil's idea to play a fast, jazzy rhythm.' As you'd expect, Collins' playing is outstanding, the jangly 12-string is a nice addition in the mix and Banks adds a terrific keyboard solo, while atmospherically it retains the overall feel of the record. It would have been a shame had it not found its way onto the album, but it's also a pity that four more minutes couldn't have been found somewhere to try 'Please Don't Touch' too. In a CD rather than a vinyl age, perhaps that compromise might have happened, and perhaps history might have been very different.

But back in the vinyl era, if side one had been beguiling enough, side two was simply extraordinary, with some of the best material of their career contained in its grooves. 'All in a Mouse's Night' is the album's slice of melodrama, its 'Robbery Assault and Battery' or 'The Lady Lies', the comic interlude to lighten the load, but again, its feel is completely in keeping with the album's autumnal mood, late at night, sheltering from the storm. A take on *Tom & Jerry* cartoons, the cat always gets it in the end, the mouse escaping to fight another day. Musically, it began as something of an epic before the band slimmed it down in the arrangement stage and took a lighter approach that perhaps better suited the lyric. It's a lovely example of the magic that happened when Banks and Hackett were playing in sync, weaving patterns around one another and, while it generally tends to be overlooked these days, it's worthy of reinvestigation.

'Blood on the Rooftops' was overlooked at the time because it didn't form part of the live act – a little too delicate perhaps for the 10,000 seat arenas they were now checking into in the United States – but it has long since been seen as a genuine Genesis classic and perhaps Hackett's finest moment, which is pitching it pretty high. Beginning with his nylon guitar introduction, stunning in itself, it sets up the song beautifully. It's all in there from the classical opening, through the Eleanor Rigby-esque character observation and even on to the television scenes that play out before him, on so many channels that, at a time when the UK only had three, it must have come from his experience in American hotel rooms. The action that unfolds is quintessentially English. It is a glorious synthesis of a 26-year-old's collected life and musical experiences. Hackett:

With 'Blood on the Rooftops', lyrically, I was trying to write something where there was no action. In other words, it's channel surfing, the action is happening all around you, you are not involved. There's political apathy, there's an avoidance of life going on, it's the man who's lived through the war saying to his son, 'I don't want to know, all I want is fantasy'. In a sense it's that. When I was writing the lyric, I didn't really know what I was writing about, all I knew was I wanted various levels of action to happen from the TV, the TV was going to be the frame of the song, yet nothing really happens. I've seen within my lifetime both my grandmother and my father reach old age, and there being a sense of them becoming an appendage to their TV. It shocked me in a way that my grandmother was prepared to watch anything on TV rather than engage with things in her own life but of course, now I look back on it, she'd had four children, survived a world war or two, why shouldn't she have earned the right to sit there and watch *Coronation Street* and all the rest? But I could never quite work out why the box was more interesting than people, why life wasn't quite fully interactive, that there was an acceptance, a sort of resignation. I felt there was a sense of danger, I was very worried about that and I think maybe that message is still very current because I do realise that many children don't really go out and play as much as they should do and relate to each other perhaps. Now, it's not just the TV; it's the digital domain taking over. It's pretty worrying that there is less integration going on than there was at one time, so maybe the song has relevance still.

It's a masterpiece in miniature; the delicacy of the opening, the care and attention that Collins, who also wrote the musical chorus, gives to the lyric, the power when the drums kick in à la 'Fly on a Windshield', the building grandeur of the Mellotron part, it's flawless.

The pairing of 'Unquiet Slumbers for the Sleepers…' and '…In That Quiet Earth' that follows is the kind of thing that might have been expected on the previous record, when post-Gabriel, you'd have expected to hear a heavily instrumental album. That it came on *Wind and Wuthering*, when the music industry would have been expecting Genesis to consolidate the success of *A Trick of the Tail*, underlines that the band were never going to be led anywhere by the nose but were going to produce the music they wanted to, when they wanted to. As Hackett told *Circus* at the time, 'The album is more of a classical piece, not because of adding a baroque synthesiser over some amplified rhythm tracks, but because of form. The album has a broader spectrum of sound and a more varied composition.'

The source of the album's title, Banks told a Colorado radio station, 'The piece 'Unquiet Slumbers for the Sleepers…' on side two originally conjured up the title *Wind and Wuthering*. We were thinking of the movie of *Wuthering Heights*, the film version with Laurence Olivier, it conjured up that kind of mood.' That first section, written by Hackett and Rutherford, picks up that ethereal atmosphere from 'Eleventh Earl of Mar' and 'All in a Mouse's Night' and develops it further, before crashing into '…In That Quiet Earth', a real Genesis wig out, the ensemble playing that they'd long done so well, full of drama, a plethora of memorable hooks, in the mould of 'Apocalypse In 9/8', needing that exultant vocal climax that it got from 'The New Jerusalem'. It gets it but in a different form…

'Afterglow' is the perfect climax to the album, even though Banks said he wrote it in pretty much the time he took to play it, only to be stricken later by the fear that he'd simply rewritten 'Have Yourself a Merry Little Christmas'. It's another enduring Genesis classic, very simple on the surface but one where more is more. Hackett still often speaks of how he was captivated by Ravel's *Bolero* as a child, the way it would steadily build and build in volume and drama. Much of Genesis' music works that way and 'Afterglow' is an absolute case in point. It's a beautiful melody from Banks right from the outset, but it gets better and better as more and more detail is added. Collins' huge bank of multitracked backing vocals – this really was the 10cc 'I'm Not in Love' comparison – is gorgeous, like sinking into a warm bath, five different notes sung by Collins and turned into tape loops on an afternoon when there was nothing else they could progress given that the 24-track machine had developed a fault and was chewing up the master tape. The emotional peak of the song's ending is the equal of any of the more celebrated moments from earlier in their career, and yet it all comes from a four-minute pop song. It was a pointer to the future, perhaps, but also a reminder that shorter was not necessarily a synonym for shallower.

The critics recognised just how good the record was from the off, Barbara Charone enthusing in *Sounds* that, 'Genesis makes Yes redundant. And the Pink Floyd too. Don't listen to me, hear it for yourself. It's addictive stuff.' *Record Mirror*'s David Brown wrote: 'It's an album to grow into, and a lot of people will take the time for their unmatched blend of music', while Chris Welch was equally supportive in *Melody Maker*: 'Rock can still have some vestige of pride left in itself when musicians like these are still working, unaffected by the clamorous pursuit of trivia elsewhere.'

Charisma managed to get the record into the shops in the UK in the week before Christmas, ensuring huge first week sales of 100,000 copies. In any other week, they would have been celebrating their first number one album, but because the chart shops didn't file their returns over Christmas, it was an achievement that only the band knew about. There's something peculiarly Genesis about that, isn't there?

1977: The Rain at Lord's Stopped Play

Genesis were busy right from the off in 1977, reopening the Rainbow Theatre in London with a run of three sold out shows beginning on New Year's Day. It was a prestigious debut for Chester Thompson, now behind the drums after Bill Bruford had departed, as had always seemed likely. Thompson had played with Frank Zappa and Weather Report, among others, and Collins was particularly excited by bringing into the fold an American player with such a strong jazz-rock background. It was a testing baptism for Thompson, who had relatively little rehearsal time because of the Christmas break, and that first show did not go according to plan. The band tried to introduce 'Lilywhite Lilith' into the set, which in turn ran straight into 'Wot Gorilla', but by the second night, both had been dropped, never to return.

Things did gradually settle down from there and the rest of the UK tour went smoothly before the band headed off for a lengthy American jaunt that would see them playing venues such as Madison Square Garden as their popularity began to increase exponentially in the States. But fans of the band elsewhere were not going to be short of things to look into, for after his self-imposed exile, in early 1977, Peter Gabriel was back.

Peter Gabriel – Peter Gabriel

Personnel:

Peter Gabriel: vocals, keyboards, flute, recorder

Robert Fripp: electric guitar, classical guitar, banjo

Tony Levin: bass, tuba, leader of the barbershop quartet

Jozef Chirowski: keyboards

Larry Fast: synthesiser, programming

Allan Schwartzberg: drums

Steve Hunter: acoustic guitar on 'Solsbury Hill', lead guitar on 'Slowburn' and 'Waiting for the Big One', electric guitar, rhythm guitar, pedal steel

Dick Wagner: backing vocals, guitar on 'Here comes the Flood'

Jimmy Maelen: percussion, synthibam, bones

London Symphony Orchestra

Michael Gibbs: arrangement of orchestra

Producer: Bob Ezrin

Cover art: Hipgnosis

Recorded at Toronto Soundstage, Morgan Studios London, and Olympic Studios London, Autumn 1976.
Released: 25 February 1977
Label: Charisma Records
Running time: 41:42
Tracklisting: 1. Moribund the Burgermeister 2. Solsbury Hill 3. Modern Love
4. Excuse Me (Gabriel/Hall) 5. Humdrum 6. Slowburn 7. Waiting for the Big One
8. Down the Dolce Vita 9. Here Comes the Flood
All songs written by Peter Gabriel, unless otherwise stated.

Once his departure from Genesis became public knowledge in the summer of 1975, Gabriel had issued a letter to the press in which he had made it clear that he had not left the band to become a solo artist – to do a Ferry or a Bowie as he termed it – but in order to get away from the music business itself and live a simpler life in which he would be in charge of the future, rather than being beholden to a band and to recording and touring schedules that were laid out across the next 18 months. Across that initial period, he explored the idea of joining a commune – also called Genesis – but the need and the desire to make music soon made itself felt. In typically bizarre Gabriel fashion, he had already co-written a song with Martin Hall for the diminutive English comedian Charlie Drake called 'You Never Know' which came out as a single in 1975 with the star-studded line up of Gabriel, Phil Collins, Sandy Denny, Robert Fripp, Keith Tippett and Percy Jones.

Songwriting itself was not enough, however, and late that year, he made some recordings at the home of old school friend David Thomas – who had recorded Genesis' earliest demos – to ease himself back into things. Becoming more serious about matters in early '76 he made demos at Trident Studios with the help of, who else, Collins, Mike Rutherford, Anthony Phillips and Brand X's John Goodsall. He also took some time that year to record an orchestral cover of 'Strawberry Fields Forever' for inclusion in the movie *All This and World War II*, which featured footage from the war with a soundtrack of various artists covering Beatles songs. If you haven't seen it, it's more bizarre than it sounds.

Gabriel was, by now, back in full flow, albeit aware of the accusations of hypocrisy that would dog him, returning to an industry that he had so comprehensively shredded on his departure from the band. Right from the outset, he was clear that a solo album was not a one-off deal but part of something longer-term: 'For me, this album is in part a run-in for the second thing. This one is much more a bunch of regular songs, whereas the next one will be the masterplan! The story is already written. It will probably be more experimental musically and conceptually.' This was perhaps a reference to the story of Mozo, hero of another rock opera he had in mind. Having been once bitten by *The Lamb*, he was twice shy of unleashing such a huge story on the public in one go, deciding that he would introduce songs from it over the course of a number of albums before performing the unified whole. The world is still waiting.

More immediately on his mind was the need to do something that would establish him as something very separate to his former band. In order to do that, he enlisted the help of Canadian producer Bob Ezrin, best known at that time for working on the more abrasive sounding Lou Reed and Alice Cooper. 'I particularly wanted to get away from my past. It would have been easy for me to come up with another European, keyboard orientated rock band. But that wouldn't have been right for me, that wouldn't have broken any new ground.'

For all that bravado, there was an uncertainty about Gabriel as he returned to serious work, his confidence dented by Genesis' success with *A Trick of the Tail*. Perceptions had now taken a 180-degree turn. From thoughts of Genesis being no more than Gabriel's backing band on his departure, the success of that album now made people wonder if Gabriel had made a musical contribution after all. A compromise of sorts was brokered, for while Ezrin was keen to use the musicians with whom he was familiar, Gabriel wanted the security blanket of taking a couple of his own people with him, Fripp and synthesiser wizard Larry Fast. It's a slightly uneasy alliance in the end, for, while there's a lot of very good material on *Peter Gabriel* – or *Car* as it later became known – consistency is not one of its virtues.

'Moribund the Burgermeister' was a deliberate attempt to cut ties with the past right from the outset, much harder in tone as it swapped back and forth between distinct sections, continuing Gabriel's interest in adding treatments to his voice. A village beset by an outbreak of St Vitus' dance is characteristic lyrical fare, and it does bear hints of 'The Colony of Slippermen' from his final Genesis album, but musically there's a cold sheen applied that would afflict a number of the songs. Perhaps it was an appreciation of the oncoming new wave, but it means there's a lack of warmth that did little to distance Gabriel from that 'mysterious traveller' persona. It's the adoption of another character, another mask, another buffer between Gabriel and the audience.

Which makes 'Solsbury Hill' all the more exciting when it follows because that has everything that 'Moribund the Burgermeister' lacks in terms of connecting with the audience. It's direct, it's personal, it has a winning hook, it establishes Gabriel in new territory, puts him naked in front of the crowd as was his professed intention. From Steve Hunter's acoustic guitar figure that opens things up, it has 'single' written all over it, but there's no compromise on the lyric, his summation of his reasons for moving on from Genesis, the need to walk 'right out of the machinery'. In contrast to the opener, this feels far more natural, not like he's trying so hard, as was the problem on the first track. 'Modern Love' has some of that too, though this is the more aggressive side of Gabriel's nature coming through, some of the ballsy approach that he had tried to inject into *The Lamb*. It was another single release, but it failed to chart, despite being the follow up to 'Solsbury Hill', which reached number 13. It was some way from his prog-rock roots, the influence of Bruce Springsteen especially evident in the keyboard part, Gabriel initially hoping to use Roy Bittan from the E Street Band on the album until their schedules proved incompatible.

'Excuse Me' was a Gabriel oddity of the kind he had previously served up for Charlie Drake in tandem with Hall, also the co-writer on this. Beginning with a barbershop quartet, then propelled along by Levin's tuba, there are some nice moments within, notably a 'Fripp-does-Django' break, but it's less than the sum of the parts. Like many musical jokes, it doesn't endure beyond a couple of listens and was probably more fun for the players than it is on multiple plays for the listener. It's a missed opportunity because it has good elements that go to waste in the hunt for whimsicality.

At the other end of the scale is 'Humdrum', ending the first side of the album on a real high. Gabriel's voice is initially low down in the mix, but it's a song of gradually building drama, full of typical wordplay and a lovely classical guitar part from Fripp. It's perhaps the closest he gets to Genesis on this album, but even then, the connection is fairly slender. More accurately, it's the closest he gets to what he is, a point picked up by his former Genesis colleague Anthony Phillips, asked to contribute a sketch of his old school friend for *Melody Maker* at the time the album came out. 'It was important that Peter went to America to record because, in fact, Mike, Phil and I did some demos for Peter here and of course, it sounded terribly, terribly like Genesis. And I thought at the time, hell, what's he gonna do? So America was absolutely necessary. I think Pete will produce a real masterpiece when he is reunited, hopefully, with his own country, 'cos he's very English'. It was an acute observation from Phillips, for too often on this album, Gabriel appeared to be more concerned with putting distance – an ocean's worth – between him and his past rather than necessarily producing winning material.

'I'll be strong / When I'm back on the Isle of Avalon' almost admits as much in 'Slowburn', Glastonbury just up the road from his home in Bath. That said, the searing, very American lead guitar from Steve Hunter elevates the song into something special before the more ambient run out of the track reprises the kind of atmosphere created at the end of 'Dancing With the Moonlit Knight'. There are some similarities with 'Modern Love', but it's the schizophrenic nature of the album that undercuts it as a whole, albeit that it does deliver on the 'expect the unexpected' tagline in the album's advertising. On tracks like those, it seems that Gabriel – and Ezrin – are looking to deliver a polished, straight-ahead rock record, but those ambitions founder on the eccentricities of 'Excuse Me', and the next track, 'Waiting for the Big One', a bar room blues which comes across as a Randy Newman pastiche, right down to Gabriel's uncanny impersonation of the singer, having one more for the road while Waiting for the Big One – nuclear apocalypse perhaps? Hunter produces yet another fine solo, making him the album's MVP, though the London Symphony Orchestra make a late bid for that honour with a powerfully dramatic introduction to 'Down the Dolce Vita'. The orchestral backing is incredibly effective and exactly the kind of thing that draws so many band members inexorably towards solo projects, that opportunity to indulge all their individual fantasies. Self-indulgent this might be, but it also works. Another take on impending apocalypse, this track features the Mozo character that Gabriel wanted to develop and who appeared again in perhaps the album's most enduring song, 'Here Comes the Flood'. As he told *Sounds*:

I was referring to a mental flood. A release, a wash over the mind, not necessarily the land. A downhill course which leads to disaster – an opening up, a telepathic society where people can read each other's minds. In such a situation, there'd be no real change for people who have been honest and open with whatever's in their minds; but those who have been two-faced and who have kept their thoughts hidden would find it very difficult. They'd suddenly be overwhelmed with people who can read what they're thinking and they'd be able to discover what other people think of them too.

It's a hardy perennial that Gabriel has returned to time and again over the years in concert, unlike much of the material which has fallen by the wayside. It's the best vocal performance on the album, though later versions which tend to feature just Gabriel at the piano, perhaps serve the song better than this production which feels like Gabriel fronting Pink Floyd.

For a while in 1977, it was another month, another Genesis-related release. In March, it was the turn of Anthony Phillips to offer fans an opportunity to discover what the band's early prime mover had been up to across the previous seven years, with *The Geese & The Ghost*, an album that might have appeared two or three years earlier had circumstances not intervened.

Anthony Phillips – The Geese & The Ghost

Personnel:
Anthony Phillips: acoustic 12-string guitar, 6-string, classical guitar, electric 6 and 12-string guitars, basses, dulcimer guitar, bouzouki, synthesisers, Mellotron, harmonium, piano, organ, celeste, pin piano, drums, glockenspiel, timbales, bells and chimes, gong, lead vocal on 'Collections'
Mike Rutherford: acoustic 12-string, 6-string, classical guitars, electric 6 and 12-string guitars, basses, organs, drums, timbales, glockenspiel, cymbals, bells
Phil Collins: vocals
Rob Phillips: oboes
Lazo Momulovich: oboes, cor anglais
John Hackett: flutes
Wil Sleath: flute, baroque flute, recorders, piccolo
Jack Lancaster: flutes, lyricon
Charlie Martin: cello
Nick Hayley and friend: violins
Martin Westlake: timpani
Viv McCauliffe: vocals on 'God If I Saw Her Now'.
Send Barns Orchestra & Barge Rabble conducted by Jeremy Gilbert.
Producers: Simon Heyworth, Anthony Phillips, Mike Rutherford
Engineers: Simon Heyworth, Anthony Phillips, Mike Rutherford
Cover art: Peter Cross
Recorded at Send Barns Studios, Woking and Argonaut Galleries, Little Venice, London, October 1974 – November 1976.
Released: March 1977

Label: Hit and Run Music
Running time: 47:19
Tracklisting: 1. Wind-Tales 2. Which Way the Wind Blows 3. Henry: Portraits From Tudor Times (Phillips / Rutherford) 4. God If I Saw Her Now 5. Chinese Mushroom Cloud (Phillips/Rutherford) 6. The Geese and the Ghost (Phillips/Rutherford) 7. Collections 8. Sleepfall: The Geese Fly West
All songs written by Anthony Phillips unless otherwise stated.

Recalling the slightly convoluted coming together of the album, Phillips said:

From the end of 1973 onwards, Mike and I went away on holiday in the winter, to Cornwall one year and then Ireland the next, and we were thinking about the record because we were writing extra material for the 'Henry' instrumental. During 1974, Mike got the green light from Charisma. There was a small advance which enabled us to set up a slightly more sophisticated studio at my parents' place. We bought two four-track TEACs and kicked off the recording towards the end of 1974, just before Genesis went off and started *The Lamb* tour. There was suddenly a bit of free time there, courtesy of Steve cutting his hand. Then in June the following year, Peter had left, nobody knew what was going on and in that gap, we moved recording to Tom Newman's barge, transferred everything to sixteen-track. We still didn't have enough tracks. Luckily, it was a pretty warm summer because we did a lot of sunbathing because the gear kept breaking down all the time! We'd get rammed by other barges, the timpani wouldn't fit on, so we'd have to use the other barge with a guy answering the phone while the timpanist was playing. It was pretty vibey stuff! Some of that material was written in 1969, but just never went into Genesis, so by the time it came out, some of that music was eight years old, it was contemporaneous with the little bits that went into 'Stagnation' and things like that. I don't think the material changed that much across those years, though I was probably a bit more refined in my playing. I wrote 'God If I Saw Her Now', 'Which Way the Wind Blows' and the main parts of 'Henry' in the summer of 1970 after I left Genesis. I had this huge outpouring of material. Mike and I then interposed the 12-string parts, the 'Misty Battlements' and 'Death of a Knight', that came later too and were a bit more refined by then. 'Collections' was from around 1970, 'Sleepfall' was later stuff.

Assorted record company issues delayed the release of the album still further, but eventually, it was ready to go, and for those wanting a slightly more sophisticated take on that early Genesis sound, it was a real treat. 'Wind-Tales' was a brief, pretty introduction, leading into 'Which Way the Wind Blows' featuring Phil Collins on lead vocals. Phillips took some criticism at the time for hanging on Genesis' coattails after Collins' success as the band's singer, but that was wholly unfair given that he had done his work on the project well before *A Trick of the Tail* was recorded. A gentle ballad suited to the things he had done to that point – 'More Fool Me', 'Silver Song' – musically, it is beautifully realised with the guitar parts feeding in and out of each other with real invention.

'Henry: Portraits of Tudor Times' is something altogether different, an epic instrumental across 14 minutes, capturing a host of moods as Henry's army prepares for war, sees overall victory and personal loss and returns in triumph and sadness. It's beautifully evocative and atmospheric, conjuring up all of those episodes without a word. The interplay between Phillips and Rutherford on 12-string guitars is quite magnificent, but there is far more to it than that, the building up of the sound picture with oboe, cor anglais and flute evoking the time and mood. Probably the only contemporaneous comparison to a piece like this would be *The Snow Goose* by Camel, high praise indeed, but Phillips is better yet, and innovative too, as he explained:

I wouldn't begin to compare this with *Pet Sounds* or *Sgt Pepper*, it's a very different kind of thing, but there are some very similar principles in the way we got different effects. Everything had to be played and then you used different techniques on what you had to alter the way it sounded. You couldn't do it with samples as you would now. We were constantly speeding things up, slowing them down – the cannon on 'Henry' is a snare slowed down an octave, for example. Nowadays, I'm as guilty as the next man of just going into the studio with a great bank of samples and just having a bit of fun rather than creating the sound in my head. I think that is a worrying trend, getting sounds is too easy and you're not getting there by thinking creatively in a different way. There's one section in 'Henry' where I've got a unison of cor anglais and a fuzz electric guitar because I knew what I was doing having done my studying of music theory after Genesis. I knew the compass of it, obviously, there was a certain amount of experimentation in placing the sounds together, but I knew that it could be a really interesting combination.

Had the album come out eighteen months or so earlier, as it might have done had it had a fair wind behind it, things might have been very different, for 'God If I Saw Her Now' would have been a potential single, whereas, in the teeth of the new wave, it would never have stood a chance. It's a pity, because it's a beautiful duet between Collins and Viv McCauliffe with a bewitching flute solo from John Hackett allied to those sparkling 12-strings. Recalls Phillips:

We were very unkind to John, actually. I knew him by that stage because we'd done the flute and oboe section on 'The Geese & The Ghost' together with my brother earlier in 1975, but then later, John came to the studio on the barge to do the 'God If I Saw Her Now' solo. I deliberately wrote out an incredibly impossible part, loads of time signature changes. He looked at it and his heart sank! I looked at him, crestfallen, and then whipped it away and gave him the real thing! I wouldn't have done it to him the first time we met, I promise, but I don't think he's forgiven me yet! It's very sad, Viv passed away some years ago and never got to meet Phil, they did their vocals separately. Their voices work so well together. Later on, as a singer, Phil became more stylised, but there's a plaintive quality on this which I think is refreshing. Nobody was saying, 'What a great song 'God If I Saw Her Now' is!' It seems to have become more appreciated as the years have passed, oddly enough. The song seems to have transcended the generations, a lot of younger people like it, which is interesting.

Like 'Wind-Tales' at the start of the album, 'Chinese Mushroom Cloud' is a link piece, but as Phillips notes, 'It was an accident. I wanted to get a sped-up 12-string and to get that, you had to record it an octave down and so when we were doing that and hearing it back, we just thought it would make a great section by itself. When the cellos hit it an octave down, it was very powerful, but it came together purely by chance.'

From a mushroom cloud to sunshine, a quality that seems to run right the way through the 15 minutes of the title track. Phillips:

It goes through moments of dark mystery, and then there's moments of pathos. I think my favourite section is where Lazo Momulovich kicks off with the cor anglais, and then it lights up. It's very of its time, the contrasts, the light and shade. The beginning of the last section, it starts with that very, very quiet little 12-string thing and then gradually builds, and then the main theme comes back, that repeat echo, and when that comes in at the end, I love that, it's like coming home. The song got its name from that repeat echo because we couldn't get a title for it; it was going to be called 'Lostwithiel' for a time. There was a technique we used to use on a six-string, playing very softly, but then we put it through a repeat echo.

Phillips himself becomes the album's third lead vocalist on 'Collections', a piano-led ballad that becomes increasingly orchestral as it tumbles into the final track, 'Sleepfall: The Geese Fly West'. What was immediately impressive was that, for all that it had been so long in the making, it was a very cohesive album with a distinct beginning, middle and an end and a very specific dynamic range – it was more than simply a collection of songs.

It does seem to have a shape and a sense to it. It ends well, 'Sleepfall' works well and it's always nice to leave people with something restful, a resolution if you like. I'm quite pleased with the way some of the themes go through it and keep reappearing, which gives it that continuity. It gives you that feel of going on a journey, but there are familiar elements along the way. For me, it has a lot of flaws, which it's bound to have when it's your own record, but overall, I like it.

And still, the music came, for in April Brand X released their second studio album, despite Phil Collins still being out on the road with Genesis, with a live record following later in the year.

Brand X – Moroccan Roll

Personnel:
Phil Collins: drums, lead vocals on 'Sun in the Night', piano
John Goodsall: guitar, sitar on 'Sun in the Night', echo
Percy Jones: bass, autoharp, marimba
Robin Lumley: keyboards, piano, Fender Rhodes electric piano, Moog synthesiser, clavinet, vocals
Morris Pert: percussion and a vast number of bits and things that he hit while the tape was running
Producer: Dennis MacKay
Engineer: Stephen W. Tayler
Cover art: Hipgnosis
Recorded at Trident Studios, London, December 1976 – January 1977.

Released: April 1977
Label: Charisma Records
Running time: 49:30
Tracklisting: 1. Sun in the Night (Goodsall) 2. Why I Should Lend You Mine (When You've Broken Yours Off Already) (Collins) 3. Maybe I'll Lend You Mine After All (Collins) 4. Hate Zone (Goodsall) 5. Collapsar (Lumley) 6. Disco Suicide (Lumley) 7. Orbits (Jones) 8. Malaga Virgen (Jones) 9. Macrocasm (Goodsall)

Brand X – Livestock

Personnel:
Phil Collins: drums (on tracks 2, 3, 4)
John Goodsall: guitars
Percy Jones: bass
Robin Lumley: keyboards
Morris Pert: percussion
Kenwood Dennard – Drums (on tracks 1 and 5)
Producer: Brand X
Engineer: Jerry Smith.
Cover art: Hipgnosis
Recorded at Ronnie Scott's, London, September 1976, Marquee Club, London and Hammersmith Odeon, London, 1977.
Released: 18 November 1977
Label: Charisma Records
Running time: 41:11
Tracklisting: 1. Nightmare Patrol (Goodsall/Dennard) 2. -Ish (Goodsall/Lumley/Jones/Pert/Collins) 3. Euthanasia Waltz (Goodsall/Jones/Lumley/Collins) 4. Isis Mourning (Goodsall/Jones/Lumley/Pert/Collins) 5. Malaga Virgen (Jones)

Moroccan Roll was a more ambitious album than *Unorthodox Behaviour*, building on the increasing understanding between the musicians that had formed across not just that first record but the gigs that followed it. With Collins committed to Genesis and everyone else having their own session engagements, finding time to get in the studio was never easy for Brand X, but it was always a worthwhile – and very popular – exercise when they did, *Moroccan Roll* reaching number 37 in the UK charts, some achievement for a record at the jazz end of the spectrum.

There was some deviation from the blueprint of the first record, notably on the opening track, 'Sun in the Night', which purportedly had Collins singing in Sanskrit, though it's likely that so attributing these wordless vocals was more of Brand X's Pythonic japery, as was the album's title – more rock'n'roll, geddit? The Indian influence was there in the music, not least in Goodsall's sitar playing. Collins took centre stage on the next two tracks, 'Why Should I Lend You Mine (When You've Broken Yours Off Already)', leading into 'Maybe I'll Lend You Mine After All'. They were both compositionally strong pieces, the former especially hypnotic with a lovely guitar figure from Goodsall. The latter is more atmospheric and features Collins on piano, picking out a variation on a theme from 'Dancing With the Moonlit Knight' and then little hints of a tune that would go on to be 'Ballad of Big' on Genesis' next album.

It's Collins back at the kit on 'Hate Zone', Robin Lumley taking the starring role with some great Moog playing, but it's a strong ensemble piece where everyone is clearly having the time of their lives, Goodsall wading and wailing in later with a ferocious guitar solo. 'Collapsar', another chance for Lumley to impress on synthesiser, is a brief interlude on the way to 'Disco Suicide'. That's the closest thing to Weather Report on this record, and perhaps the most clearly commercial piece on there, despite being nearly eight minutes long. Another brief link piece came by way of Jones' bass doodle 'Orbits', leading to the more fully realised 'Malaga Virgen', which suggests that Brand X were moving towards a slightly more arranged direction. Goodsall's 'Macrocasm' brings the album to a strong end, veering from the manic to the sublime to the frenetic, quintessential Brand X.

Collins actually flew back to London from a day off during Genesis' European tour to play a gig with the band at the Marquee Club, a show that was recorded, 'Euthanasia Waltz' making it to the *Livestock* live album that Brand X put out at the end of 1977. He also featured on '-Ish' and 'Isis Mourning (Parts 1 & 2)', both recorded at Ronnie Scott's in September 1976, with Kenwood Dennard appearing on the other two tracks.

For all the Brand X involvement, Genesis was still at the centre of his focus, not least because they had an EP coming out prior to returning to England for a string of shows at Earls Court.

Spot the Pigeon

Personnel: Tony Banks, Phil Collins, Steve Hackett, Mike Rutherford
Producer: David Hentschel & Genesis
Engineered by: David Hentschel

Cover art: Hipgnosis
Recorded at Relight Studios, Hilvarenbeek, September 1976.
Assistant engineer: Pierre Geoffrey Chateau
Remixed at Trident Studios, London, October 1976.
Assistant engineer: Nick 'Cod' Bradford
Released: 20 May 1977
Label: Charisma Records
Running time: 13:22
Tracklisting: 1. Match of the Day (Collins/Banks/Rutherford) 2. Pigeons (Banks/
Rutherford/Collins) 3. Inside and Out (Rutherford/Collins/Hackett/Banks)

As Collins explained to *Sounds* at the time, 'We actually had too much
material for *Wind and Wuthering*; one track was too long for inclusion
on the album and didn't quite fit into the feel of the complete piece and
there are two shorter, commercially orientated songs.' These three formed
the *Spot the Pigeon* EP that came out in May 1977 and, illustrating the
burgeoning appeal of the band, it peaked at number 14 in the UK charts. It
was a mixed bag in truth, for 'Match of the Day' features a Collins lyric that
centres around the experience of going to a football match, one he was
so unhappy with that at one point, he tried to excise it from the Genesis
story, refusing to allow it to go on the *Archive #2* box. It was restored to
the later 2007 box sets, and while you can understand his reservations,
especially with the ad-lib conversation at the end of the song, it's not quite
the disaster he suggests. With its light, bright acoustic guitars, it does have
a certain good-hearted charm about it, the same being true of 'Pigeons', a
very simple song by Genesis standards, but undeniably catchy, even if the
methods of exterminating pigeons make for unusual song lyrics.

It's pretty obvious why neither were included on the album, for
sonically, they were something of a departure for the group, standing very
much apart from the grandeur of the other material, but 'Inside and Out'
was very unfortunate not to make the cut. Hackett's lyric opens with a
young man going to jail, perhaps on false allegations, the second half of
the song explaining that once you've been inside, even after you've done
your time, there's no escaping the stigma. Musically, it's in two sections
too, the first part based on archetypal jangling 12-strings, then the second
part where the song goes into overdrive, accelerated but still pin-sharp
12-string playing, a sparkling lead line from Hackett, beautiful bass runs
from Rutherford, a mesmerising synth solo from Banks. It's sublime
ensemble playing that they introduced into the live show later on the
Wind and Wuthering tour, a hidden gem in the catalogue.

Once the tour wrapped up in July, it was time for the band to reconvene in the studio and to work their way through a couple of year's worth of concert tapes in order to put together a new live album.

Seconds Out

Personnel: Tony Banks, Phil Collins, Steve Hackett, Mike Rutherford
Guest musicians: Chester Thompson, Bill Bruford
Producer: David Hentschel & Genesis
Cover art: A&D Design
Recorded at the Palais de Paris from 11 to 14 June 1977 (The Cinema Show recorded at the Pavillion de Paris on 23 June 1976).
Released: 14 October 1977
Label: Charisma Records
Running time: 95:31
Tracklisting: 1. Squonk (Rutherford/Banks) 2. The Carpet Crawl 3. Robbery Assault and Battery (Banks/Collins) 4. Afterglow (Banks) 5. Firth of Fifth 6. I Know What I Like (In Your Wardrobe) 7. The Lamb Lies Down on Broadway 8. The Musical Box (Closing Section) 9. Supper's Ready 10. The Cinema Show 11. Dance on a Volcano (Rutherford/Banks/Hackett/Collins) 12. Los Endos (Collins/Hackett/Rutherford/Banks)
All songs written by Banks/Collins/Gabriel/ Hackett/Rutherford unless otherwise stated.

There was plenty of enthusiasm going into the mixing of the record, Hackett saying on Capital Radio in June that, 'Some of the live tapes we've already mixed, there are versions that far surpass the studio versions in terms of just spirit. If you get a good live version of something, it's so much better than any studio version because you're just feeding off the audience.' In that, he was right, for *Seconds Out* endures as one of the best live albums of the era, full of powerful performances from right across the Genesis catalogue. Although *A Trick of the Tail* was heavily, and understandably, represented, there were a host of old classics that Collins had now made his own, including 'The Carpet Crawl' and 'I Know What I Like'. The mountain for him to climb was, of course, 'Supper's Ready', but he handled it with aplomb, while the performances from the rest of the band were equally intense. Thompson had settled in on drums by the time they'd reached Paris towards the end of the tour, giving more heft to the music, but it remains a shame that only one performance with Bruford – 'The Cinema Show' – was released, for his playing on the previous tour had given a different tilt to things. For all that, *Seconds Out* is an impeccable live album, also acting as a terrific 'story so far' document for those fans who had only just come to the band in the post-Gabriel era.

Even so, it didn't please everyone, in particular Steve Hackett who, in early July, midway through mixing the album, decided that the time had come for him to leave Genesis behind. Speaking to *The Source* for an American radio special on the band in 1980, he explained:

> We were in there mixing the live album and it was he who shouts loudest, whoever was at the mixing console was having his own way, everyone was jostling for position, not enough faders to go round. We were mixing 'Supper's Ready', which in itself was something I'd already done to the best of my ability once in 1972 on *Foxtrot*. I didn't feel doing a rehash was doing anybody any favours or breaking new ground. At that point, I felt I had to move on.

It's unlikely that *Seconds Out* was the real bone of contention though, more like the final straw. Above all, the taste of being captain of the ship on his solo record had inevitably coloured things when he had to step back into band life where everybody was fighting their corner and compromise is part of the job description:

> I did find it hard to step back into Genesis and I did agonise about the decision to leave two years before I did. There was also the problem they didn't want someone with a parallel solo career going on and they were worried that the focus would come down too heavily on one member of the band again. I got a lot of stick for the album that I'd done and the album I was going to do. Then we got into arguments about songwriting because I knew the lion's share would not come my way, and I really felt that I needed the safety valve of doing albums on my own or I was going to go crazy. When you're working with the same people all the time, you know what ideas will please them, but the radical ideas are sometimes the ones you most want to do. Really, it was time to go.

The issue over songwriting was the clincher and there had been some heated discussions towards the end of the *Wind and Wuthering* tour about how that would be carved up on the next record and whether there was space for Hackett to make a second solo album alongside that one. Once again, it was the irresistible force and the immovable

object that had confronted them with Gabriel three years earlier.
The other three guys in the band were probably right that with a
successful American tour behind them in 1977, another year of absolute
concentration on Genesis might help them make the real breakthrough
in the States, establish them as a huge global group, and buy them the
opportunity to finally take the foot off the gas, slow down a little and
perhaps look into those solo ventures. If they slowed the pace now, all
that hard work might be in vain and they might have to start from square
one again. Equally, the new wave was taking its toll on contemporaries
such as ELP and Yes, and disappearing from view now might be a fatal
mistake. But from Hackett's viewpoint, there was a block to him getting
as much of his material as he wanted onto their albums and, if that was
the case, he needed the opportunity that a solo career offered to get
that material out to the public. Equally, while Genesis prided themselves
on their self-sufficiency, Hackett was interested in working with other
people, both to bring in new ideas and to get the best person for the job
working on the songs – using Randy Crawford as a singer on his next
album was to prove an example of that.

In essence, it's the same story as Gabriel's and, to a lesser extent,
Phillips' departure – young men growing up, growing in different
directions, all of them reaching a point where they're increasingly self-
confident, increasingly unwilling to compromise. When that happens, as
Phillips points out, something has to give:

After a while in any kind of collective, people start to feel that they
don't get enough of a voice, that's natural, I think. When I was in
the band, we had four composers, which was a tough set up – two
composers tend to fall out often enough, so having four all wanting to
get material through is ultimately unmanageable and, of course, they
found that again later on. If you have strong ideas, it's inevitable that
you feel at some stage you're not getting your share of the cake or
you get three against one on some songs, you get to the point where
you're bartering over material – 'you can have your verse if you take
my chorus'. When it worked, it worked fabulously well, but within it,
it does have the seeds of disaster. Ultimately, Genesis came to a much
more manageable set-up. With Phil doing all the vocals, Mike having all
the guitars and Tony all the keyboards, everybody had their separate
territory and it became easier to handle. But when I was there, there
was too much overlapping, and then I guess that continued in the

same vein for Steve when he came in, though it would perhaps be even harder for him initially because he was an 'outsider' and a very quiet, shy personality.

The well-worn tale is of Collins seeing Hackett on the way to the studio to carry on mixing and stopping to offer him a lift, only for Hackett to tell him he would call him later. On arriving at the studio, Banks and Rutherford told him that Hackett had left, whereupon they continued work. It seems a fairly offhand way to deal with it, Rutherford saying in the *1976-82* box set interviews, 'It was a relief when he phoned me up because we sensed he wasn't as committed as we were and when that happens, you'd rather they left.' But in harsh, practical terms, the show had to go on, and Genesis were already gearing themselves up for the next album, recording of which would start almost as soon as they had mixed *Seconds Out*.

Seconds Out came out in October, timed to coincide with the announcement of Hackett's departure and to suitably strong reviews, Chris Welch noting that the band were 'at the peak of their creative powers ... but even as we speak, a new Genesis album is being prepared, so it won't be long before we hear what fresh miracles they have to lay on our ears...'.

1978: So Glad You Saw Fit To Pay a Call

...And Then There Were Three...

Personnel: Tony Banks, Phil Collins, Mike Rutherford
Producer: David Hentschel & Genesis.
Engineered by: David Hentschel
Cover art: Hipgnosis
Recorded at Relight Studios, Hilvarenbeek, September – October 1977.
Assistant: Pierre Geofroy Chateau
Mixed at Trident Studios, London, October 1977.
Assistant: Steve Short
Released: 31 March 1978
Label: Charisma Records
Running time: 53:27
Tracklisting: 1. Down and Out (Collins/Banks/Rutherford) 2. Undertow (Banks) 3. Ballad of Big (Collins/Banks/Rutherford) 4. Snowbound (Rutherford) 5. Burning Rope (Banks) 6. Deep in the Motherlode (Rutherford) 7. Many Too Many (Banks) 8. Scenes From a Night's Dream (Collins/Banks) 9. Say It's Alright Joe (Rutherford) 10. The Lady Lies (Banks) 11. Follow You Follow Me (Rutherford/Banks/Collins)

With Steve Hackett gone, the remaining trio were left with the question of whether or not to replace him with another guitarist. The experience of Peter Gabriel's departure gave them a strong lead on the best answer – if you could remain self-sufficient, then why bother?

There were many reasons for that, the strongest of them picking up on the point made by Anthony Phillips in the previous chapter. Bringing in another player, potentially another songwriter, would only mean the same arguments over the cut of the songwriting cake surfacing once again. On those grounds alone, better to try to soldier on as a trio with Rutherford handling the lead guitar role. But there was more to it than that, the nebulous concept of chemistry playing a big part in it all. For some time, Tony Banks, Phil Collins and Mike Rutherford had proved themselves to be a strong, self-contained unit who were on the same wavelength not just musically but as people. Hackett had never quite fitted in with the same ease, and bringing in a fresh outsider might create similar issues. No, in this case, three was the magic number. And why not? Those were the three that had been largely responsible for powerful instrumental moments such as 'Apocalypse In 9/8' and 'The Cinema Show', that musical compatibility and telepathy perhaps locking in as far back as 1970 when Genesis were working as a four-piece.

None of which avoids the fact that the departure of Hackett was a pivotal moment for the band, more so than the loss of Gabriel in many ways. After Gabriel had gone, the following albums still had that identifiably Genesis sound. In that sense, Genesis lost more when Hackett left than when Gabriel had, Banks noting later that Hackett was more attracted to experimenting with the music, to exploring the weirder end of things than Rutherford and Collins, who were drawn towards simplifying things a little more – that's a sweeping generalisation of course, but it holds some water. With Hackett gone, Banks lost that ally and a few of the more idiosyncratic edges of the band were shaved off.

Did they lose much in songwriting terms? That's a more nuanced argument, for while Hackett had already proved his worth in that field and would go on to do so again and again on his solo records over the years, Genesis were never short of material and with Collins writing more and more, the pot would remain full to overflowing. Would future albums have been improved by the addition of 'Spectral Mornings' or 'The Steppes'? Well, what albums wouldn't be? But would they have survived the auditioning process and, even if they had, would they have made it to record in the same form? Unlikely. In that sense, the parting of the ways was, as with Gabriel, perhaps the best, even the only solution, for if nothing else, it meant we got even more great music to enjoy. But what Genesis unquestionably lost was a great guitarist whose contribution wasn't to scatter great technique across the grooves, but instead to play exactly what was needed in the service of the song, from the gentlest acoustic work, through the most lyrical, liquid playing and on to raw savagery. Hackett was a pioneer on guitar, always innovative, experimental, looking to take the instrument into new areas and to coax new sounds from it. There is no doubt that Rutherford was every bit his equal as a great acoustic and 12-string player, but he never really found a voice on lead guitar to equal that of Hackett.

While the loss of Hackett clearly did make a difference to the way ...*And There Were Three...* sounded – a bigger difference than their erstwhile guitarist had imagined, perhaps only understanding in hindsight just how significant his influence had been – it's important not to run away with the idea that this was the only reason for the beginnings of a shift in style for the band. The *Spot the Pigeon* EP had suggested change was in the air, for 'Pigeons' and 'Match of the Day' were both different in sound and tone to the rest of the material that came from the *Wind and Wuthering* sessions. Those two had been written by Banks, Collins and Rutherford and suggested a drift towards a different direction. Whether that would have continued had Hackett stayed, it's hard to say, but they were definite pointers to the style adopted on the new album.

The thing that many listeners pointed to as a big change was the fact that there were 11 songs on the album, as though this was unpardonable – there had been 11 on the first two sides of *The Lamb Lies Down on Broadway*, 12 across sides three and four, so it wasn't quite the seismic shift it was represented as. It was a deliberate choice going into the record, Rutherford telling *Sounds*, 'Maybe people will be slightly frustrated that we haven't extended our songs the way we normally do. But I think that by cutting down on the length of some of those songs, we've been able to get more variety on this album... It's very difficult for us to keep trying to be different, to avoid being a parody of ourselves.'

There was a sense of that in the album opener, 'Down and Out', opening on a wash of synthesiser not a million miles away from 'Eleventh Earl of Mar' before Rutherford leans into his first lead riff and Collins comes in like a volley of cannons firing from over the hill. It's a different kind of drum sound than hitherto, sharper, harder but in a typically idiosyncratic time signature that drops a beat. Lyrically it's a knowing kind of song, understanding the way in which big business, including the record business, was becoming increasingly ruthless, this the story of an executive from out of town coming in to fire the established management and bring in a fresh face. Maybe there was a bit of allegorical paranoia going on here, for there was certainly a musical changing of the guard going on, baby, bathwater, the whole lot being thrown out. It was a fate that Genesis were looking to escape and in songs like 'Down and Out', they were giving a hint as to how they might do it. It was more tightly focused, though clocking in at well over five minutes for all that. Even so, the solos were tightened, in part perhaps because Rutherford was still feeling his way into the lead role, but Banks' contribution on a variety of keyboards was still mightily impressive, and Collins had never quite thrashed the living daylights out of his kit as he did in the closing section. It wasn't exactly The Clash, but this was Genesis packing a punch, retooled for a new age.

Throughout their career, from start to finish, much of the best Genesis material was written by the group or chunks thereof, each bouncing off the other to come up with something greater than the sum of the proverbial parts. By the time this album came around, that philosophy had been largely parked; partly the consequence of everyone wanting to stake their claim in the post-Gabriel world, partly because they were no longer youngsters who could head off to country houses and work together. Writing was now something they generally did at home in gaps between touring and recording and increasing family commitments. Indeed, the group writing on this album came together late on, once they were already in the studio, with Rutherford writing three songs on his own, Banks offering four. They were high-quality offerings, Banks, in particular, maintaining the extraordinary peak that he had reached on *Wind and Wuthering*. First up was 'Undertow', a track that he was to return to over the following year, first using a snatch from it as part of the soundtrack to the film *The Shout* that he composed with Rutherford, and then using another theme from it on his solo album. Little wonder, because it's a lovely song that features a superb vocal from Collins, beginning to show that Gabriel-esque ability to wrap himself in a song, not merely sing it. The smile you can hear in his voice on the 'Wine flows from flask to glass to mouth' is a glorious little detail. Rutherford offers some nice guitar lines as the chorus rises to a crescendo, a brighter tone to his playing than the more languid work of Hackett, while Banks' new Yamaha electric grand, which was to prove an important instrument over the next few years both in the studio and in concert, began to make its presence felt here. It's a beautiful song, one of the album's highlights, though not built for live work, the contrasts between the gentle verses and the more strident choruses too much of a shift, especially for the stadia they were booked in to play in the States.

'Ballad of Big' was the second of the group-written songs, Collins – later to become recognised as one of the leading authorities on the story of the Alamo – penning a Wild West lyric, the tale of big Jim Cooley who 'died like all good cowboys, with his boots on, next to his men'. The words come from a legion of John Wayne and Glen Ford movies – as would 'Me And Virgil' from the *Abacab* sessions later – but musically, it's in the direction that *Spot the Pigeon* hinted at. A slightly unholy alliance of three distinct sections, one penned by each of the members, it promises a bit more than it delivers because there's a suggestion of a real powerhouse beating inside that never quite makes it to the surface – the reins are being held too tightly somehow. The end section sees Rutherford getting to grips with the Roland guitar synth for the first time, he and Banks manoeuvring around one another.

There's a slightly obvious pacing to the first side of *...And Then There Were Three...* for after the rumbustious 'Ballad of Big', another ballad slips into the running order in the form of 'Snowbound', a pretty little song from Rutherford. There's some interesting production trickery on this, Collins' drums slowed down to give a much flatter tone while Banks produces a haunting keyboard flurry, all swirling notes that are the audio equivalent of a snow globe, a clever piece of musical imagery. The softer sections of the song are in the same territory as 'Your Own Special Way', built around acoustic guitar, very much in Rutherford's comfort zone but played quite beautifully. Again, Collins' vocal is outstanding, underlining just how he improved from album to album in those early days of him being the lead singer. His harmonies and backing vocals are beautifully pitched too, always illuminating the main line of the song.

The first side ends with perhaps its strongest song, Banks' 'Burning Rope'. It started out as a fully-fledged epic that could very easily have turned into something along the lines of 'One for the Vine', clocking in at a dozen minutes or more, but he consciously wielded the axe to bring it in at just over seven. If this had been released on *A Trick of the Tail* or *Selling England by the Pound*, it would have been lauded as a classic of the catalogue, but history has too often judged this album, and its constituent parts, as the end of Genesis as a progressive force, an impression not helped by the album sleeve which is an absolute stinker, a real Hipgnosis-by-numbers effort. It's palpable nonsense, not just in the context of this album but in what was still to follow from the band, and 'Burning Rope' shows it up for the willful refusal to listen that it is. Certainly, you could excuse the album as a whole of coming up slightly short sonically on the basis of Rutherford's fairly tentative lead guitar work, but in terms of ambition, all the Genesis hallmarks are present and correct – and in 'Burning Rope', you even get a really strong guitar solo. Interestingly, Banks explained in *Chapter and Verse* that it was a written solo that Rutherford played note for note, not something where he simply let fly the way Hackett did on 'Fountain of Salmacis' or 'Firth of Fifth', reinforcing Rutherford's limitations on this record, but even so, it serves the song beautifully. And once again, you have to marvel at just how great a drummer Collins was throughout the 1970s. Lyrically, it picks up the preoccupations already on show in 'Undertow', the importance of seizing the day, living in the moment, but it is as a composer and player that Banks is at his most eloquent on this song, a tour de force fit to rank with his best work.

Rutherford was back at the songwriting helm for the start of side two, showcasing the slightly heavier end of his tastes on 'Deep in the Motherlode', just as he had on 'Squonk' or 'Back in NYC'. Another Wild West tale – did they only get the cowboy channel on TV in Hilvarenbeek? – this one is about the gold rush, packing up the covered wagons and heading west. There's a nice atmospheric section midway through that changes the pace effectively, but the predominant feeling from the song is that it really swings – Collins could have done worse than include a version of this song on his *A Hot Night in Paris* big band album in 1998.

'Many Too Many' ranks highly among any of the Genesis ballads from any era. Spun off as the album's second single in the UK, it only reached number 43, a surprisingly low placing, not least because the single included a couple of non-album tracks. Rutherford finds some effective, and affecting, lead lines on the track, not least on the lengthy fade out, while Banks contributes both a lovely piano introduction and some fine synth playing later on, notably a great Moog string part. It's another one of those Genesis songs that got away, something that should feature more highly when reflecting on their music. They tried to reintroduce it to the audience in 2008 when, to coincide with the release of the *When in Rome* DVD, they issued a 12 track CD free with *The Mail on Sunday* in the UK and included 'Many Too Many', indicating that they had subjected the song to some reappraisal.

'Scenes From a Night's Dream' was a song that was nearly lost to the cutting room floor, as Rutherford explained in *Sounds*. 'The music is by Tony and the words by Phil. This went through a funny change. We always liked it, but Tony didn't like the lyrics he had for it and went off them – more than the rest of us actually – halfway through. Then Phil came back with some different lyrics, a slightly different melody and some answering harmonies.'

Collins had got the lyrical idea from a book of cartoons that he had bought for his brother, the newspaper cartoonist Clive, who later produced the biographical cartoons for the special 7" edition of 'In the Air Tonight'. It dated back to the early 1900s, featuring Nemo, a young boy, and the tales of the dreams he had every night. It's a strong addition to the album, bringing a light, breezy feeling to proceedings after the more introspective 'Many Too Many'. Collins' work on the layers of backing vocals and harmonies is stunning, conjuring up a suitably dreamy landscape. The whole thing has that sunny Genesis jangle to it that they would use to great effect again on tracks such as 'You Might Recall' further down the line.

Light and breezy was not a description you'd apply to 'Say It's Alright Joe'. Rutherford's stab at a Frank Sinatra 'In the Wee Small Hours', drunk alone at the bar at 3am song, the barman desperate to close up for the evening, only to be forced to hear yet another story about love and loss. It opens by wallowing in self-pity, about to drown in its own pathos, but the roaring chorus sections conjure up a kind of drunken delirium. Collins embroidered the live renditions of the song by turning the stage set into his own personal bar, propping himself up against Banks' keyboards with a dimly lit lamp and shade and a glass of something possibly stronger than Pepsi. It was a nicely subtle theatrical touch that certainly enhanced the performance of a song that might otherwise have had no chance of surviving in the big arenas.

On the other hand, 'The Lady Lies', a glorious piece of typical Genesis melodrama, was the perfect song to play in front of those big crowds. Collins would exhort the crowd to boo and hiss the villain, who he would illustrate by twirling an imaginary moustache and 'overacting rather badly' as he would note in his concert introduction. It's another of those slices of Genesis humour, piling layer upon layer – it's the story of a man who can't resist temptation, even when he knows it will lead him to his own doom, so it draws on the siren's song, on the myth of Salmacis, on the silent movie baddie tying the helpless maiden to the train tracks to lure the hero into his trap. But then, 'who can escape what he desires'? Lyrically it might be a comic opera, but musically there are wonderful moments on it, from Banks' slinky opening vamp through Rutherford's glorious bass playing, a terrific percussion section from Collins on the choruses. It's a song that might well have survived longer on the road than it did – just two tours in the set, 1978 and 1980 – and is another minor classic.

It's the album's final song that became its defining moment though, 'Follow You Follow Me' splitting the core audience after it had the temerity to reach number seven in the UK singles charts. It was almost a throwaway, Rutherford explaining to *Sounds*:

We deliberately planned to end the album on a lighter note, in contrast to our usual, heavy, pompous Armageddon-here-we-come sort of thing. It's meant to be something of an afterthought. I look upon 'The Lady Lies' as the end of the album. This is a wistful postscript. As a single, I don't think it's quite as strong. With some groups – Queen and 10cc for example – the best tracks they do are their singles. Our strongest tracks don't make good singles.

The record-buying public were very keen on it after the radio stations gave it plenty of airtime. As Banks said later in *Chapter and Verse*, that was all hugely important for their longevity.

The most exciting moment for me in the studio was when Mike played a big flanged guitar riff and I started playing a few chords along to it; suddenly the combination sounded fantastic, this very simple little thing … it was a song that made you feel warm. It was a happy song … We were lucky we had the hit single with that song because it gave the positive impression that we survived all the changes we'd been through; punk music was coming in and was supposed to be doing away with groups like us. But at exactly that moment, we had our first hit single.

The song has endured too, continuing to get radio play, while at the time, Collins was thrilled to hear that it was getting played on the Weather Report tour bus, taking it as a signal that, 'We must be doing something right!'

All told, *…And Then There Were Three…* was a fine album, reaching number three and staying in the UK charts for 32 weeks. It was perhaps stronger in the songwriting than in the execution this time, for there's no question that Rutherford's novice status on lead guitar meant the overall sound was a little thin and too dependent on the keyboards, that lovely interplay of sounds that Banks and Hackett had so often created noticeable by its absence. For all that, they had weathered the storm of the latter's departure, Chris Welch giving the record the enthusiastic thumbs up in *Melody Maker*: 'An album as good as any they have made in recent post-Gabriel years.' That judgement might not have stood the test of time, but it was closer to the mark than Steve Clarke's in *New Musical Express*: 'There are signs on *…And Then there Were Three…* that Genesis might well be advised to rethink drastically – perhaps even call it a day … hitherto, unlike their assumed peers Yes and ELP, Genesis have remained free of any charges of obsolescence, but unless their next album – if indeed there is one – is an improvement on this, those charges will soon be made.'

It was a Genesis spring in 1978, for hard on the heels of the band's album came solo efforts from Peter Gabriel, Anthony Phillips and, first out of the box, Steve Hackett.

Steve Hackett – Please Don't Touch!

Personnel:

Steve Hackett: electric and acoustic guitars, vocals, keyboards, percussion

John Hackett: flutes, piccolos, keyboards, bass pedals

Tom Fowler: bass

Chester Thompson: drums, percussion

Phil Ehart: drums, percussion

Randy Crawford: vocals

Richie Havens: vocals, percussion

Steve Walsh: vocals

James Bradley: percussion

Graham Smith: violin

Hugh Malloy: cello

Dave Lebolt: keyboards

John Acock: keyboards

Maria Borvino: vocals

Dan Owen: vocals

Producers: Steve Hackett & John Acock

Engineer: John Acock

Assistant engineers: Chip, Rob, Mark and Rafe

Cover art: Kim Poor

Recorded at Cherokee Studios, Hollywood; Kingsway Studios, Wembley; Record Plant, New York City; De Lane Lea, London, November 1977 – February 1978.

Released: 14 April 1978

Label: Charisma Records

Running time: 38:35

Tracklisting: 1. Narnia 2. Carry On up the Vicarage 3. Racing in A 4. Kim 5. How Can I? 6. Hoping Love Will Last 7. Land of a Thousand Autumns 8. Please Don't Touch 9. The Voice of Necam 10. Icarus Ascending

All songs written by Steve Hackett.

It was a feisty Steve Hackett who attacked the launch of *Please Don't Touch!*, getting a few frustrations off his chest in a *Sounds* interview with Sylvie Simmons, distancing himself from his former band. 'I had a lot of arguments with Genesis. In the end, it got totally ridiculous, to the point where gone was any personal respect.' Beyond that, though, he had clearly grown tired of the live circuit, feeling that it was stifling creativity. 'An album is the most personal statement I can make to anybody. It's a lot more personal than getting up on stage and repeating the performance. A lot of people think live performances are very important. I personally think The Beatles really started happening as a band as soon as they gave up live performances … it's like writing a book compared to reciting a book.'

Certainly, *Please Don't Touch!* was not crafted with live performance in mind because freed of the confines of working with the same group, he assembled an impressive cast of musicians to join him, the kind he could never gather together on stage. This was a one-off vinyl happening and, across four months and two continents, recording went on with admirable attention to detail on every track. Working in London and in the USA was significant and a bedrock of the album's initial philosophy, as he explained:

The fact that the people involved were from different sides of the Atlantic, coming together on the project, was fundamental to the core of the album. I felt people made European sounding albums or American sounding albums and you didn't get too much mingling of the two. I always felt Steve Walsh from Kansas had a very strong voice and I ended up working with him and that gave the record a different quality which I really wanted to get. It did have more songs, and intentionally every track was different from all the others. There were a few ballads – I prefer to call them slow songs – but they went off into various flights of fancy, at tangents to the others. I tried to line up as many opposites as I could. It's like an octopus, where you have a centre, but all the tentacles are spread far and wide.

It was a marked change from *Voyage of the Acolyte*, Hackett ironically matching Genesis in writing shorter pieces, ten songs across less than 39 minutes, but like his old band, there was no lack of quality amid the quantity. It was a much more song-based record than its predecessor and nor did it have so many of those jazzier elements that had marked that one out. It was a little more conventional maybe, but the material and the performances were of such quality, who cared?

Steve Walsh of Kansas was the first guest to make his mark, vocalist on 'Narnia', which opened with a summery guitar refrain from Hackett, instantly marking it out as single material. Based on the C.S. Lewis books – cult classics then, mainstream cinema today – the single would be ripe for re-release now, if singles were still a thing. Hackett accurately described what Walsh brought to the song: 'He is clean and precise; it's very optimistic, very youthful American. A gleaming, efficient thing.'

English lit. was source material for 'Carry On up the Vicarage' too, Kenneth Williams meets Agatha Christie, introduced by a tinkling musical box and the sound of Victorian toys, then featuring a heavily treated Hackett vocal, and including a secondary line that sounds like it was done under the influence of helium. A fairground organ maintains the playfully sinister tone of the song, but like so many songs that are built around a jokey idea, it doesn't endure as well as the rest of the material. 'Racing in A', on the other hand, recaptures some of the feel of 'Ace of Wands' from the first album, with some beautiful guitar phrases in the opening section, Walsh coming in to provide a strong vocal. That's all the more impressive given the structure of the lyric makes for quite a staccato delivery in the verses in particular. The chorus has a touch of Todd Rundgren about it, but it's the guitar that really shines on the song, not just in the electric burst at the start but in a lovely acoustic coda that sets up the next track.

Reaching for the tried and tested, 'Kim' is a pretty duet between acoustic guitar and flute, John Hackett being given his moment and taking that opportunity with both hands, a beautiful performance of a haunting melody. The production is interesting, both instruments seemingly coming at you as if from a distance, heard floating across a field rather than being right in front of you.

Richie Havens had been the support act when Genesis played Earls Court in June 1977 and Hackett had quickly struck up a friendship with him. Seizing the opportunity to work together on this album when he was recording in Hollywood, Havens made the pilgrimage across country from New York to join him in the studio.

Richie Havens got straight off a six-hour flight, got picked up at the airport, insisted on travelling in the back of the van, arrived at the studio, learnt 'How Can I?' and did an incredible performance. He seemed indefatigable. He was an amazing source of energy, wonderful. To be honest, it's 'Across the Universe' revisited. I was aware of it and had Richie not been so enthusiastic about doing it, I probably wouldn't have done it. But he did all those Beatles songs, so why not get him to do one written with The Beatles in mind?

It's a beautiful vocal, world-weary, lived in, complemented perfectly by Hackett's sparse guitar.

'Hoping Love Will Last' introduced Randy Crawford to a new audience, this song coming out a year before 'Street Life' made her and The Crusaders real stars around the world. It's very much a departure for Hackett, not just a straight love song, but done in a soul music setting. The string section was something, 'I had great difficulty writing', Hackett admitted on his YouTube channel. 'It's Graham Smith who was with String Driven Thing in the main. It was my first attempt at writing for orchestra, but the Genesis guys were very complimentary about this. Then [Randy] sounds just like Aretha Franklin when she opens up her pipes! Wonderful singing. Chester Thompson played brushes on it, I didn't ask him but he could feel it needed a trio meets quartet kind of thing.'

'Land of a Thousand Autumns' which bleeds into 'Please Don't Touch' are perhaps more of what was expected of the solo Hackett. Shifting time signatures, some meaty, manic guitar playing, a hint of Zappa, all progressive life is there and you can see how it might have fitted into Genesis as the next logical step on from 'Los Endos'. 'The Voice of NECAM' was the third part in the trilogy, the main theme played on what sounds like a pipe organ, before a forest of vocals on tape loops takes over, then into some beautiful nylon guitar playing, the calm after the storm.

Havens returns for 'Icarus Ascending', the track which Hackett had originally envisaged using him on – 'How Can I?' was just something they had time to fit in when he was in the studio. It fits his smoky voice perfectly, through a song in three distinct sections. The standard song part goes into a quirky middle section where the band goes through one style after another, from reggae to lounge, to jazz, and then back to the song which churns and builds, a little like 'Shadow of the Hierophant'; but this time, there's the added bonus of Havens' voice on top of it, improvising an ending as the band keeps on playing. It's a potent end to a strong album from Hackett, charting at number 38 in the UK, a slight fall off from *Voyage of the Acolyte*, but encouraging enough after leaving Genesis behind. The reviews were promising too, Phil Sutcliffe writing in *Sounds*, 'Hackett's awareness of dynamics is probably the single quality which shapes *Please Don't Touch!* into a record that holds you right until it lets you go'.

The album wasn't without issues. Given its galaxy of performers, most with their own careers to go back to, just how did you take this music on the road, for whatever Hackett's disinclination in that direction, record companies in the UK and the US were soon pressing him to get out and promote it. He resolved the issue in October, recruiting a band for a European tour and to then work with him as a unit on his next record that would be released the following year.

Anthony Phillips was the next out of the gate with his own second album, released a month after Hackett's.

Anthony Phillips – Wise After the Event

Personnel:
Anthony Phillips: vocals, harmonica, guitars, keyboards, sundries, drums and bass on 'Greenhouse', orchestral arrangements on 'Regrets'
Michael Giles: drums
John G. Perry: bass
Jeremy Gilbert: keyboards
Mel Collins: soprano sax, flute
Robin Phillips: oboe
Rupert Hine: percussion, backing vocals, locks, probs, modes, vibraphone, drums and bass on 'Greenhouse'
Alan Perkins: synthesiser
Rodent Rabble: clicks, claps and crampons
Gilbert Biberian: orchestra conductor
David Katz: orchestra assembling
Producer: Rupert Hine
Engineers: Richard 'Papercup' Austen, Alan Perkins, Steve Taylor
Cover art: Peter Cross
Recorded at Essex Studios, London; with the Manor Mobile at the Farmyard, Buckinghamshire; CBS Studios, London, October – December 1977.
Released: May 1978
Label: Arista
Running time: 55:27
Tracklisting: 1. We're All As We Lie 2. Birdsong 3. Moonshooter 4. Wise After the Event 5. Pulling Faces 6. Regrets 7. Greenhouse (Phillips/Gilbert) 8. Paperchase 9. Now What (Are They Doing to My Little Friends?)
All songs written by Anthony Phillips, unless otherwise stated.

Given the delays that Phillips had endured before *The Geese & The Ghost* was finally released, the turnaround on *Wise After the Event* was relatively rapid, out and in the shops inside fifteen months. But that wasn't to say it was a serene process, for it was anything but. His initial focus had been an instrumental album based around the story of *Tarka the Otter*, but the counsel he was receiving at the time suggested that the 1978 marketplace required a focus on songs. At this distance, it's hard to recall just what an impact the new wave had on everything, but if you look at the field of progressive rock, long songs, instrumentals, anything of great complexity was shunned for several years. Everything was slimmed down across that period, even among the biggest names. With recording time a costly business, the record labels could call the tune, particularly when it came to artists who weren't established, as Phillips pointed out:

It's interesting thinking back to those days of big, expensive studios and all of that, and nowadays where you can make a record in your spare bedroom and mix it on your laptop on the train while you're going off somewhere. It's the democratisation of music, which I think is fantastic. It's easy as we get older to be curmudgeonly about things, 'it was all better in my day', and I do find plenty to worry about in this technological age; that we don't talk to each other any longer, that everything is so computer-based, and if you aren't up to speed with it, you get hung out to dry, which is particularly worrying for the older generation. But that aspect of it is great, because if you go back to the '70s, if you didn't toe the record company's line, you simply couldn't get your ideas down – if you were a classical composer, at least you could notate it, but a rock band needed the record company. Now, you can realise your ideas without having to kowtow to a record company, and that is great. The plutocracy era of equipment has gone as well. In the '80s, the cost of a Synclavier or a Fairlight was more than I was making in a year! Only the very rich and successful people could afford that, so it was a terribly uneven playing field. Socially, we still have this big gap between the rich and the poor, but for musicians, the gap has become much smaller in terms of what is accessible, and that has to be a good thing. But back in the 1970s, if you wanted to make a record to a good standard, using a good studio and so on, it was an expensive business, and he who pays the studio bill calls your tunes!

It's a mixed bag of a record, not least because Phillips, especially at that stage, was uncertain about taking on the role of singer, certainly across a full album project. There are moments when he handles it superbly and others where you can hear his own uncertainty in the role and that inevitably colours the record, as did the demands to be commercial and to produce hit singles. That was not a natural discipline for him – nor any of the other Genesis members until the 1980s, any single activity that they enjoyed coming as a happy by-product of what they were doing naturally. The irony is that there is nothing on *Wise After the Event* that sounds anything like as commercial as 'Silver Song' or 'God If I Saw Her Now'.

'We're All As We Lie' is a case in point, for although it has nice elements in it, they are truncated before they have a chance to really make an impact – Mel Collins' soprano sax part has come and gone before you get a chance to really appreciate it, for example. 'Birdsong and Reprise' has much more going for it, and it's probably no coincidence that it's a song pushing up towards the seven-minute mark. The 12-string sound roots it in the same territory as the first record, there's a delightful guitar solo that offers Phillips the freedom to express himself more fully than on the opener, and his vocal sounds much more assured as if he is more at home with the material, perhaps because it's a piece that dates back to just after he left Genesis rather than being newly written for the project.

'Moonshooter' was a new song, just like 'We're All As We Lie', and more successful than the opener. The piano riff leads into a nice chorus, but in a year of Elvis Costello, Blondie and *Saturday Night Fever*, it's too well mannered to leap out of the speakers and grab an audience by the throat, though it also suffered from the lack of the orchestral parts that were scored but never recorded when time ran out on the session. The title track was the album's major concession to Phillips' more natural method of writing, a near eleven-minute piece that features some wonderful Rickenbacker 12-string playing, notably through a suitably majestic instrumental section midway through, the song culminating in a lengthy and atmospheric coda that leads the listener into 'Pulling Faces', another of the new songs and the one which sounds most like a potential single, Mike Giles' drum track giving it a nice energy, John G. Perry complementing him nicely on bass. It has a touch of 10cc about it but without the same character in the vocal that you would get from Eric Stewart or Lol Creme.

'Regrets' did reap the benefit of the orchestral treatment, opening as a tender piano piece before the strings were introduced, the orchestra swelling to crescendo as the song built before coming full circle and ending on plaintive piano and voice again. It was a piece with some potential, a power ballad that might have earned some radio play, but while Phillips handles the vocal well enough, it lacks that real charisma that makes the difference between a good performance and a hit performance.

The other song that missed out on orchestral effects because of time constraints was 'Greenhouse', which sees Phillips doing a good take on a Lennon-esque vocal, the verse having more than a trace of 'I Am the Walrus' about it. It continues the general theme of the album, a concern for the environment, the future of the planet and its creatures. It seems strange to think of it now, but back in 1978, such concerns were marginalised and largely dismissed as the kind of thing that only old hippies worried about. Phillips was 40 years ahead of his time. Again, it underlines the importance that timing and fashion play in success – release a record with such concerns today, and the press would be all over it.

'Paperchase' sees some of Giles' most aggressive drumming on the record, and it is a really attractive song, the chiming 12-string, a lovely bass pattern from Perry and some nice piano embellishments all combining particularly well, the song's internal dynamics always keeping the interest. 'Now What (Are They Doing to My Little Friends?)' was inspired by a TV documentary that Phillips had seen – and been horrified by – about the culling of baby seals, and he gives a passionate vocal performance as a consequence, accompanied by a beautiful piano part and a shimmering performance by Jeremy Gilbert on harp, the track ending with a sense of foreboding. With the title track, it's perhaps the highlight of the record, and it's telling that those two are the longest songs on it. Good storytelling, musically and lyrically, sometimes needs that space to convey what it has to say, but the climate was not conducive. The review in *Sounds* noted, 'I guess Genesis/Camel fans will like it. For the rest, it's music to crash a sink full of plates and cutlery about to.' Not the most helpful description for someone wondering how best to spend their hard-earned £3.99. *Melody Maker* opined, 'Throughout the album, there are plenty of pleasant melodies to set one humming, and there isn't a raucous note in it. But it's clearly not intended to be just fairly pleasant and mildly soporific, which is exactly what it is.'

Next up was Peter Gabriel, with his second self-titled album, the idea being that the albums were like a series of regular magazines where you differentiated between one and another via the cover photos.

Peter Gabriel – Peter Gabriel

Personnel:
Peter Gabriel: vocals, Hammond organ, piano, synthesiser
Robert Fripp: electric guitar, acoustic guitar, Frippertronics
Tony Levin: bass, Chapman stick, string bass, recorder arrangements, backing vocals
Roy Bittan: keyboards
Larry Fast: synthesiser, treatments
Jerry Marotta: drums
Sid McGinnis: electric guitar, acoustic guitar, steel guitar, mandolin, backing vocals
Bayeté: keyboards
Tim Cappello: saxophone
George Marge: recorder
John Tims: insects
Producer: Robert Fripp
Cover art: Hipgnosis
Recorded at Relight Studios, Hilvarenbeek; The Hit Factory, New York November 1977 – February 1978.
Released: 3 June 1978
Label: Charisma Records
Running time: 41:29
Tracklisting: 1. On the Air 2. DIY 3. Mother of Violence (P. Gabriel/J. Gabriel) 4. A Wonderful Day in a One Way World 5. White Shadow 6. Indigo 7. Animal Magic 8. Exposure (Gabriel/Fripp) 9. Flotsam & Jetsam 10. Perspective 11. Home Sweet Home
All songs written by Peter Gabriel, unless otherwise stated.

From that cover onwards – Gabriel seemingly scratching away a chunk of his portrait with his nails – it was clear that this was a darker record in every sense, going much deeper than his debut had done. It wasn't the only change. Although American musicians played a big part again – Tony Levin and Larry Fast were joined by Jerry Marotta, Sid McGinnis and, at last, Roy Bittan – there was a much more European sensibility at play this time, with Gabriel enlisting Robert Fripp as producer, as well as player. The first album had paradoxically played into both Gabriel's self-confidence and self-doubt. He was clearly pleased to have carried it off, had enjoyed a bonafide hit single and had played a comparatively short but well-received concert tour on either side of the Atlantic. At the same time, that album had lacked consistency in terms of material, which had run the gamut from the brilliant to the mundane, while the willingness to touch as many bases as possible meant that he hadn't really carved out a cohesive identity. The second album would be a little more focused.

It opened up in familiar mode, with 'On the Air' and 'DIY' both channelling the aggression and edge of *The Lamb Lies Down on Broadway*, as well as its subject matter to a certain extent. Perhaps this was because both tracks featured the Mozo character, actually name-checked for the first time on the opening track, communicating his existence to the world via a pirate radio signal, just as Rael had done with his spray can of paint. Even Fast's intro to 'On the Air' had a hint of Banks' opening to 'The Lamb Lies Down Broadway' about it, evidence that having mapped out some new territory on that first record, Gabriel was no longer so sensitive about sounding like his old band – and why should he, given he had made up 20% of its number? For all that, he couldn't help having another little dig at his former colleagues in 'DIY' – 'When things get so big, I don't trust them at all / If you want to keep control, you've got to keep it small. DIY.'

If the opening salvo had been a nod in the direction of the past, then 'Mother of Violence', co-written with his then-wife Jill, suggested directions for the future. It's a sumptuous song with a delicious vocal from Gabriel and glorious piano from Bittan, deceptively low key in tone, featuring his perennial preoccupation with the way in which the micro feeds the macro and vice versa. It's warmly unsettling, from the buzz of insects that begins it, through the lush arrangement, to the refrain that questions what we are being told, and how the only thing left to believe in is fear, which begets violence, at home and on the streets. Despite being recorded in 1978, it increasingly feels like the theme tune for the 21st century. An easy flippancy was still both a Gabriel strength and temptation, as underlined in 'A Wonderful Day in a One Way World'. Reminiscent of 'The Grand Parade of Lifeless Packaging', a chance encounter with Einstein in a deserted supermarket doesn't impress the singer who, offered eternal youth, decides, 'It's money I serve'. Again, Gabriel seems preoccupied with, if not a lack of free will, then at least a willing uniformity amongst the population, happy not to question, but to go along with the dominant way of thinking, refusing to rock the boat – the brother John school of thought.

'White Shadow', first unveiled on his 1977 tour, has an eerie quality about it. It features a heavily treated vocal and some excellent guitar work from Fripp on acoustic and electric. The original vinyl pressing, where this was the final track on side one, included a locked groove; you would be treated to some closing Fripp ad infinitum until you finally got up and removed the stylus yourself. Which is a lot more fun than streaming it, let's face it.

'Indigo' had also seen the light of day on the '77 tour, albeit under the title 'A Song Without Words'. It ushers in side two, a yet darker selection of songs, defining the terrain that he would refine further on his third album in 1980, that of damaged mental states. 'Indigo' is a contemplation of impending death, most likely through the serious illness of old age given its reference to the model being 'out of date' and a yellowed liver, but you could read it as a suicide note of sorts too. 'Animal Magic' heads in a different direction, a timid young man joining up for the Army – 'the professionals' as the recruiting adverts of the time, screened during war films, had it – only to find himself on the streets of Belfast amid The Troubles that disfigured life in Northern Ireland for the last 30 years of the 20th century. He comes home transformed by the experience, though whether that's for the better or not is very much left to the imagination.

'Exposure' was the co-write with Fripp, and was also the name of the guitarist's solo record that came out around the time, part of his self-proclaimed trilogy that also included his production of Daryl Hall's *Sacred Songs*. Drenched in Frippertronics, the song is the very definition of claustrophobia, a cloying vocal gasping for air, at odds with the lyric that's desperately demanding space. 'Flotsam and Jetsam' follows that up, the same sinister element to it as would seep into 'Intruder' in due course. It has a stalkerish feel, love overbalancing into unhealthy, then dangerous obsession, but perhaps it's less evil than that. Throughout his career, Gabriel has talked about his inability to show his true emotions in one to one situations, to touch people, to embrace them, and there are traces of that in this lyric, a frustration at his failure to communicate on a personal level, ironic for a singer, painful in a relationship where the other person in the story seems much more capable: 'We both know it, Christ you show it.'

'Perspective' is a return to a more crunching rock sound, a longer version of the song appearing on the original 'DIY' single release before being truncated for the album. It has that new wave edge to it, a choppy guitar riff, a pogoing rhythm, all of which played into Gabriel's attempts at repositioning himself across the year, including playing a support slot at a Battersea Park festival for The Stranglers, who were, Jean-Jacques Burnel apart, all older than he was. With shaven head and wearing a hi-vis jacket, Gabriel looked the part, though he might have undermined himself by playing 'Me and My Teddy Bear'.

The album ends on a harrowing note in 'Home Sweet Home', the tale of a struggling family, desperately short on money and penned in a high-rise flat. Life becomes so unbearable, and hope of change in such short supply that one day the singer comes home from work to find his wife has thrown herself and their child out of the window. Life isn't finished with him yet though, and on receiving what he sees as the tainted insurance money, he goes out to fritter it away at the casino, only to win the kind of fortune that would have transformed their lives, but which is now meaningless.

As an album, it is streets ahead of the first, illustrating a new direction for him in the years ahead. A solid band, based around Levin, Fast and Marotta, was taking shape, and they would serve him well in the coming years. His willingness to see a unit coalesce suggested that Genesis was now long behind him, happy to find himself in another band, but one where he was very much in charge of the show.

As a live act, his old band, now augmented by American Daryl Stuermer on guitar and bass, were seen but briefly in the UK in 1978, but it was a monumental show that they played, the Knebworth Festival on 24 June 1978 in front of 100,000 fans. The show, along with a couple of others in Europe, were the subject of a BBC documentary about the band, their music and the huge scale of their touring operation, which was said to cost $25,000 a day to keep on the road. The giant festivals certainly helped defeat that cost, while the release of 'Many Too Many' as a single, although not a major hit, got plenty of radio play and boosted sales of the album again. Two new songs were unveiled as the B-side to the single. 'The Day the Light Went Out' was a typical Banks workout in every sense, dominated by the synth sounds that had been so central to the album, the lyric inspired by science-fiction, just as his writing had so often been, all the way back to material like 'Watcher of the Skies'. 'Vancouver' was a collaboration between Rutherford and Collins, the guitarist writing the tune in, oddly enough, Vancouver. It has the same gentle flavour as 'Open Door', another B-side of a couple of years later, but lyrically, Collins chose to essentially rewrite The Beatles' 'She's Leaving Home', only this time with a happy ending, the girl not leaving in the end, but instead staying with her family, peace breaking out in the homestead. Perhaps that was wishful thinking on the part of the singer as he reflected on his own domestic life.

The plan for the year was Europe in the summer, along with three separate American tours, the idea being that playing in shorter bursts should ease the strain of touring. In fact, the opposite happened, the breaks so short that they seemed to be perpetually on the road, and by the time the tour closed, personal lives were beginning to suffer, notably that of Collins. That would prove significant, both in the short and longer term...

1979: A Serious Undertaking

Genesis' original plan for 1979 had involved writing sessions early in the year for an album that was scheduled to be released in the late summer, ahead of a 'back to the roots' theatre tour of the UK in the autumn. The latter was planned to act as an antidote to the massive production they carried around the world with them, playing to enormous audiences both indoors and out through 1978. But the best-laid plans…

Phil Collins' workaholic schedule that saw him not just working with Genesis but Brand X too, and then doing whatever session work he could still fit in, had put his marriage under real strain, and by the latter stages of Genesis' world tour, which climaxed in Japan in late November and early December 1978, it was in tatters. Very early in 1979, after his wife and children had left the UK to be with family in Vancouver, Collins had resolved to follow her to try to patch things up. He was ready to go and live in Canada and called a band meeting to say, 'If the band can write and record in Vancouver, I'm still in the group. If not, I'm out.'

In the face of such an ultimatum, the reaction of Tony Banks and Mike Rutherford was rather more considered than the band as a whole had been in similar circumstances in the past. Their solution was to shelve Genesis' plans for nine months and for Collins to use that pregnant pause to try to repair his personal life while they went off and made solo albums. They would then reconvene later in the year and see how the land lay. Peter Gabriel might have allowed himself a wry smile at this newfound understanding of matters domestic, while Steve Hackett would have been forgiven for asking how it was that just eighteen months after leaving the band, in part because there was no time for solo projects, here they were taking the better part of a year out to do just that.

Both of them would have had a point, but equally, times had changed for the group, largely because of the impact of 'Follow You Follow Me' as a hit single and the fact that they had, after six long years of toil, cracked the American market. Any band that managed that had earned itself the luxury of a year's break, safe in the knowledge that their audience would almost certainly still be there when they returned.

Moreover, now that they had slimmed down to a trio, they were at the point where they really could not afford to lose anyone else, where they had all become pretty much irreplaceable. Had Collins left in '79, perhaps Chester Thompson might have been persuaded to take over behind the kit, and they might even have drafted in Daryl Stuermer as a full-time member to play guitar alongside Rutherford, but they would have been back in the same predicament as they were in 1975. Who was going to sing? After all the trials and tribulations that had attended that process, they were in no hurry to repeat it. The self-contained three-piece that had made ...*And Then There Were Three...* had quickly shown itself to be the ideal set-up in terms or writing and recording, one with real long-term potential, whatever that album's flaws. Banks and Rutherford were understandably – and quite rightly – keen to give that line-up every chance of surviving.

But if the band were on hiatus, it didn't mean that 1979 would be a quiet year on the Genesis front, although Gabriel did give the first indications that the pace of his writing and recording would start to slow in the coming years. Looking to release his third album that year, it was so far delayed that he had to pull together a pick up band in the summer of '79 to fulfil concert obligations such as a slot at the Reading Festival in August. The band included, among others, Van der Graaf Generator's Dave Jackson on sax, John Giblin on bass and Phil Collins on drums, the two Genesis singers performing a gorgeous duet on 'Mother of Violence' and then trading lines on 'The Lamb Lies Down on Broadway', Collins remembering the lyrics rather better than the man who had written them. Gabriel's groundbreaking third record would not emerge until the following year, and would prove a seismic event for both him and Collins.

Anthony Phillips was having no such problems in producing material, and he was back with his third solo record in April 1979.

Anthony Phillips – Sides

Personnel:
Anthony Phillips: guitars, keyboards, lead vocals, cello, bass
Michael Giles: drums
John G. Perry: bass
Dale Newman: lead vocals
Dan Owen: lead vocals
Ray Cooper: percussion
Frank Ricotti: timpani
Morris Pert: Monotron, congas
Mel Collins: tenor saxophone
Rupert Hine: percussion, cor anglais
Producer: Rupert Hine

Engineers: Richard Austin, Andy 'Poppadom' Pierce, Nick Bedford, John 'Herbie' Sutcliffe, Slick Huddersfield, Vic Grimsby, Dick Halifax, Steve Short, Colin Green, John Brand
Cover art: Peter Cross
Recorded at Essex Studios, London; Matrix Studios, London; Trident Studios, London; Pye Studios, London, October – January 1979.
Released: April 1979
Label: Arista
Running time: 46:19
Tracklisting: 1. Um & Aargh 2. I Want Your Love 3. Lucy Will 4. Side Door 5. Holy Deadlock (Phillips/Hall) 6. Sisters of Remindum 7. Bleak House 8. Magdalen 9. Nightmare
All songs written by Anthony Phillips, unless otherwise stated.

Still being required by the record label to produce music with some commercial reach, whatever that means, *Sides* was a far better stab at it than *Wise After the Event* had been, the poppier end of the material better constructed and more convincing, while Phillips also gave himself scope to stretch out on some of the other pieces, neatly dividing the album into two sides of his tastes, the more commercial end on one side, the more experimental, progressive aspect on the other. As he admitted:

It had to be something of a compromise. Everyone was saying, 'You have to do songs, no instrumentals, it's got no balls!' It was just rubbish. Music has light and shade. If you've got a heavy rock song, that's how you treat it, something softer goes in that direction, why does everything have to have balls?!? *Sides* was going to be called 'Balls' originally, that's why the football table is on the cover. We had to change the title because they wouldn't wear it. Peter Cross spent so much time on the cover, it is so detailed, like all the others. He had the lyrics, so you can see all the different elements within his artwork. It's an enormous shame that eventually he stopped doing the covers, but the money had dried up, and they were simply too expensive to do any longer.

Phillips exorcised that frustration on the opening track, 'Um & Aargh', clearly his code for A&R, the thinly-veiled retelling of his conversations with a record company desperate for him to play to the lowest common denominator, while he was asking, 'Don't people have minds of their own?' It's a much more focused track than anything on its predecessor, concise and catchy enough to be released as the single – attention to detail, such as the lyrics, was never a great strength of record companies. It could have been a hit, but as Phillips noted in the song, 'Your image is incomplete'.

He tried to circumvent that by basically inventing Mike & The Mechanics seven years before Mike Rutherford got round to doing it. Accepting that his voice fitted some songs and not others, he drafted in Dan Owen and Dale Newman to sing some songs on the record, the idea being that they might also front things in the event of any commercial success. Owen was the singer on 'I Want Your Love', typical of the kind of ballad that people like Andrew Gold were doing good business with at the time. The 'I'm not superstitious / Your love is the richest' is a beguiling chorus, and there are some sparkling guitar moments on there too; it's hard to see what else Phillips could do to have a hit – had Phil Collins being fronting this with his increased profile, it could have been a top ten single. Phillips was back at the microphone for 'Lucy Will', the song built around a catchy acoustic guitar figure. It's another sturdy piece of songwriting and clearly very personal to the writer, but perhaps leaving all the singing in the hands of others might have offered a more cohesive feel?

As it is, 'Side Door' is back in the hands of Owen as singer, though perhaps the most significant contribution is Mel Collins on tenor sax. The jauntiness of the tune feels a little bit forced, where on 'Holy Deadlock', a co-write with Gabriel collaborator Martin Hall, it all feels rather more natural. It's very much in the 10cc mould, which seems to have been the guiding light for a lot of that first side of the album. But 10cc had the advantage of six years of hits behind them, something which helped them, for a time, in the teeth of the new wave. Phillips was not unaware of the problem.

It was a very tricky time, like the old Catholic priests having to hide in the priest hole. Anything with any classical influence and you had to hide it under the table. I remember Morris Pert saying that he had to keep his classical career on the quiet or he'd be up in front of the Stasi. You got the wretched *NME* people attacking you, it was just schoolboy nastiness really, but they were given the pulpit by some very irresponsible people. I don't blame the musicians at all, I'm sure if I'd been ten years younger, I'd have been doing the same, if not as nihilistically I hope. Then you had the irony that bands like The Police and The Stranglers were people who hadn't made it first time around – Andy Summers had auditioned to replace Brian Jones after all!

Turn the album over and you had something that was altogether more progressive, simultaneously looking back to his roots in Genesis and forward to his soundtrack work. The instrumental 'Sisters of Remindum' could very easily have been a section of a longer song, going through different moods and atmospheres, showcasing Phillips' ability as both writer and musician, and it's the juxtaposition of this kind of material along with the more song orientated first side that makes *Sides* a success, something still worth returning to today. Instead, amid the punk fallout, a lot of good music fell by the wayside, including 'Bleak House', featuring Dale Newman on vocals. It's a moody ballad, much in the same area that Tony Banks would later explore on his later solo records, sadly coming up against the same kind of brick wall of acceptance in a market ever more desperate for instant gratification. 'Magdalen' is another longer song that twists and turns across its near eight minutes and, while Giles and Perry are a sound rhythm section, you do wonder what Collins and Rutherford would have made of this, for the potential is there for it to really come alive. 'Nightmare' certainly does that, perhaps the standout track on the album. The opening figure owes something to 'Compression', a B-side of Mike Rutherford's from the *Smallcreep's Day* project a year later, on which Phillips played keyboards. That, in turn, had come out of an unused Genesis jam when they were writing for *Selling England by the Pound*, so perhaps he had introduced that to Phillips when they were preparing *The Geese & The Ghost*? However it all came together, it is a terrific piece, as progressive as it gets, restlessly churning through ideas, by turns melodic and aggressive, all musical life is here; its only downside is that it fades out after seven minutes when there's a lot more life left in it. If it had had the Genesis badge on the bonnet, it could easily have been a huge stage favourite. But brand names matter and Phillips didn't have one.

When we got to *Sides*, I had two other sides of material, a long synth piece that I used a snippet of on one of the re-releases, 'Holly Piece', and then there was a long 12-string piece, so I was still doing that kind of material, but it got excised for the more poppy stuff. Without wanting to sound pompous, I was exploring what I thought was a natural combination of rock instrument styles with 'classical' instrument styles. I'm not talking about the rock band on one side playing with the orchestra on the other side, I mean integrating them. That's what my period of studying had taught me and I loved experimenting with the combination of the instruments. But that dried up with punk. Those longer pieces, people had been willing to experiment with things a little more perhaps, certainly with instrumentals, which were pretty imaginative. Some of them became overblown and unwieldy and in the latter part of that first prog era, you have got albums that are too complicated for some people. But I think it was from sound motives, people experimenting, trying things out, just to try to get the best out of the music. I don't think it was trying to be clever for the sake of it. But it is a lost era because we then went into that extraordinary reverse gear with punk. Looking back on it, what happened seems barely believable. I don't think there was anything wrong with punk, but what was deeply wrong was the record companies all cashing in on it and knifing everyone in the back and throwing them aside as yesterday's heroes, which was disgraceful. It was very un-English, because we were normally pretty discriminating. It became this one-party system, this monotheistic idea.

Not content with releasing one record, though, *Sides* came with a bonus. The first 5,000 copies included a bonus album, *Private Parts & Pieces*, a collection of acoustic pieces, on a variety of guitars or on piano, sometimes sketches of ideas, other times more fully worked and realised.

Anthony Phillips – Private Parts & Pieces

Personnel:
Anthony Phillips: 12-string guitar, classical guitar, piano, Fender Stratocaster, pin piano, harmonium, vocals
Harry 'Piranhaphone' Williamson: graphics on 'Tibetan Yak-Music'
Producer: Anthony Phillips and Harry Williamson ('Tibetan Yak-Music')
Cover art: Peter Cross
Recorded at Send Barns, Woking, 1972 – 1976.
Released: April 1979 (free with first 5,000 copies of Sides)
Label: Arista
Running time: 56:46
Tracklisting: 1. Beauty and the Beast 2. Field of Eternity (Phillips/Rutherford) 3. Tibetan Yak-Music 4. Lullaby – Old Father Time 5. Harmonium in the Dust (or Harmonious Stratosphere) 6. Tregenna Afternoons 7. Reaper 8. Autumnal 9. Flamingo 9. Seven Long Years
All songs written by Anthony Phillips, unless otherwise stated.

It is a wilfully uncommercial record, initially released by Passport in the
United States in November 1978, before gaining its UK release along with
Sides. It's hard to see how else it could have been released in the UK of
the time, given it was clearly not a rock record and yet it did not fit into
the obvious classical niche. But that it was released and later begat a series
that is now 11 volumes strong was one of the great strokes of fortune of
Phillips' career, as he readily acknowledges. 'Being able to release *Private
Parts & Pieces* as an album that came with *Sides* was a huge slice of luck
for me because it established a sort of conduit for my more acoustic,
homespun stuff, and doing those records as a series was very affordable
too, because nobody had to pay for me to go into a big studio for days to
make those.'

It had its obvious attractions for the Genesis collectors in that 'Field of
Eternity' was a co-write with Mike Rutherford and 'Reaper' was written
immediately after he left the group, but it is far more than just being a
jumble of odds and ends. Instead, it offers a compelling window onto
Phillips' world in the early '70s, helping make sense of his decision to
leave Genesis while showing the trajectory he followed thereafter, to the
point at which he began releasing his own albums.

> I was very lost for a while when I left them, I didn't know what to do. I
> did experience a 'Road to Damascus' moment with classical music – I
> hate that term because it is so meaningless, and it still puts so many kids
> off, as it did me. I'd always associated it with rather staid and precise
> music, ornamental but not very emotional, very straitlaced if you like,
> which to me still covers music from the classical period. But later on, as
> the harmonies become more modern, it's extraordinary. The first time
> I heard *Claire de Lune* by Debussy, I thought, 'My God, this sounds like
> The Beatles!' Then I realised I'd got it the wrong way round, he'd got
> there first! The big turning point was hearing Sibelius, the *Karelia Suite*,
> it was amazingly tuneful, it was beautiful, and I wanted to learn how he'd
> created that. That was what made me determined to study, and from
> there, to write the material that I perhaps became best known for.

There are some stunning moments across the collection on which Phillips
excels both as composer and player. A decade later, with instrumental
music gaining greater interest among more open-minded rock fans, this
album really did begin to find its audience – and so it should because it
works as a record that you can relax with, can wallow in or to which you

can pay rapt attention to pick out all the tiny details that make it bear repetition.

Phillips' replacement in Genesis was also busy in early '79, bringing out his third solo record in May of that year.

Steve Hackett – Spectral Mornings

Personnel:

Steve Hackett: electric and acoustic guitars, Roland GR-5000 guitar synthesizer, lead vocals, backing and harmony vocals, harmonica, koto

Pete Hicks: lead vocals

Dik Cadbury: bass, backing and harmony vocals, Moog Taurus bass pedals, violin.

Nick Magnus: keyboards, Vox String Thing, Novatron, clavinet, Fender Rhodes and RMI electric pianos, Minimoog, Mini-Korg 700, Roland string synth, harpsichord

John Hackett: flute, bamboo flute, Moog Taurus bass pedals

John Shearer: drums, percussion

Producer: John Acock and Steve Hackett

Cover art: Kim Poor

Recorded at Phonogram Studios, Hilversum, Netherlands, January – February 1979.

Released: May 1979

Label: Charisma

Running time: 39:03

Tracklisting: 1. Every Day 2. The Virgin and the Gypsy 3. The Red Flower of Tachai Blooms Everywhere 4. Clocks: The Angel of Mons 5. The Ballad of the Decomposing Man (Featuring The Office Party) 6. Lost Time in Córdoba 7. Tigermoth 8. Spectral Mornings

All songs written by Steve Hackett.

Spectral Mornings was the album that saw Steve Hackett settle into what would become an identifiable style and pattern over the following few years. Both *Voyage of the Acolyte* and *Please Don't Touch!* had been one-offs in their distinct ways, the first a debut that tested the water, the second an opportunity to work with a diverse palette of guests. But for all that he had voiced his disdain for live work in the promotional interviews around that second album, the reality was that if he was going to build an audience for his solo work, he would need to get out on the road, and the logical way of doing that was to form some kind of regular band. He did that for his late '78 tour and, buoyed by the reception they received, they headed into the studio in the Netherlands at the start of 1979, an experience not unlike recording *Wind and Wuthering* with Genesis. Confronted by ferocious winter weather, they were essentially confined to barracks for the duration, Hackett recalling that they worked hard and partied just as enthusiastically as they pieced the album together:

I was recommended to a studio in Holland, a place called Hilversum, a Phonogram studio, and there's also a radio station there. We were out in this huge area of Holland, knee-deep in snow, 50 degrees below zero, just after Christmas, and we started on the album. The fact we were in a captive environment didn't seem to make any difference, everyone just had a really good time. We couldn't really go anywhere because of the weather, but it seemed that because of all these things, the album did take on a character of its own, and I was pleased with it. I had a band by then that liked working together, liked the fact that for one reason or another, we were doing good business. Some of the things we put together [for the October/November 1978 tour] became cornerstones of what was to be the next album, which I thought of in terms of a band album. Even though I was the writer in the main, there was a band feel to it, and a lot was done spontaneously, as a result of people throwing ideas in. The band loved to jam, which was a very natural sounding thing. Even when we did other songs – we did 'I Know What I Like' sometimes – it was a really good version. There was just something very natural about the way we worked together, and that aspect of the band I liked very much.

The album offered up a number of songs that are still hardy perennials in the Hackett live catalogue 40 years and more later, including the opening track, 'Every Day'. It's about a dark subject, drug culture and the dangers thereof, Hackett's anguished, howling guitar sound conjuring up the pain and loss. Writing of the way someone in the grip of addiction may be physically present, it's a harrowing song once you dig into it, featuring some electrifying playing.

'The Virgin and the Gypsy', based on the D.H. Lawrence novel, was partly left over from the previous album. It's an intricately plotted song featuring layers of 12-string guitars and Hackett's beloved harmony vocals. It's very much in the English folk tradition but updated for modern instrumentation, including guitar synthesizer and also features Pete Hicks debuting as lead vocalist to good effect. The problem that would beset him, even more than it had Gabriel in Genesis, was what does a singer do when for 75% of the time, the band is playing instrumental pieces?

The double-tracked flute from John Hackett has a slightly Asian flavour to it and that leads nicely into 'The Red Flower of Tachai Blooms Everywhere'. Hackett plays koto on this instrumental that is rooted firmly in Japan or China. It's musically very descriptive, conjuring up images of elderly people doing their daily exercises in unison to the accompaniment of the tune. It is very much the calm before the storm, though, for 'Clocks – The Angel of Mons' takes no prisoners. Opening on a doom-laden bass pedal refrain, once John Shearer kicks the drums in, Hackett channels an air raid through his guitar, wreaking havoc in the musical telling of the story of British troops supposedly being saved by supernatural forces at Mons in the early weeks of the Great War.

'The Ballad of the Decomposing Man' carries on in the same tradition as 'Carry On up the Vicarage' from the previous record. The everyday tale of working folk, the first half deals with the standard drudgery of day to day life before heading into the calypso 'Office Party' section, the idea of needing the chance to blow off steam every now and again simply to survive the boredom. 'Lost Time in Córdoba' is another Hackett staple, a duet between guitar and flute in the same vein as 'Kim', beautifully performed by the brothers Hackett.

'Tigermoth' picks up the Great War theme again, this time concerning the dogfights between British and German airmen. The Mellotron provides the dramatic backdrop, Hackett's jagged guitar lines taking on the role of the machine guns as the battle rages. The treated vocal that comes in during the second half of the song captures period and place particularly well, as well as the stupidity of war – you serve Kaiser or King through an accident of birthplace, nothing to do with conviction. The lullaby ending is intriguing too – is that the defeated pilot picking up his harp and wings, or is it the innocents back home, sleeping soundly, blissfully unaware of the carnage?

The album climaxes on the title track, perhaps Hackett's single best piece of music from right across his career. Originally intended as a song, once Pete Hicks heard the instrumental version, he told Hackett that 'Spectral Mornings' was just fine as it was and not to tamper with it. Hicks was right, for everything on this recording exists in service of the guitar and a vocal would have merely got in the way. It's a gorgeous performance, plain and simple. Hackett proclaimed that this was, 'A period of high confidence for me. It was very well received, we had a very successful tour and then did really well at the Reading Festival too. It's a period I look back on fondly.' Rightly so, for *Spectral Mornings* was the record that established Hackett as a solo artist, something separate from Genesis, a musician to be appreciated and assessed on his own merits.

It was a rather less positive period for Phil Collins, however. Having headed for Vancouver in an attempt to save his marriage, he was soon back in England after things had not improved. Finding Banks and Rutherford already embroiled in the production of their solo albums, and so with no Genesis album immediately in the offing, to fill his time, he plugged back into Brand X for their fourth studio album, Collins having played no part in 1978's *Masques*.

Brand X – Product

Personnel:
Phil Collins: drums, percussion, vocals, drum machine
John Goodsall: guitar, vocals
Percy Jones: bass
Robin Lumley: keyboards, sounds
John Giblin: bass
Peter Robinson: keyboards, sounds, vocals
Mike Clark: drums
Morris Pert: percussion
Producer: Brand X, Colin Green, Neil Kernon
Engineers: Colin Green, Neil Kernon, Phil Collins
Cover art: Hipgnosis/Elgie
Recorded at Startling Studios, Ascot, April 1979.
Released: 14 September 1979
Label: Charisma Records
Running time: 46:40
Tracklisting: 1. Don't Make Waves (Goodsall) 2. Dance of the Illegal Aliens (Jones) 3. Soho (Goodsall/Collins) 4. Not Good Enough – See Me! (Jones/Robinson) 5. Algon (Where an Ordinary Cup of Drinking Chocolate Costs £8,000,000,000) (Lumley) 6. Rhesus Perplexus (Giblin) 7. Wal to Wal (Jones/Giblin) 8. ...And So to F... (Collins) 9. April (Giblin).

A revolving door of eight different musicians made up the band this time, recording in shifts at Ascot at one point. It's a surprisingly together-sounding record in the circumstances and by far their most commercially focused. It was to prove Collins' last real hurrah with the band – the following year's *Do They Hurt* was a tidying up of outtakes from these sessions – and you can understand why it was heading that way even before he found huge success with *Face Value* in 1981. While Genesis was gradually loosening up – a process that was to accelerate through *Duke* and *Abacab* – Brand X were beginning to head towards material that was less about improvisation and more about composition and about songs. As Collins was to say later, 'The two bands met in the middle.'

'Don't Make Waves' is an obvious example of that because it's not a million miles away from a song like 'Behind the Lines'. Obviously, Collins' vocal means there will always be similarities to Genesis, but John Goodsall's song owes a lot to the rockier end of the spectrum than their jazzier leanings of yore, Goodsall admitting that he was increasingly influenced by bands like Boston. 'Dance of the Illegal Aliens' was more traditional Brand X fare, Percy Jones' bass bubbling along in the line-up that featured Mike Clark on drums. But it's 'Soho', the co-write between Goodsall and Collins, that really shows where Brand X were heading, a real stab at a hit single. It was to be a particularly significant recording, for unlike the rest, it was made at Collins' home, as he explained to *Melody Maker*. 'We recorded it on an eight-track system which I have at my place and since the transfer from eight to 24-track was successful, I'll hopefully be doing some more work there.' It was the turn of the 'other' Brand X again on 'Not Good Enough – See Me!' and this takes a turn back towards the jazzier end of the spectrum, Goodsall the thread running through it all, providing a searing guitar break.

Opening side two, 'Algon' returns to the Collins/Goodsall/Giblin/Lumley quartet, and this time they centre things around mood and atmosphere, a nice grasp of dynamics. It's typically tricksy but loses nothing for that, albeit that the review in *Sounds* complained that, 'They sometimes pack in too many ideas and tend to restrict the natural flow'. Following that, 'Rhesus Perplexus' suggests that they'd been paying attention to the emerging Pat Metheny Group, while 'Wal to Wal' makes surprisingly strong capital out of a trio featuring two bassists and a drum machine, the first time Collins had recorded with one.

It's Collins who provides the album with its standout piece, '...And So to F...', which he would later feature in his solo concerts. *Melody Maker* reported that it 'is a simple theme rooted somewhere in Genesis-land that the individual talents of Brand X make their own'. It was a pretty impressive high on which to sign off with the band, Giblin's 'April' offering a low key coda to it all.

By the time the album came out in September 1979, Collins was already at work on the next Genesis record, although there was a brief hiatus in October when Tony Banks was required to do some brief promotional work for his first solo album pieced together earlier in the year.

Tony Banks – A Curious Feeling

Personnel:
Tony Banks: keyboards, guitar, bass, percussion
Chester Thompson: drums, percussion
Kim Beacon: vocals
Producer: Tony Banks and David Hentschel
Engineer: David Bascombe
Cover art: Hothouse/Ainslie Roberts
Recorded at Polar Music Studios, Stockholm, Sweden, Spring – Summer 1979.
Released: 12 October 1979
Label: Charisma
Running time: 52:54
Tracklisting: 1. From The Undertow 2. Lucky Me 3. The Lie 4. After the Lie 5. A Curious Feeling 6. Forever Morning 7. You 8. Somebody Else's Dream 9. The Waters of Lethe 10. For a While 11. In the Dark
All songs written by Tony Banks.

As already noted, prior to embarking on their solo records, Banks and Rutherford had collaborated on writing some soundtrack music for the John Hurt and Alan Bates film *The Shout*. The main theme for that – heavily underused in the finished movie – was taken from 'Undertow' on *...And Then There Were Three...* but Banks felt that there was more to be done with that piece of music and so 'From the Undertow' became the jumping-off point for the album. It's very typical of his work in Genesis around that period, a melancholy and eerie quality to it that is to some extent resolved in the closing seconds when there's a feeling of the sun coming out.

That leaks into 'Lucky Me' when Kim Beacon comes into the mix and instantly lifts the mood. The lead singer with Charisma act, String Driven Thing, his was the voice that stood out from the mountain of tapes that Banks sifted through, and he was a great choice for the material. Subsequent events – Beacon died in 2001 – have added an extra layer to his performance, Banks saying now that, 'Over the years, he's become the character in the story in my mind. He had a lovely voice, he was very enthusiastic and he did a great job.'

The character in question is the narrator of what is a concept record, initially based on the book *Flowers for Algernon* by Daniel Keyes. That's the story of a caretaker, essentially a simpleton, who undergoes an experimental surgical technique to increase his intelligence. This works initially, tripling his IQ from 68 to the 200s, but eventually, the effect wears off, and ultimately he is left with an even lower IQ than he had started with. Banks got in touch with the author to ask permission to use the novel as the basis for his album and was told that while that was fine, Michael Crawford was about to front a musical version of the book, *Charlie*, in the West End. Had that been a success, then it would have overshadowed Banks' record, which would have also seemed to be trying to ride on its coattails. It meant that Banks then reworked a number of the lyrics to avoid being an exact copy. 'The general feel is the same in the sense of what happens to the character. My story's not as good, but it has the same emotive quality to it.'

'Lucky Me' was written on guitar, nothing new for Banks, as has already been discussed. What was new was that this time, he was going to play all the lead guitar and bass himself as he explained an interview for *Cherry Red TV*:

> I was very happy picking guitar on things like 'Lucky Me', but lead guitar, mostly it ended up sounding like a synthesizer anyway. Bass was surprisingly difficult to play, I had to put foam under the strings to stop them vibrating, but I kept the parts very simple and just about got away with it. I probably lacked confidence because I wasn't sure about working with other musicians. I got Chester Thompson involved because he was a good friend, we'd worked together in Genesis for a couple of years and I knew he was sympathetic to the kind of music I was doing, and he did a great job.

'Lucky Me' features the character in the here and now, explaining how he has lost his memory, and much of his mind, and has only vague ideas that things were once different, but he's happy in his lack of responsibility and in the absolute simplicity of his daily life. 'The Lie' then flashbacks to his childhood when he used to make little bets with fate, all of no consequence until he says that if he never falls in love, he wants to be wise and famous. Fate pricks up its ears – this is a 'serious undertaking' – and seals the deal, saying that if he does fall in love, 'You'll not only not be wise / You'll lose your memory and most of your mind.' The song motors along on a lovely piano piece, Thompson then joining the dance until the song pivots in the middle, Beacon voicing Fate in the central moment of the record.

The contemplative 'After the Lie' sees Beacon's character growing in intelligence to the point where he is now a genius, his opinion highly sought after. 'A Curious Feeling' itself, also written on guitar, sees Banks stepping out of the story in part in order to have a dig at politicians who claim to have all the answers. The song has a lovely swing and swagger to it and might have been a good choice as a single – 'For a While' was the one that was eventually selected – but as Banks admitted, having a hit wasn't really on the agenda. 'There were no barriers on making this album, I didn't have to have a single, I was just able to write as I wanted.'

That was very much the case in the instrumental sections such as 'Forever Morning', a dramatic six-minute piece that overlays synthesizer lines on a piano track. Sonically, it's very much of a piece with the work he was doing on ...*And Then There Were Three...* and it again hints at 'Undertow', ideas cascading one after another.

'You' is where the spanner is placed in the works, as our hero falls in love with a girl he has known since childhood. Simple in composition, featuring a lovely 12-string guitar figure and a glorious vocal from Beacon, it dissolves into an instrumental coda, Banks' extraordinary keyboard solo capturing the sudden turmoil that he goes through as Fate turns up to claim his prize. It's some of the most exciting and enduring playing of his career, culminating into one of those great climaxes familiar from 'The Musical Box', though without Gabriel singing over the top of it this time.

There's not a bleaker song in the Banks canon than 'Somebody Else's Dream', Beacon suddenly horrifyingly aware that his memory and his mind are slipping away, that all his hopes and dreams are disappearing with them, before his very eyes, the singer giving a powerfully charged performance. All these years on, where the ravages of dementia have become more recognised within society, it has a new reading as something of an illustration of that horrible process too, 'the oncoming night'. 'The Waters of Lethe' follows, the title taken from the river of forgetfulness in the Greek underworld. It's another emotional instrumental and Banks' favourite track on the record. 'It's a very stirring melody, it's got those big chords in the middle which work really well. And it's got the only real piece of lead guitar on the album on it.' From there, 'For a While' has a nice, loping groove to it, a bittersweet song of regret, the pain of imminent loss. Like a lot of material on *The Lamb Lies Down on Broadway*, it's a pretty song that could have had a life away from the album, but its subject matter is too closely identified with the parent album to have a real chance of independent success.

Album closer 'In the Dark' returns us to the present day, Beacon making it clear that he doesn't want to be told the details of his life story, that he prefers to live in the dark, that the truth would be too painful to contemplate. There are plenty of wider applications for that lyric, of course, but it rounds off the story in the right fashion, brings us full circle with that same sense of melancholy that opened the record.

Recording took place in Sweden, in ABBA's newly built Polar Studios. Banks used David Hentschel as co-producer, but he fell ill with mumps when they arrived and was out of action for a week. Tape op and engineer Dave Bascombe, now renowned for his work with Tears For Fears, Human League and many others, was right at the beginning of his career then, but with studio time booked he was thrust into the position of engineering the sessions for a week as they looked to get some music down on tape. It was a good place for him to start, for the album charted at number 21 in the UK and has been reissued on two occasions since, forming the cornerstone of Banks' solo catalogue.

Mike Rutherford followed him into Polar Studios shortly after to record *Smallcreep's Day*, released early in 1980, and the 1970s came to a close for Genesis with the three-piece band reunited once more, blazing the same trail to Stockholm to record *Duke*, their first album of a new decade. But that's another story...

Epilogue

As the 1970s came to a close, it had been an extraordinary decade for Genesis, both together and apart. The band that had gone into 1970 without a record deal had ended it with a top ten single, albums that sold in huge quantities and had joined the rock elite such as the Rolling Stones, Pink Floyd and Led Zeppelin in headlining the Knebworth Festival in front of 100,000 people. They were similarly revered throughout mainland Europe, so popular indeed that they could no longer play in Italy for fear of sparking riots. In the USA, they were selling increasing numbers of records and packing out giant arenas in all the major markets. And yet in spite of that, they were perhaps the biggest cult band in the world, still very much the jealously guarded property of their fans, still barely registering in the mainstream press.

The 1980s would put a stop to that.

At the start of the decade, you'd have got pretty long odds that, musically speaking, it was going to be defined by a drum break. But when Peter Gabriel set the ball rolling by decreeing that there would be no cymbals on his third record and his erstwhile colleague Phil Collins responded with the drum pattern that kicked off the first track, 'Intruder', they were on the way to creating history, redefining their lives and that of Genesis. Collins took that drum sound with him into his first solo record, applied it to a song called 'In the Air Tonight' and, having lit the blue touchpaper, stepped back and watched the fireworks that followed the release of that single and its parent album *Face Value*.

That immediately lifted Collins into a different league, away from the band and any of his colleagues as solo artists, a star far bigger than Gabriel had ever been during his time in Genesis. Tony Banks was both hilariously dry and admirably candid when he admitted that although he was pleased to see that his friend was a success, he didn't mean 'that big a success!' But with all of them now entering their thirties, there was greater acceptance and maturity about it all, and Collins' solo success became the fuel that propelled Genesis on to greater mainstream acceptance too.

What Collins' emergence as a writer – and as a star – did mean was that Genesis was to become much more of an even split between Banks, Collins and Mike Rutherford, and that was not without its controversies, certainly among the fans who had been with them for many years. When *Abacab* was released seven months after *Face Value*, it represented too much of a change in tack for some, the inclusion of the Earth Wind &

Fire horn section, so beloved of Collins, a bridge too far, as was the punk parody 'Who Dunnit?' The band were booed when they played the new material in Leiden in the Netherlands, but album sales increased, the bulk of the old fans sticking around, Collins' success bringing in new ones who had previously had no idea that he was in Genesis – had maybe never even heard of the band – but who largely enjoyed what they found.

As the decade wore on, Collins only seemed to be more ubiquitous, making his own records, playing with Robert Plant, producing and touring with Eric Clapton and plenty more. But still, Genesis were part of his plans, the self-titled album that spawned 'Mama' and 'That's All' adding to their popularity. Banks and Rutherford continued to release solo albums meanwhile, albeit to nothing like the same interest. Banks' frustration centred on his inability to engineer a parallel career as a composer of film soundtracks, while Rutherford concluded that working entirely solo wasn't for him and instead created a band vehicle, Mike & the Mechanics, which enjoyed early success with 'Silent Running' and 'All I Need Is a Miracle' in 1986.

The period from mid-1986 through to the summer of 1987 was to be the single most remarkable year in Genesis history, for it saw the band release *Invisible Touch*, a platinum-selling album around the globe, spawning an American number one single in the title track, along with four more hit singles. Their world tour took them to Australia for the first time, saw them play some of the biggest indoor and then outdoor arenas in the United States and culminated in a record four shows at Wembley Stadium in the summer of 1987. They could, with some justification, claim to be the biggest band in the world.

Not only were Genesis doing incredible business, but the former members of the band were enjoying their time in the sun too. Steve Hackett formed a short-lived alliance with Yes guitarist Steve Howe in GTR, and their single, 'When the Heart Rules the Mind', was a massive American hit too. Meanwhile, Gabriel was not going to be upstaged forever. His third and fourth solo albums, again called *Peter Gabriel*, had been among the most innovative and influential of the early '80s, but sales had been no better than respectable. Gabriel was seen more as worthy and interesting, rather than as a rock star, something reinforced by his founding involvement with the world music festival WOMAD in 1982, an artistically brilliant and financially catastrophic event that brought him to the point of personal bankruptcy, and found him on the receiving end of some very dark threats from creditors. The financial morass was only resolved on 2 October 1982 when, in the pouring rain and autumnal cold of a Saturday night in Milton Keynes, Jonathan King introduced to the stage a band that had initially formed at his old school. A coffin was brought on, from which appeared Peter Gabriel, joining Tony Banks, Mike Rutherford, Phil Collins, Chester Thompson and Daryl Stuermer, Six of the Best, for an evening of songs from an era that already seemed long gone even then, their ranks swelled to seven when Steve Hackett joined them for the encore. It'd been a long, long time. Hadn't it?

After all that, as Gabriel's long-term drummer Jerry Marotta noted, 'He went into what became *So*, determined to have some hits and to be a star again.' He managed that and plenty more, aided and abetted by a promo video that defined the genre, 'Sledgehammer', also reaching number one in the United States.

While Genesis were reaping the benefits of success, it was to prove a double-edged sword, especially in terms of their frontman. The offers for Phil Collins came pouring in thicker and faster than ever, including the chance to star in films, such that Genesis could not reconvene until 1991. *We Can't Dance* was again well received and was, perhaps, a better album than *Invisible Touch* in many respects, but as they finished up a relatively brief world tour in the summer of 1992, it did seem as if Genesis might be nearing its end. Collins finally concluded that was so, the announcement of his departure coming in 1996.

Banks and Rutherford got together to write new material, found they were happy with the early results and ultimately recruited singer Ray Wilson from Stiltskin to join the fold. The result was a more than serviceable first album together, 1997's *Calling All Stations,* which hinted at undeniable potential for the new band, which had included Nir Z on drums on much of the record – Nick D'Virgilio also appeared on it but was not in the live group on their European tour. Their timing was awry this time though and after their American tour was cancelled through lack of ticket sales, the curtain came down on the band. There have been compilations, box sets and one reunion tour with Banks, Collins and Rutherford since, with another delayed by Covid, but as a recording act, Genesis looks to have had its day.

Like the story that we wish was never-ending, we know some time we must reach the final page…

Bibliography

Unless attributed otherwise in the text, quotes from Anthony Phillips (April 2015), Steve Hackett (May 1988 and May 2013) and Jerry Marotta (March 2015) come from interviews conducted by the author.

Hackett, S., *A Genesis in My Bed*

Banks, T., Collins, P., Gabriel, P., Hackett, S., Rutherford, M., *Chapter & Verse*

Giammetti, M., *Genesis 1970-1975: The Peter Gabriel Years*

Bowler, D., Dray, B., *Genesis: A Biography*

Macfarlane, S., *Genesis: On Track*

Gallo, A., *Genesis: The Evolution of a Rock Band*

Gallo, A., *Genesis: I Know What I Like*

Macphail, R., *My Book of Genesis*

Collins, P., *Not Dead Yet*

Gallo, A., *Peter Gabriel*

Bright, S., *Peter Gabriel: An Authorised Biography*

Easlea, D., *Without Frontiers: The Life & Music of Peter Gabriel*

Bruford, B., *The Autobiography*

Fielder, H., *The Book of Genesis*

Rutherford, M., *The Living Years*

Beat Instrumental, Disc, Melody Maker, Mojo, New Musical Express, Prog, Sight & Sound, Sounds, ZigZag.

www.thegenesisarchive.co.uk

www.worldofgenesis.com

Youtube – Hackettsongs, BillFilm, *Rock History Music*

Genesis – *1970-75, 1976-82, 1983-1998* box set interviews

Genesis - *on track*
every album, every song

Stuart Macfarlane
Paperback
160 pages
44 colour photographs
978-178-952-005-7
£14.99
USD 21.95

**Every track recorded
by the legendary
British band.**

From schoolboy band to sold-out stadium tours and worldwide album sales of over 100 million, Genesis were one of the defining progressive rock bands of the seventies, playing a huge part in shaping the genre. Over a career spanning forty years from formation to the world reunion tour of 2007, they developed and adapted through many changes, some of which polarised their existing fans but attracted countless new ones. While *Foxtrot* and *The Lamb Lies Down on Broadway* helped define progressive rock, it was the three-piece line up of Tony Banks, Mike Rutherford and Phil Collins that became the real hit-makers, with albums like *Invisible Touch* and *We Can't Dance* and massive hit singles like 'No Son of Mine' and 'Land of Confusion'.

Fifteen studio and six live albums later, including five consecutive number ones in the UK and five consecutive top tens in the USA, fans still live in the hope of yet another reunion tour. This book takes the reader on a journey through their entire catalogue, taking each album in turn and examining every track. It is compiled from the viewpoint of a lifelong fan, and it is hoped that the book stirs many old memories, as it has done for the author, as well as providing some insight for more recent fans of the band.

Peter Gabriel - *on track*
every album, every song

Graeme Scarfe
Paperback
160 pages
40 colour photographs
978-178-952-138-2
£14.99
USD 21.95

**Every album recorded
by this British pioneer
of progressive music.**

If Genesis, according to British comedian and fan Al Murray 'were the progressive rock band who progressed', then Peter Gabriel as a solo artist would be the member that progressed the most. Who would have thought that listening to early Genesis would eventually take the listener to Senegal, Armenia, South Africa and beyond, via the artistic endeavours of their former vocalist?

This is a journey through Peter Gabriel's solo albums, his live recordings and soundtrack compositions. During his forty-year plus solo career, Gabriel has become a worldwide pop star via his early, self-titled albums and his seminal 1986 record

So. He has had hit singles throughout his career, including the bucolic 'Solsbury Hill' in 1977 and the poignant 'Don't Give Up'. He also helped pioneer video creativity with the song 'Sledgehammer'. In doing so, he has reached beyond his progressive rock origins to achieve a level of popularity and respect that other musicians from that genre could only dream about. You may have heard many of these songs before, but there's always something new to be found by digging in the dirt. This is the perfect guide to his music for new listeners and long-term fans alike.

What on earth is going on? In the words of the Burgermiester: 'I...will...find...out.'

Yes in the 80s
Decades

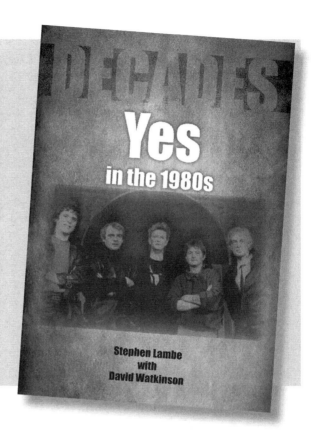

Stephen Lambe with David
Watkinson
Paperback
192 pages
80 colour photographs
978-178-952-125-2
£16.99
USD 24.95

**An in-depth
examination of this
famous progressive
rock band's most
turbulent decade.**

When Yes ran into problems recording their tenth album in Paris at the end of 1979, it was almost the end. Yet in the 1980s, the band rallied, firstly as part of an unlikely collaboration with new wave duo The Buggles, then with *90125*, the most successful album of their career, which spawned a number one hit in the USA with 'Owner Of A Lonely Heart'. The band failed to capitalise on this success, however, lingering too long over its successor *Big Generator* and by the end of the decade, Yes had effectively split into two versions of the same group.

With most authors concentrating on the group's 1970s career, *Yes in the 1980s* looks in forensic detail at this relatively underexamined era of the band's history, featuring rarely-seen photos researched by author David Watkinson. The book follows the careers of all nine significant members of the group during a turbulent decade which saw huge highs but also many lows. Not only does it consider the three albums the band itself made across the decade, but also the solo careers and other groups – including Asia, XYZ, The Buggles, Jon and Vangelis and GTR - formed by those musicians as the decade wound towards a reunion of sorts in the early 1990s.

Decades Series
Pink Floyd In The 1970s – Georg Purvis 978-1-78952-072-9
Marillion in the 1980s – Nathaniel Webb 978-1-78952-065-1

On Screen series
Carry On… – Stephen Lambe 978-1-78952-004-0
David Cronenberg – Patrick Chapman 978-1-78952-071-2
Doctor Who: The David Tennant Years – Jamie Hailstone 978-1-78952-066-8
Monty Python – Steve Pilkington 978-1-78952-047-7
Seinfeld Seasons 1 to 5 – Stephen Lambe 978-1-78952-012-5

Other Books
Derek Taylor: For Your Radioactive Children – Andrew Darlington
978-1-78952-
Jon Anderson and the Warriors - the road to Yes – David Watkinson
978-1-78952-059-0
Tommy Bolin: In and Out of Deep Purple – Laura Shenton
978-1-78952-070-5
Maximum Darkness – Deke Leonard 978-1-78952-048-4
Maybe I Should've Stayed In Bed – Deke Leonard 978-1-78952-053-8
The Twang Dynasty – Deke Leonard 978-1-78952-049-1

and many more to come!

Would you like to write for Sonicbond Publishing?

At Sonicbond Publishing we are always on the look-out for authors, particularly for our two main series:

On Track. Mixing fact with in depth analysis, the On Track series examines the work of a particular musical artist or group. All genres are considered from easy listening and jazz to 60s soul to 90s pop, via rock and metal.

On Screen. This series looks at the world of film and television. Subjects considered include directors, actors and writers, as well as entire television and film series. As with the On Track series, we balance fact with analysis.

While professional writing experience would, of course, be an advantage the most important qualification is to have real enthusiasm and knowledge of your subject. First-time authors are welcomed, but the ability to write well in English is essential.

Sonicbond Publishing has distribution throughout Europe and North America, and all books are also published in E-book form. Authors will be paid a royalty based on sales of their book.

Further details are available from www.sonicbondpublishing.co.uk. To contact us, complete the contact form there or email info@sonicbondpublishing.co.uk